Morgenthau

Hans Morgenthau

Realism and Beyond

William E. Scheuerman

polity

First published in 2009 by Polity Press

Polity Press
65 Bridge Street
Cambridge CB2 1UR, UK

Polity Press
350 Main Street
Malden, MA 02148, USA

ISBN-13: 978-0-7456-3635-1
ISBN-13: 978-0-7456-3636-8(paperback)

A catalogue record for this book is available from the British Library.

Typeset in 10.5 on 12 pt Palatino
by SNP Best-set Typesetter Ltd., Hong Kong
Printed and bound in Great Britain by MPG Books Ltd, Bodmin, Cornwall

The publisher has used its best endeavours to ensure that the URLs for external websites referred to in this book are correct and active at the time of going to press. However, the publisher has no responsibility for the websites and can make no guarantee that a site will remain live or that the content is or will remain appropriate.

Every effort has been made to trace all copyright holders, but if any have been inadvertently overlooked the publishers will be pleased to include any necessary credits in any subsequent reprint or edition.

For further information on Polity, visit our website: www.polity.co.uk

For Lily

Contents

Acknowledgments

I was inspired to write this book by a wonderful conference that took place in the autumn of 2004 at Gregynog Hall outside Newton in Wales. Organized by Michael C. Williams, Department of International Politics, Aberystwyth, and devoted to a reconsideration of the intellectual legacy of Hans J. Morgenthau, the meeting brought to my attention the need for an updated survey of Morgenthau's ideas sufficiently attuned to contemporary intellectual and political trends. My special thanks to Michael for the invitation to participate, as well to the many speakers for their fascinating insights on Morgenthau and his views.

Audiences at Chicago, Cornell, Indiana, McGill, and Vanderbilt Universities have graciously served as guinea pigs as I tried out my sometimes heterodox ideas on Morgenthau. I am also indebted to the journal *Review of International Studies* for allowing me to integrate some sections of an article originally published there into chapter I, and also *Constellations* for permitting me to reuse (in chapter II) some materials which originally appeared in its pages. Jeffrey Flannery of the Library of Congress provided easy access to the Morgenthau Archives, and Luke Mergner at Indiana University helped dig up copies of Morgenthau's harder-to-find writings. Emma Hutchinson at Polity has been an exemplary editor in every respect. Finally, I thank the two anonymous referees at Polity for their astute comments, criticisms, and suggestions on an earlier draft.

My father was briefly a student of Morgenthau's during the early 1970s. In fact, trying to figure out how my dad – who, like many in his generation, was radicalized by the events of the 1960s – could think so highly of an erstwhile "classical Realist" like Morgenthau undoubtedly played a role in my decision to write this book. I know that my dad – the first in his family to attend college, hailing from an apolitical and somewhat anti-intellectual working-class family – remains grateful for Morgenthau's support during a crucial juncture in his life. If I have done any justice to Morgenthau's thinking in these pages, perhaps I can help repay a family debt.

This book is dedicated to my daughter Lily, who has accompanied and – by capably allying herself with her older sister Zoe – frequently interrupted its composition. Lily's feisty spirit and contagious smile have provided much-needed respite from working on the volume and thinking about the many frightening historical conjunctures (e.g. Nazism, the cold war, the Vietnam War, and the specter of nuclear war) to which my research necessarily drew me. Lily has also helped remind me of how much remains at stake in a political universe still haunted by many of the same problems – just to mention two: democratic decay and nuclear proliferation – which rightly preoccupied Morgenthau in the final decades of his long career.

Abbreviations

For the *key* or *main* texts authored by Morgenthau, the following abbreviations have been used. To facilitate transparency, the relevant abbreviation and page number(s) appear in the main body of the text. So "(*IDNI*, 114)," for example, refers to p. 114 of *In Defense of the National Interest*. For *Politics Among Nations: The Struggle for Power and Peace* (*PAN*), the edition used is also noted.

IDNI   *In Defense of the National Interest* (1951)
IRWG   *Die internationale Rechtspflege, ihr Wesen und ihre Grenzen* (1929)
NFP   *A New Foreign Policy for the United States* (1969)
PAN   *Politics Among Nations: The Struggle for Power and Peace* (1st edn., 1948; 2nd edn., 1954; 3rd edn., 1960)
PAP   *Purpose of American Politics* (1960)
"PFIL" "Positivism, Functionalism, and International Law" (1940)
SM   *Scientific Man Vs. Power Politics* (1946)
VUS   *Vietnam and the United States* (1965)

For the *collections of essays* authored by Morgenthau, the following abbreviations have been used.

DDP   *Decline of Democratic Politics* (1962)
DP   *Dilemmas of Politics* (1958)
IAFP   *The Impasse of American Foreign Policy* (1962)
RAP   *The Restoration of American Politics* (1962)
TP   *Truth and Power: Essays of a Decade, 1960–70* (1970)

Full bibliographical information (including, of course, the title of the relevant essay or book chapter referenced) is provided in the endnotes or bibliography.

Substantial use has been made of archival materials from the Hans J. Morgenthau Papers (HJM) at the Library of Congress, Washington, D.C. (with "B" referring to the box or container number).

Finally, endnotes with full biographical information are provided for all other materials, including publications by Morgenthau infrequently cited or used.

Introduction:
Morgenthau's uneasy Realism

Realist international theory continues to exercise extraordinary influence on policy makers and intellectuals. A complete list of Realist practitioners would read like a *Who's Who?* of modern foreign policy.[1] Henry Kissinger would surely be positioned atop the list, but it would also encompass many other prominent public figures. Realism's present theoretical representatives include luminaries as otherwise intellectually diverse as the US political scientist Kenneth Waltz and Italian political philosopher Danilo Zolo. Historians have traced Realism's impressive intellectual roots to Niccolò Machiavelli, Thomas Hobbes, and Max Weber.[2] Realism represented the predominant theoretical orientation among especially postwar US scholars of international politics for decades. Although the end of the cold war and worldwide debates about reforming the UN placed Realism on the defensive in the 1990s, with the 9/11 terrorist attacks, US hostility to international law, China's ascent, resurgent Russian nationalism, and disorder in the Middle East, Realism appears to have undergone both a political and intellectual come-back. In the United States, some prominent defenders of the Iraq War have alluded vaguely to Realist ideals, whereas leading critics of the invasion of Iraq have appealed even more forcefully to Realist principles.[3] In ongoing debates concerning global governance, Realism provides a rich intellectual goldmine for those skeptical of cosmopolitanism and its ambitious blueprints for international reform.

So how then might we define Realism? The question is more complicated than first seems apparent, and scholars have invested substantial energy in trying to come up with a useful summary of its main tenets.[4] Matters are complicated by the fact that Realism, like any great intellectual movement, comes in different shapes and sizes. Fortunately, political theorist Michael Joseph Smith has provided a succinct working definition:

> the Realist picture of the world begins with a pessimistic view of human nature. Evil is inevitably a part of all of us which no social arrangement can eradicate: men and women are not perfectible. The struggle for power – which defines politics – is a permanent feature of social life and is especially prominent in the relations between states. In the realm of international politics, states are the only major actors, and no structure of power or authority stands above them to mediate their conflicts; nor would they peacefully consent to such a structure, even if it could be shown to be workable. States act according to their power interests, and these interests are bound at times to conflict violently. Therefore, even if progress toward community and justice is possible *within* states, the relations *between* them are doomed to a permanent competition that often leads to war. However deplorable, this permanent competition remains an unavoidable reality that no amount of moral exhortation or utopian scheming can undo.[5]

Of course, what counts as "real" in contrast to "ideal," like beauty, is always in the eyes of the beholder.[6] But the Realist tradition in international political theory typically highlights the imperfectibility of human nature, inevitability of political conflict, indispensable role of states in preserving a modicum of political order and morality, and the competitive and potentially violent nature of interstate relations, as well as the improbability of far-reaching global reform, let alone the achievement of what Immanuel Kant, Realism's greatest philosophical nemesis, famously described as "perpetual peace," to be secured by a worldwide or cosmopolitan legal order.

Modern Realist theory has been espoused and sometimes updated by myriad authors. Besides Waltz and Zolo, Raymond Aron, E. H. Carr, John Herz, and Reinhold Niebuhr, as well as contemporary political scientists like Robert Gilpin and John Mearsheimer, immediately come to mind. The provocative "English School" of international relations arguably includes substantial overlap with Realism as well. Yet twentieth-century Realism's intellectually most impressive and certainly most influential figure remains the German-Jewish émigré Hans Joachim Morgenthau (1904–80), aptly described by Stanley Hoffmann as the "pope of Realism." When Hoffmann noted that "if our discipline [i.e. US international relations] has any founding father, it is Morgenthau," he was accurately describing Morgenthau's huge impact on the study of international politics, especially in postwar America.[7] One recent study has employed the latest quantitative methods to prove that Morgenthau's intellectual agenda effectively dominated the scholarly study of international relations in the United States well into the 1970s.[8] Realism remains a multisided movement, and even though contemporary Realists enjoy touting their purported advances vis-à-vis Morgenthau and other so-called "classical" (or human-nature-centered) Realists, by any account Morgenthau belongs among its intellectual giants. Not only did Morgenthau write two of postwar Realism's most influential books, *Politics Among Nations: The Struggle for Power and Peace* (1948) and *In Defense of the National Interest* (1951), but he penned about a dozen others, as well as hundreds of scholarly articles on an astonishing range of topics. Unlike most academics, Morgenthau also became a much sought-after public intellectual, and his oftentimes pithy commentaries on foreign affairs appeared regularly in popular magazines and journals, as well as newspapers like the *New York Times*, from the 1950s onwards. When he passed away in 1980, not only was Morgenthau the founding father of the dominant US approach to the study of international politics, but major public figures like Henry Kissinger described him affectionately as a teacher and mentor.[9]

When I began this study, I did so believing that Morgenthau's enormous influence called for an intellectually rigorous but accessible survey of his ideas. My original plan was to buttress the conventional view of Morgenthau as a provocative but ultimately conservative Realist thinker, highlighting the ways in which his theory sometimes fruitfully challenged contemporary cosmopolitanism, to which I am broadly sympathetic. To make a long story short, I accepted the conventional view that Morgenthau was an intriguing but institutionally backwards-looking thinker, hostile to global reform and the quest for a novel world order. The fact that a practitioner of traditional *Realpolitik* like Kissinger could consider Morgenthau his mentor did not seem surprising. The German-born Morgenthau, after all, had been influenced by political icons like Bismarck and right-wing strands in central European thinking about power politics. On this view, Morgenthau had imported this continental tradition into Anglo-American intellectual and political discourse. His theory, I initially believed, encapsulated the rare strengths as well as the abundant weaknesses of classical European power politics and *Realpolitik*.

Even today, this interpretation remains influential.[10] Morgenthau's ideas are now widely associated with a Realist tradition whose origins are located in Machiavelli, Hobbes, as well as more recent figures like Bismarck and Schmitt.[11] Morgenthau, we are regularly reminded, devalued the place of morality and even law in international affairs, and he evinced deep animosity towards the quest for novel modes of political and legal organization beyond the nation state. He disdained "moralism," "legalism," and especially "utopianism" in international thought. He merely applied a rather old-fashioned defense of the Westphalian system and traditional power politics to the novel exigencies of the cold war.

As is often the case with conventional wisdom, this view contains some valuable insights. Morgenthau was at least partially influenced by conservative central European ideas about foreign affairs, including those of the right-wing authoritarian thinker Carl Schmitt. In many ways, his reflections fit neatly under Michael Smith's concise definition of Realism. Morgenthau built on a pessimistic philosophical anthropology, underscored the irrepressibility of political conflict in human affairs, and regularly expressed skepticism about many models of global reform. At times, his reflections incorporated an undeniable nostalgia for the traditional state system, whose demise he lamented. For many understandable reasons, Realists have looked to Morgenthau for inspiration. By the same token, cosmopolitan defenders of international reform have occasionally considered him a worthy opponent, but understandably not a fruitful source for constructive thinking about the prospects of global governance.

Despite its strengths, this conventional picture is badly flawed.[12] In fairness, Morgenthau was partly to blame for the widespread tendency to simplify and even caricature his ideas. He was a blunt writer who loved rhetorical flourishes. This made his work accessible (as well as popular among university teachers putting together course readings), but it allowed readers to overlook the richness and nuances of his highly idiosyncratic international theory.[13] Unfortunately, those with a theoretical or philosophical bent have tended – in my view, incorrectly – to deem Morgenthau a simple thinker, easily pigeonholed as a relatively straightforward Realist and then comfortably removed from closer observation. In addition, the disciplinary divide, especially in the United States, between the empirical study of international relations (i.e., the subfield of IR) and political theory has exacerbated the difficulties of accurately assessing his work. Like his good friend Hannah Arendt, Morgenthau himself bridged or at least ignored the disciplinary divides of postwar political science, whereas most of his successors, especially in North America, have not. As a result, political theorists and philosophers neglect Morgenthau, accepting uncritically the conventional view of him as a "Realist IR theorist," while international relations scholars interpret him as a forerunner to (purportedly) more scientific versions of recent Realist theory. Not surprisingly, they tend to occlude Morgenthau's ambitious normative aspirations. The result is not only a badly skewed portrayal of Morgenthau, but also a significant body of literature that reproduces the artificial separation between political theory and international relations he fought energetically to overcome.[14]

Throughout his long career, Morgenthau engaged deeply and widely with some of the most important voices in political and legal theory. His intellectual socialization as a young lawyer in Weimar Germany, during which he responded powerfully to Hans Kelsen, Schmitt, and especially creative voices in left-wing legal sociology, left deep marks on his thinking. During the 1940s, as he established himself at the University of Chicago as an up-and-coming young scholar of international politics, his writings demonstrated not only a deep affinity for Max Weber and the theologian Reinhold Niebuhr, but also an impressive familiarity with the mainstream of western political and moral thought. In the final decades of his career, as a renowned public intellectual fearful of the possibility of nuclear annihilation, he turned to the German existentialist philosopher Karl Jaspers for guidance. When he anxiously pondered the fate of democracy in his adopted American home, Kelsen, Alexis de Tocqueville and perhaps Arendt served as conversational partners.

Even the conventional "Realist" label proves troublesome when applied to Morgenthau. Until the start of the Second World War, he indeed advocated a "realistic" approach to the study of international law. Yet his proposed method had little in common with Realist international theory as conventionally interpreted after 1945. Instead, it was directly shaped by left-wing legal sociology and the ideas of Morgenthau's key mentor from the late 1920s and early 1930s, the politically progressive Weimar labor lawyer and legal scholar Hugo Sinzheimer. During the 1940s and especially in major works like *Scientific Man Vs. Power Politics* (1946), Morgenthau refused to describe his own intellectual endeavors as Realist, instead subjecting Realist and proto-Realist international thinking to a scathing critique. It was really only with the publication of *In Defense of the National Interest* (1951), and then the second edition of *Politics*

Among Nations (1954), that Morgenthau finally situated his own theoretical project under the Realist rubric. Since this was Morgenthau's most influential intellectual and professional moment, it is hardly surprising that most of his readers have readily accepted the commonplace view of Morgenthau as a more-or-less conventional Realist. However, by the early 1960s, he was again emphasizing the conceptual limitations of Realism, arguing that the prospects of nuclear war required a fundamental rethinking of international relations theory capable of reintegrating the neglected insights of what Realists too often had dismissively dubbed "utopianism." Morgenthau, in fact, *defended* far-reaching reforms to the Westphalian system of states, insisting that ultimately only a world state could save humanity from the perils of nuclear war. To be sure, he always remained hostile to what he considered unduly naïve models of international reform. Yet he also openly endorsed the *functionalist* model of international reform proposed by another émigré from central Europe, David Mitrany, whose ideas were already playing a decisive role in the emergence of a novel supranational polity in Western Europe. At an early date, Morgenthau greeted the movement towards a unified Europe with enthusiasm.

Morgenthau was always an *uneasy Realist*, unsatisfied with conventional interpretations of the tradition and its intellectual forerunners and at times unsure whether his work should even be described as a contribution towards it. To his enormous credit, he at least occasionally acknowledged that Realism, as generally conceived, was poorly suited to some of the novel challenges of our times. Although this exegesis will surprise many readers, it offers not only a more accurate, but also a theoretically more fruitful, interpretation of Morgenthau's far-flung and admittedly sometimes tension-ridden writings. First, it encourages contemporary Realists to reconsider unquestioned assumptions about not only the genesis of their own ideas, but also their generally dismissive views about far-reaching international reform. Their intellectual father, I suspect, would have been justifiably alarmed by many of the morally complacent and institutionally conservative intellectual strands found among his offspring. At many junctures in this study, I defend Morgenthau against his Realist children.

Second, this reinterpretation should lead contemporary cosmopolitan advocates of international reform to reconsider Morgenthau's legacy. To be sure, some of Morgenthau's reservations about ambitious proposals for global governance relied on problematic theoretical assumptions. His theory raised at least as many new questions as it successfully answered old ones. Traumatized by the rise of Nazism and the Holocaust, Morgenthau was a deeply skeptical thinker who doubted that human beings capable of the horrors of Auschwitz were destined to produce a pacific global order in the near or even foreseeable future. Yet his own forthright defense of a world state at least points to the possibility of a fruitful dialogue between Morgenthau and contemporary cosmopolitanism. Like the most impressive voices in present-day cosmopolitanism, he underlined the necessity of linking far-reaching social and political reforms to the establishment of new modes of supranational organization.[15] A plausible version of cosmopolitanism will have to take Morgenthau's insights seriously. Of course, the intellectual divide between cosmopolitanism and Realism is likely to remain large. By the early 1960s, however, Morgenthau himself at least *suggested* the prospect of a novel international theory synthesizing Realist and cosmopolitan ideas. Even if he ultimately failed to achieve that synthesis, a closer look at Morgenthau's legacy will hopefully invite some readers to undertake it.

The organization of this volume is both thematic and roughly chronological. Biographical details have been woven into the exegesis of Morgenthau's ideas, but the emphasis remains on his thinking.[16] I also take Morgenthau's contributions as a political commentator and popular pundit seriously, believing that they illuminate many facets of his thought otherwise easily missed by focusing exclusively on a handful of major publications.

Chapter 1 situates Morgenthau in the Weimar context and especially the politically progressive and creative intellectual environment of Frankfurt, Germany, where Morgenthau started his career as a practicing lawyer and aspiring scholar of international law while working intimately with Sinzheimer, Germany's leading left-wing labor lawyer. Morgenthau's Realism always drew on diverse intellectual sources. However, I underline the progressive and sometimes even radical roots of his Realism in order to compensate for the overstated tendency in recent secondary literature to emphasize the impact of conservative and indeed reactionary writers on Morgenthau. Without properly understanding Morgenthau's initial dependence on left-wing German legal sociology, we cannot appreciate either his subsequent theoretical development or the politically progressive impulses which consistently motivated his thinking.

Chapter 2 then turns to Morgenthau's first decade in the United States, when, particularly in *Scientific Man Vs. Power Politics*, he formulated a morally demanding political ethics. With some justification, Realism is often accused of downplaying the rightful place of morality and ethics in international politics, and of closing its eyes to the pathologies of the modern nation state. These criticisms may be apt when unleashed against competing variants of Realism. Yet they misrepresent Morgenthau's ideas and the appealing moral impulses behind them. During the 1940s, Morgenthau angrily decried the contribution of the nation state to the demolition of noble yet ever more fragile universal moral values. Even if skeptical of most proposals for extending global governance, he did not celebrate the Westphalian system or the nation state. He also insisted that political actors deserving of our praise should be expected to grapple with the harsh realities of power relations on the international scene while *simultaneously* maintaining fidelity to a strict moral code. Morgenthau's political ethics from the 1940s, in my view, remains surprisingly powerful.

Chapters 3 and 4 examine Morgenthau's influential 1950s writings in which he unabashedly aligned himself with Realism. Chapter 3 argues that Morgenthau's widely discussed *In Defense of the National Interest* represented an attempt to solve internal intellectual and political puzzles generated by his ambitious version of political ethics from the 1940s. Like other commentators, I worry that Morgenthau's reflections on the national interest were problematic and even contradictory. They overstated its centrality to intelligent foreign policy, in part by generally obscuring the constitutive role of political and cultural identity in the determination of the national interest. The claim that foreign policy makers simply should follow the lodestar of the national interest was misleading. Chapter 4 thematizes Morgenthau's most widely read work, *Politics Among Nations*, focusing on how even this unambiguously Realist text nonetheless transcended conventional theoretical categories. Readers have tended to neglect the book's central argument that the admirable and unfulfilled quest for world peace necessitates the establishment of world government. In contradistinction to Realists who concede the desirability of world government but argue aggressively against its realizability, Morgenthau pointed to a number of steps to be taken in order to move humankind at least somewhat closer to its achievement. A world state could only come about by time-consuming piecemeal reforms focusing on concrete regulatory needs that nation states could not successfully tackle on their own. For good reason, however, he worried that humanity might incinerate itself in a horrific nuclear war before a novel political order could be established.

Chapters 5 and 6 examine neglected but illuminating junctures in Morgenthau's late career. During the late 1950s and 1960s, Morgenthau joined the ranks of the growing number of intellectuals deeply alarmed about the prospects of atomic warfare. Inspired by insights from existentialist philosophy, he now argued even more forcefully in favor of the desirability of supranational government, regularly insisting that the previously utopian ideal of a cosmopolitan order had become a realistic *necessity* in the atomic age. Morgenthau's analysis of the unprecedented threats posed by atomic weapons to human survival encouraged him to rethink, albeit unsuccessfully, core Realist ideas. During this period, Morgenthau also formulated many prescient – and unfairly forgotten – insights about the perils of the nuclear arms race, deterrence, and conventional nuclear strategy. For those who worry that international relations theory has yet to come to grips with the historically unprecedented possibility of humanity's self-destruction, Morgenthau has much to offer. On these matters in particular, his theory is superior to that of his Realist offspring, who condone and even celebrate nuclear proliferation to a degree that would have terrified him.

During the 1960s, Morgenthau became one of America's most prominent academic critics of the Vietnam War. His far-reaching criticisms of the Vietnam debacle did not, as some have suggested, represent an abrupt break with his earlier theorizing. On the contrary, his arguments against the war built on the sound intuition, first hinted at in *Purpose of American Politics* (1960), that an effective US foreign policy required far-reaching political and social reform at home. I interpret *Purpose of American Politics* as a struggle to circumvent the weaknesses of Morgenthau's earlier reflections on the national interest, suggesting that he had probably become aware of the limitations of his previous neglect of the role of political and cultural norms and ideals in its formulation. Especially during the 1960s, Morgenthau openly proposed "radical reform" to US democracy, whose deep ills he held responsible for the inanities of US foreign policy in Vietnam and elsewhere. He also formulated a surprisingly robust vision of democratic politics, directly linking – in sharp contradistinction to competing variants of Realism – domestic political and social conditions to the successful pursuit of the national interest.

Some US neoconservatives are now advocating a synthesis of Realism with a renewed appreciation for the distinctive moral identity of the American polity. In this view, Realism is fine as far as it goes, yet it misses the special and indeed universal appeal of American values. As Condoleezza Rice put it with her usual lack of subtlety during the 2000 US presidential campaign, "American values are universal. People want to say what they think, worship as they wish, and elect those who govern them."[17] At least on the surface, some of Morgenthau's reflections from the 1960s parallel this more recent attempt to combine Realist intuitions with an awareness of America's special moral and political traits. In stark contrast to the neoconservatives, however, Morgenthau's open acknowledgment of the core moral components of the national interest simply strengthened his resolve to advance political and social reform at home, as well as new forms of supranational government abroad. As neoconservatives refer selectively and misleadingly to Morgenthau while pursuing domestic and foreign policies inimical to everything for which he stood, we could do worse than to recall Morgenthau's own more thoughtful discussion of what he similarly described as America's universal appeal.

1

Radical roots of Realism

David Held has recently offered a concise summary of Realist international theory:

> Realism posits that the system of sovereign states is inescapably anarchic in character; and that this anarchy forces all states, in the inevitable absence of any supreme arbiter to enforce moral behavior and agreed international codes, to pursue power politics in order to attain their vital interests. This *Realpolitik* view of states has had a significant influence on both the analysis and practice of international relations, as it offers a convincing prima facie explanation of the chaos and disorder of world affairs. In this account, the modern system of nation-states is a "limiting factor" which will always thwart any attempt to conduct international relations in a manner which transcends the politics of the sovereign state.[1]

If we accept this initial definition of mainstream Realism (and I see no reason why we should not), the young Hans J. Morgenthau was no Realist. In fact, he rejected central attributes of Realism as conventionally understood, including the claim that the modern state system could not be transcended in favor of a normatively superior alternative to it.

To be sure, Morgenthau described his own intellectual project as a quest for a "realistic" theory of international relations. His central thematic preoccupations from the very outset of his intellectual career were the pathologies of existing international law and the dominant positivist approach to analyzing it. Those pathologies,

Morgenthau believed, could only be understood if we developed a hard-headed theory of international politics attuned to the dynamics of power and its tendency to distort law's underlying normative aspirations. Only a realistic assessment of power relations on the global scene could sufficiently explain the actual operations of the international legal order.

How then could one begin to develop such a theory? The young Morgenthau repeatedly called for what he characterized as a *sociological* approach to the study of international law. As late as 1940, he classified his own theoretical endeavors as a contribution to legal sociology. In formulating his version of the sociology of international law, he relied on a substantial body of interwar left-wing legal scholarship. Morgenthau's early political and legal thinking not only clashed substantially with core tenets of postwar Realist theory (including, as we will see, some elements of his own mature rendition of it), but built directly on an unabashedly left-wing model of peaceful social reform via legal means.

This interpretive claim seems surprising. How could Morgenthau's tough-minded Realism possibly claim left-wing intellectual roots? Did the Weimar left decisively shape postwar US international relations theory? This reading should appear somewhat less jolting, however, after we have examined a widely neglected yet revealing conjuncture in Morgenthau's prewar intellectual biography. Between 1928 and 1931, Morgenthau not only worked closely with one of the major voices in left-wing Weimar jurisprudence, Hugo Sinzheimer, but also developed close ties with a number of Sinzheimer's protégés, all of whom were outspoken socialist lawyers who subsequently gained prominence as left-wing political and legal scholars. Well after the destruction of the Weimar democratic left and its vision of peaceful legally based reform for which Sinzheimer and his disciples fought, Morgenthau remained close to Sinzheimer, and he always counted him among the central forces in his intellectual development. Even though Sinzheimer is a nearly forgotten figure today, of little interest except to a dwindling band of left-wing labor lawyers, his work and its impact on Morgenthau demand a careful look.[2]

Roots of Realism in the Weimar left

In May 1928, the 24-year-old Hans J. Morgenthau joined Sinzheimer in Frankfurt as a *Referendar* in his law office, as well as his assistant at the University of Frankfurt, where Sinzheimer was a member of the law faculty.[3] Morgenthau's decision to work under Sinzheimer provides early evidence of the fierce intellectual and political independence which later so often landed him in rocky waters. Despite a conservative familial background, Morgenthau opted to pursue his legal ambitions under the guidance of one of Weimar's most famous left-wing lawyers, a well-known Social Democrat (in an overwhelmingly right-wing and even authoritarian profession), a former member of the Reichstag regularly subjected to vicious antisemitic attacks for daring publicly to challenge the most retrograde features of German wartime policy,[4] and perhaps the key legal mind behind the quest for novel forms of labor and social regulation crucial to German Social Democracy's quest for a peaceful transition from capitalism to democratic socialism. Sinzheimer was the main architect of the Weimar Constitution's controversial promulgation of ambitious social rights: Article 151, for example, called for a new economic order organized in conformity with "the principles of justice," Articles 157 and 159 recognized the rights of labor and labor unions, and Article 165 established worker participation in economic decision making and pointed the way towards a restructuring of economic life in a democratic socialist direction.

Although Morgenthau apparently at first assumed he would remain with Sinzheimer in Frankfurt for a mere six months, he stayed on for nearly three eventful years, in which he practiced law alongside Sinzheimer, published his first articles as well as a book on international law, and decided to pursue an academic career as a theoretically minded legal scholar specializing in international jurisprudence. All of this occurred in the context of the decay of Weimar democracy and rise of Nazism. Sinzheimer quickly served as a confidant on a whole series of intellectual, professional, and personal matters well after Morgenthau left Frankfurt in 1932, with Morgenthau developing heartfelt admiration for someone he later described as "passionately and eloquently devoted to the legally defined interests of the underdog – the worker exploited and abused and the innocent helplessly caught in the spider web of criminal law."[5] When Morgenthau fled Europe for the United States, it was Sinzheimer who saw him off from the docks of Antwerp.[6] Nearly forty years later, when German legal scholars were organizing a conference to mark the centenary of Sinzheimer's birth, Ernst Fraenkel – another *Referendar* of Sinzheimer's who went on to an illustrious career as a political scientist in postwar Germany – wrote to Sinzheimer's daughter to tell her that the conference organizers hoped to attract Morgenthau to participate, as a prominent member of what he dubbed the "Sinzheimer School."[7]

Morgenthau's 1978 autobiographical reminiscences suggest that the years in Frankfurt represented an intellectual liberation from the generally stultifying atmosphere of the German schools and universities he previously had attended. He recounted the lively intellectual climate of Weimar-era Frankfurt, where religious-minded socialists like Paul Tillich argued with Sinzheimer, Karl Mannheim was lecturing on sociology,[8] and Marx and Freud were heatedly discussed at the Institute for Social Research (where Sinzheimer occasionally lectured). In addition, he became "life-long friends" with "a group of distinguished people [who] worked in that [i.e., Sinzheimer's] office" – including Fraenkel, as well as Franz L. Neumann and Otto Kahn Freund – all of whom similarly served as Sinzheimer's *Referendar* and later became prominent leftist scholars.[9] One can imagine Morgenthau amid this group of talented young lawyers heatedly discussing the future of Weimar democracy and its special status as a political and social order transitionally situated, or so Sinzheimer and his left-wing students believed, "between capitalism and socialism."[10] A 1934 letter from Morgenthau to Sinzheimer, who as a famous Jewish socialist was forced to flee Germany for Holland, offers a vivid statement of the significance of Sinzheimer's mentorship. After explaining to Sinzheimer that he had failed to respond to his letters only because they never made it to Geneva, where Morgenthau spent his first years in exile, he notes:

> [h]ad I been so inclined, I could have broken off written relations, but never the inner relations existing between us, which can never be severed. For I was not only your employee. I also breathed the intellectual and moral air that emanated from you. Giving up the ties that such an influence creates would mean giving up my own personality.[11]

Morgenthau's autobiographical comments also reveal what lessons he later drew from the tragic figure of Sinzheimer, who spent his best years trying to exploit the new legal possibilities for social reform provided by the Weimar Constitution, before being forced to leave his homeland. Morgenthau retrospectively observed that the courtroom battles they fought together for the economically and socially disadvantaged "were marginal to the crucial issues with which society had to come to terms. What was decisive was not the merits of different legal interpretations but the distribution of political power." Notwithstanding Sinzheimer's lawyerly brilliance and the fact that the relatively progressive language of the Weimar Constitution meant that left-wing lawyers could often provide effective justifications for their views in court, he and his associates operated in the context of a "political system that had stacked the cards against him and his cause."[12] Not surprisingly, these experiences left Morgenthau with a deep skepticism about the transformative possibilities of law in the context of profound social antagonisms and deep inequalities in power. That skepticism later served as a fundament of Morgenthau's *postwar* version of Realism. The *young* Morgenthau, however, seems to have shared his teacher's faith in the possibility of taming inequality by legal means.

Sinzheimer's multifaceted writings defy easy summary, yet their basic starting point was straightforward enough.[13] Like many on the left, Sinzheimer thematized the tension between *formal legal freedom and equality* and the *social or empirical reality of dependence and inequality* in the capitalist workplace. From the perspective of the law, the laborer and entrepreneur face each other on formally free and equal terms. In social and economic reality, however, this relationship is plagued by dependency and structural inequality. In contrast to those on the orthodox left who took this gap as evidence for the bankruptcy of bourgeois formal law, Sinzheimer considered the tension potentially productive. To be sure, the starting point for social and legal reform required the open recognition of the ideological and mystifying role performed by legal devices in the context of a deeply unjust social and economic status quo. Yet this acknowledgment need not lead to a one-sided debunking of the law. The normative promise of modern law and its implicit commitment to defensible ideals of freedom and equality in fact provided immanent possibilities for overcoming this troubling gap.

Despite the failure of most elected parliaments before the First World War to recognize the special needs of labor, Sinzheimer observed, decisive steps were already being taken towards developing a distinctive body of what he described as *autonomous* labor regulation. Even though labor in Germany still lacked a statutory, let alone constitutional, basis for its demands, a growing union movement was forcing employers to reach novel agreements concerning workplace conditions, wages, and a host of related matters. Organized social groups, in short, were independently developing a system of self-regulation in response to novel social trends. The task at hand, Sinzheimer argued, was not only to advance this process to the advantage of labor, but also to make sure that it possessed a sufficiently sturdy legal and constitutional framework. Any sensible system of labor law had to concede that decision making between labor and capital should take place in a relatively decentralized matter; many points of conflict between labor and capital were best tackled by specialized agreements between particular groups of employers and employees. However, statutory and constitutional legislation could successfully complement this process of autonomous decision making: well-designed legal and constitutional guarantees for the rights of labor, as well as new constitutionally based modes of both decentralized (i.e., workplace-centered) and centralized worker representation in economic decision making, could firmly ground a legally viable as well as egalitarian system of labor regulation to a greater extent than autonomous self-regulation between employers and employees would prove able to achieve.

Sinzheimer defended an ambitious model of works councils as well as a national "economic council" which would allow for substantial labor participation in overseeing the economy. In contrast to those inspired by the Soviet experience, he envisioned new institutional sites for worker participation as a *complement* to the main instruments of liberal democratic decision making. A political system dominated solely by worker soviets, he predicted, in opposition to the communist left, necessarily contained anti-democratic and authoritarian implications. If Germany instead could move in the direction of the model he proposed, the factual power advantages typically enjoyed by capital could be effectively checked and labor's dependent status corrected. The gap between formal legal freedom and equality and the harsh realities of capitalism could be reduced and ultimately overcome without abandoning the lasting normative achievements of modern law. Amid the new "class balance between labor and the bourgeoisie" produced by the German Revolution of 1918, Sinzheimer apparently hoped, the right moment had come for aggressively advancing this reform agenda.[14]

In hindsight, Sinzheimer's main intellectual achievements are probably twofold. First, he played a major role on the European continent in establishing labor law both as a distinctive body of law and as an object of legitimate scholarly interest. Previously, labor relations had been seen as falling under the general sphere of private law and thus, in principle, no different from other arenas of the law regulating private relations between legally equal and free subjects.

Sinzheimer grasped that labor was a special commodity because it "has no other container than human flesh and blood" and thus could not be conflated with a piece of real estate, for example, or other forms of property.[15] Because labor was an unusual commodity, labor law correspondingly possessed a special status within the legal order as a whole: it represented the very centerpiece of a social democratic reform project, whose main function was the liberation of wage labor from the illegitimate tutelage of capital.

Second, Sinzheimer was an early proponent of the sociology of law, which he conceptualized in a socially critical fashion. Influenced by Karl Marx and Max Weber, as well as the Austro-Marxist Karl Renner, Sinzheimer insisted that German legal scholarship should broaden its horizons beyond a traditional focus on the study and exegesis of positive law: a deeper understanding of the role of social factors in law's operations was called for. Only a rigorous empirical or sociological examination of the law could provide a necessary understanding of its social context and, in particular, the relationship between law and the capitalist workplace. As Sinzheimer learned from Renner, legal norms might remain formally unchanged, yet suddenly serve fundamentally novel social functions.[16] A gap could always emerge between a formal rule and the "real" rule of law. Sinzheimer's own research in labor law suggested that changing social conditions might lead to new autonomous forms of legal self-regulation. Worried that the decisive "problem of the 'transformation' of social changes into new norms" had been neglected, Sinzheimer stressed how social "reality influences the conceptual groupings of existing norms," as well as how norms emerge spontaneously in response to social change.[17] The sociology of law called for an analysis of the fundamentally dynamic or historical character of the nexus between legal norms and reality.[18]

This embrace of the sociology of law, however, by no means implied discarding conventional legal methods and ideals altogether. Sinzheimer remained faithful to an array of traditional legal ideals and approaches. A sociological approach to law supplemented but did not replace a relatively conventional view of the proper study and interpretation of the law. Sinzheimer apparently was a skilled and even eloquent "lawyer's lawyer," who not only was an agile courtroom performer, but also insisted that his legal apprentices undergo a rigorous schooling in the intricacies of the black letter of the law and relatively traditional positivistic ideas about legal interpretation, while sharing with them his own anxieties about the dangers of excessive judicial and administrative discretion.[19] Sinzheimer accurately observed that in the Weimar context, where right-wing authoritarians possessed extensive influence over the judiciary and state bureaucracy, such discretion too often served the cause of reaction by increasing the disproportionate influence of political groups hostile to progressive social legislation.[20]

Morgenthau and Sinzheimer

In a short unpublished notice from 1935 written appreciatively in honor of Sinzheimer's sixtieth birthday, Morgenthau accurately summarized the core intuition underlying his teacher's theory: "at its base is the legal theoretical insight that the abstract concepts of freely and equally contracting persons that dominate German civil law no longer accord with the changed structure of capitalist society," and, consequently, such legal forms must fail, given the real-life "dependence of the industrial worker." As a result, new legal forms must be established in order to realize meaningful freedom and equality for the working classes. Morgenthau noted that Sinzheimer had long been fascinated by the tension between the "abstract individualism of bourgeois law" and the "realistic, that is, social relations-oriented" facts of legal experience.[21]

Morgenthau's brief summary of Sinzheimer's project represents a useful starting point for making sense of his *own* prewar theoretical contributions.

In 1929, the 25-year-old Morgenthau published his first book, based on his dissertation, devoted to determining the necessary limits of judicial and arbitral functions in international law.[22] Entitled *Die internationale Rechtspflege, ihr Wesen und ihre Grenzen* ("The Nature and Limits of the Judicial Function in International Law"), its central preoccupation was the distinction between two varieties of international conflict: *disputes* ("Streitigkeiten") could normally be resolved by international legal devices such as courts and arbitration boards, whereas *tensions* ("Spannungen") eluded effective legal resolution. Tensions expressed fundamental political divisions possessing an especially *intense* and explosive character. Consequently, it was naïve and potentially counterproductive to expect them to be effectively resolved by judicial or arbitral devices. Tensions allowed to masquerade as disputes, Morgenthau suggested, represented a disruptive force in international law. To assert that tensions – for example, the potentially explosive conflict between France and Germany during the 1920s concerning the occupation of the Rheinland – could be easily resolved by judicial or arbitral devices was illusory. When such attempts were pursued, the intensity of the political conflict at hand simply underwent augmentation, and judicial or arbitral devices served alien and counterproductive goals transcending their necessary limits.

A close reading of the text reveals Sinzheimer's indelible impact. First, the volume's basic method was directly inspired by the view that legal scholarship should pay attention to the gap between law and empirical or social reality. According to Morgenthau, traditional dogmatic and positivistic legal analysis was incapable of making sense of the phenomenon of international tensions because it ignored their roots in the misfit between the normative structure of law and the real social conditions of international politics. The fundamental dilemma of international law, he argued, was its *static* character. While domestic law rested on an elastic normative framework by means of which law could be readjusted (e.g. by means of new legislation) in accordance with changing social realities, international law codified the political status quo without offering reliable norm-based legal instruments by which affected parties could efficiently recalibrate legal devices in accordance with changed real-life conditions: "The development of international law stopped at precisely that juncture where the most fundamental function of a legal system commences" (*IRWG*, 75).[23] International law directly expressed the configuration of social and political relations which obtained when the relevant norms were promulgated. Politically explosive tensions emerged as a direct result of the gap between the static (and inevitably anachronistic) structure of international law and ubiquitous changes in real social conditions. In this view, non-justiciable political tensions were most likely to appear when shifts in social relations conflicted dramatically with international law.

Because international law had yet to develop a flexible framework by means of which alterations in social relations could be given proper legal form, it remained an underdeveloped normative system prone to tensions capable of culminating in interstate violence. How else might those states hoping to change the international status quo do so, in light of the fact that the path of peaceful legal evolution had been closed to them? Demand for change was inevitable given both the manifest inequalities of international politics and the dynamic character of social and political reality. Why should weaker states be expected to abide for all eternity by norms privileging the great powers? In the domestic setting, legal systems failing to offer meaningful possibilities for peaceful legal adaptation faced the specter of revolution. Rising social groups might seek to overthrow ruling groups by force if necessary. Because static law was commonplace in international relations, however, the possibility of violent upheaval was vastly more pronounced there.

Significantly, the young Morgenthau refused to embrace the conclusion that explosive tensions constituted an irrepressible necessity in international politics. On the contrary, he argued that international law should be transformed into a dynamic system which, like its domestic corollary, would allow for significant adjustments to power relations by peaceful legal means. Morgenthau admitted that this demand raised a host of difficult questions. Nonetheless, his 1929 book concluded with a heated polemic against those who deemed reform impossible, dismissing their views as ahistorical and "metaphysical" (*IRWG*, 148). More recent Realism's deep hostility to supposedly "idealistic" attempts to reorganize the interstate system was not only absent here, but the young Morgenthau in fact ridiculed opponents of fundamental global reform.

Die internationale Rechtspflege, ihr Wesen und ihre Grenzen creatively applied Sinzheimer's chief programmatic insights to the international field. Like Sinzheimer, Morgenthau complemented doctrinal legal analysis with a sociological or realistic account of law. He also focused on an attribute of social reality that so fascinated Sinzheimer and his leftist disciples: the fact of inequality – in this case, between and among states – ultimately took center stage. The first and most elementary sense in which Morgenthau's thinking underscored the virtues of realistic analysis reproduced Sinzheimer's intuition that legal analysis must be supplemented by an empirical or sociological analysis of the power inequalities in which law operates. Sinzheimer's theory began with the gap between formal legal ideals of freedom and equality and the harsh social facts of inequality and dependence in the workplace. In a conceptually analogous vein, Morgenthau contrasted the abstract legal ideals of international law (including the doctrine that each state is legally sovereign and equal) to the stark realities of the international arena, where the great powers typically dominated.[24]

The same argumentative move is found in a provocative 1932 survey of German legal thought since the nineteenth century, where Morgenthau accused the mainstream of German legal thought of disingenuously fleeing the harsh realities of political life. In the essay, Morgenthau exhibited deep respect for legal positivism and especially the work of Hans Kelsen, while nonetheless criticizing Kelsen's positivism for allegedly closing its eyes to the necessity of a hard-headed realistic or sociological account of international law capable of forthrightly analyzing real-life power relations. Revealingly, he emphatically distinguished his "realistic" sociological approach from Bismarckian power politics, which he openly criticized.[25] In a short 1933 article for a Zurich newspaper, Morgenthau pointed out that the gap between legal concepts and social reality was *greatest* in the international sphere, concluding that the sociological or realistic approach was likely to prove most fruitful there: Sinzheimer's method was especially suited to the analysis of international law since its norms tended to exhibit an even greater distance from the dynamics of social reality than those at the national level.[26]

Echoing Sinzheimer, Morgenthau's Weimar-era work also repeatedly highlighted what his left-wing lawyer friends described as the ideological functions of formal law amid real-life inequality.[27] Yet this by no means forced him to overlook the normative potential of formal law, notwithstanding his acknowledgment of the deep pathologies of existing international law. In his 1929 volume, for example, Morgenthau extended Sinzheimer's legalistic reformism to the international sphere. Just as Sinzheimer had hoped that legal reality might be successfully recalibrated in accordance with the altered social realities of present-day capitalism, Morgenthau hinted at the possibility of a "relatively just and for all parties valid" system of international law meshing better with changing social relations in the international arena (*IRWG*, 150). One clear implication of this proposal was that a reformed international legal system might permit rising states, against which the great powers have likely stacked the legal deck, to change the international order by peaceful means. Law, it seems, could play a constructive role in allowing for peaceful shifts in power relations. Just as Sinzheimer's legal reformism aimed to render violent revolution unnecessary on the domestic front, so too might a new international legal order minimize the dangers of interstate violence.

A major conceptual difference nonetheless separated Morgenthau and his Weimar writings from Sinzheimer and his left-wing pupils: Morgenthau always kept a safe distance from Marxism's imposing theoretical rudiments. Perhaps his main object of scholarly interest, interstate relations, struck him as less amenable to Marxist analysis than the capitalist workplace, on which his legal colleagues had fastened their scholarly attention. In any event, we can now better understand precisely what Morgenthau meant when in 1978 he admitted that, under Sinzheimer's guidance, he "learned a great deal from Marx," even though he never could "abide that particular type of Marxist who considers Marxism to be a closed intellectual system."[28] Even though Morgenthau never endorsed Marxist ideas, the fundamental structure of his early thinking owed much to Sinzheimer's unorthodox Marxist-inspired analysis of the gap between legal and social reality.

Two additional features of Morgenthau's 1929 study closely followed Sinzheimer. First, it reproduced Morgenthau's mentor's legalistic instincts and anxieties about judicial discretion, suggesting that open-ended legal norms which invited broad discretion in the international arena overlapped with the phenomenon of tensions. When tackled by means of inappropriate judicial devices, politically explosive conflicts necessarily undermined the integrity of the law: fundamental conflicts were covered up by vague legal clauses, and judicial rulings lacked the objectivity which they possessed during the normal operations of adjudication.[29] To the extent that Morgenthau's argument implied that reform might reduce the likelihood of dangerous international tensions, it held out the possibility of actually strengthening traditional legal virtues (e.g. generality and regularity) in the international arena.[30] In Morgenthau's theory, as in his mentor's, a realistic or sociological analysis of power complemented a model of the rule of law which remained, in crucial respects, relatively conventional.

Second, Morgenthau endorsed Sinzheimer's view that dynamic or temporal factors deserved a central role in the realist or sociological analysis of law. A core programmatic attribute not only of his book, but of *all* Morgenthau's Weimar-era writings, was his demand for a dynamic or flexible international law better adjusted to changing social and political conditions. In 1929, he also published his first two articles, an appreciative account of the place of Gustav Stresemann in German foreign policy, as well as a short critical report on the annual meeting of German international lawyers, both appearing in a left-wing legal journal, *Die Justiz*, co-edited by Sinzheimer. In the Stresemann essay, Morgenthau praised the former German Foreign Minister for breaking with the widespread hostility among his countrymen to international law, while simultaneously refusing to succumb to naïve ideas about international law blind to the real conditions under which it operates. In effect, Morgenthau enlisted Stresemann as an ally in his own defense of an alternative international order: Stresemann's political acumen derived from an appreciation of the fact that international law could only successfully serve pacific purposes if it were to become a dynamic normative system attuned to the dictates of political and social change.[31] Here again, Morgenthau criticized the widespread faith in power politics ("Machtpolitik") among his fellow Germans, bluntly asserting that the very idea of *Realpolitik* was a worthless tautology since "all politics is 'real' if it is politics at all."[32] In his report on the meeting of German international lawyers, he criticized their deliberations for failing to illuminate what he self-confidently described as the core issue of the entire field of international law, namely the need for a major restructuring so as to heighten its dynamic character.[33]

In light of the mature Morgenthau's relative skepticism about the transformative power of international law, his early demands for a reformed international legal order inevitably seem surprising. Nonetheless, it would be mistaken to dismiss them as nothing more than a sin of youth, a momentary lapse of good judgment, immediately jettisoned for purportedly sounder and more familiar ideas associated with orthodox variants of Realism. His reformist ideas also make an appearance in a lengthy unpublished manuscript from 1931, where Morgenthau repeated his view that the gap between static international law and the changing social conditions of the international arena represented the main source of explosive conflict, and that such conflicts could only be warded off by establishing a dynamic legal system. In fact, that manuscript closed by insisting on the necessity of tying major changes in international law to far-reaching alterations to the economic order. Only a new economic system, Morgenthau declared during the darkest days of the Great Depression, could counteract the self-destructive enthusiasm for warfare which had resulted in so many millions suffering the horrors of the First World War. Unless new possibilities for creative and self-affirming activity were provided in everyday life, warfare would disastrously continue to seem like an attractive escape from the debilitating and depersonalizing economic status quo. Echoing his Frankfurt friends' radical views, Morgenthau declared that:

[i]n the economic sphere the change in conditions must be total. Because of modern wage slavery; because of the closing of every opportunity for the masses to prove themselves and improve their station according to regular methods; because of the impossibility for the overwhelming majority of men to be able to complete something

responsibly and by full employment of their personality about which they might say, here is my achievement, my work; because of the degradation of the human being to an object . . . because of their irrevocable damnation to a depersonalized machine . . . Because of these conditions a leaden and tired hopelessness has emerged, the true sister to an explosive desperation, which sees war as a savior, as a great uplifting force. To change this situation and to bring about a renewal is a task which the best men of our times have taken upon themselves as their fate.[34]

Although Morgenthau never shared his Frankfurt colleagues' enthusiasm for Marx, he sympathized with their desire for far-reaching social and economic reform. He also shared their faith in the possibility of significant legal reform as a way of advancing social change. By transplanting the Weimar democratic left's legal reformism to the global arena, Morgenthau anticipated the possibility of major shifts in the traditional European state system and a clear break with the tradition of *Realpolitik* with which it had been linked for centuries.

Morgenthau's sociological functionalism

Along with Sinzheimer and the other socialist Jewish lawyers to whom he was closely linked in Frankfurt, Morgenthau was forced to flee Germany with the rise of Nazism. His first stop was Geneva, where he both deepened his critique of orthodox international law and explored in detail the philosophical intricacies of Kelsen, its most important interwar theoretician. He then spent a brief but eventful period in Madrid, before finally making his way to the United States in 1937, initially gaining a position at Kansas City University. Within a mere five years, Morgenthau had witnessed at close hand the destruction of *two* new European republics, their replacement by closely allied but competing models of right-wing dictatorship, the promulgation of vicious anti-semitic legislation, the Spanish Civil War, and first-hand harassment by Nazi agents planted in his classroom. Since Geneva also served as headquarters for the League of Nations, Morgenthau was able to gain an intimate grasp of its practical impotence as the interwar system of international law collapsed in the early and mid-1930s.[35]

Despite these traumatic events, Morgenthau's intellectual project remained fundamentally congruent with his pre-1933 writings. As late as 1940, Morgenthau conceived of his realistic alternative to mainstream international law primarily as a contribution to the sociology of law. This becomes clear when we turn to a pivotal 1940 article, "Positivism, Functionalism, and International Law" ("PFIL"), aptly described by the international lawyer Francis Anthony Boyle as "one of the most stimulating ever published in the *American Journal of International Law*" (hereafter *AJIL*). As Boyle points out, the essay delineated an impressive research program pretty much abandoned by Morgenthau after "the horrors of World War II."[36] Once again, its chief arguments mesh uneasily with mainstream postwar Realism.

In the *AJIL* essay, Morgenthau described his own method as a variety of *functionalist* analysis. Yet Morgenthau's employment of the term "functionalism" entailed no rejection of what since 1929 he had consistently characterized as an identifiably realistic or sociological alternative to mainstream international law: " 'realist' jurisprudence is, in truth, 'functional' jurisprudence" ("PFIL," 274). Here as well, Morgenthau used the terms "realist" and "sociological" interchangeably ("PFIL," 264). But he now avoided the term "realist" because of its potentially misleading connotations: Morgenthau worried that it might encourage US readers to place him in the camp of American Legal Realism, or, even worse, to infer an association with Nazi ideologues who were also advocating a "realistic" view of law. Even though Morgenthau shared the Legal Realists' longstanding concern that orthodox jurisprudence ignored the sociological context of legal action, they tended to go further in discounting fundaments of the modern legal tradition and rule of law. Morgenthau wanted to explain why the realities of power at the international level undermined key features of the rule of law, but he refused – probably to his credit – to embrace the deep legal skepticism soon associated with Legal Realism.

The self-characterization "functionalist" in fact aptly captured a constitutive feature of Morgenthau's prewar intellectual project. For him, the relationship between law and social reality was fundamentally tension-ridden: because social relations were dynamic and ever-changing, law always lagged behind social change. The constantly altering contours of modern social life inevitably posed deep challenges to the quest for stability and predictability in the law. Especially in the international arena, where we lack what Morgenthau since 1929 had described as dynamic devices for adjusting law to evolving social relations, the gap between legal and social reality proved particularly troublesome. While domestic law typically possessed a flexible normative-legal framework by means of which legal relations were updated in accordance with altered social needs (i.e., new legislation), international law codified the political and social status quo without typically creating effective mechanisms for revision. As he had tried to show in *Die internationale Rechtspflege, ihr Wesen und ihre Grenzen*, explosive conflicts emerged in international politics precisely because of the structural misfit between the relatively static character of international law and the unavoidably dynamic contours of social existence. A less dramatic but no less urgent consequence of this misfit was that the normative framework of international law often appeared formally unchanged, while in reality it served novel political and social *functions*. Because formal alterations to international law were difficult to achieve, social actors outfitted standing rules with new functions as a way of establishing some rough equilibrium between law and social reality. Particularly in the international arena, legal rules tended to serve new purposes or gain unexpected meanings rarely anticipated by those who originally engineered them:

> Thus, one is able, for instance, to distinguish three different periods in the history of the Treaty of Locarno. Those three periods are characterized by three significant changes in the normative content of the rules, resulting from changes in the political [or social] context, although the wording of the rules remained unchanged. The Covenant of the League of Nations, as a whole, as well as particular provisions . . . have been submitted to similar modifications as a result of factual sociological developments and not of legislative changes. ("PFIL," 271)

Not coincidentally, this understanding of functionalism was commonplace among the left-wing Frankfurt legal sociologists who influenced the young Morgenthau.[37]

The 1940 *AJIL* essay failed to endorse many of the familiar features of Realism as it was commonly conceived, especially after 1945. To be sure, it acknowledged the frailties of certain ambitious proposals for reform at the international level. Yet nothing in its core arguments excluded the possibility of fundamental legal reform. In fact, Morgenthau's sociological method, in which *social change* occupied a preeminent analytic and explanatory role, clearly deviated from the standard Realist tendency to downplay both the desirability and feasibility of fundamental reform to the international system. Still writing in 1940 as a reform-minded lawyer, albeit one who clearly believed that the admirable quest to minimize international violence by legal means could best be advanced by breaking with legal orthodoxy, Morgenthau offered a surprisingly sympathetic account of many of its features. His main target was legal positivism and by no means international law or reform *in toto*. Even though the article began with the characteristically polemical comment that "great humanitarians and shrewd politicians [who] endeavored to reorganize the relations between states" were akin to "sorcerers of primitive ages" who "exorcise social evils by the indefatigable repetition of magic formulae," Morgenthau still paid heed to modern public international law's fundamental quest for peace ("PFIL," 260). His central point was only that a realistic or sociological interpretation of international law could better accomplish that goal than legal positivism, whose intellectual pathologies, he believed, plagued the real-life operations of the interwar international order.

With some justification, Morgenthau accused positivists like Kelsen of mapping out a distorted picture of legal reality, in which law was artificially separated, on the one hand, from ethics and mores, and, on the other hand, from the factual realities of social power. In his appropriately labeled "pure theory of law," Kelsen had argued that if the autonomy of law were to be appropriately theorized, legal analysis would have to break radically with ethics and politics, on one side, and the social sciences, on the other. Too often, Kelsen posited, legal science had been subordinated to problematic moral theories and crude modes of social analysis so as to transform it into a cheap weapon for competing political ideologies.[38] Although mindful of the value of this basic methodological move, Morgenthau argued that it was overstated, and the *AJIL* essay built on a massive unpublished 1934 manuscript devoted to Kelsen's theory, "The Reality of Norms," in order to relativize the strict positivist divisions between law and morality, on one side, and law and social reality, on the other side.[39] Without collapsing law into morality or ethics, or disfiguring law's significance as a relatively independent normative system, a realistic analysis recognized two crucial points. First, law was indeed separate from morality and ethics, yet "the intelligibility of any legal system depends upon the recognition of . . . fundamental principles which constitute the ethical substance of the legal system" ("PFIL," 268).[40] Second, the actual operations of law could only be fully understood "within the sociological context of economic interests, social tensions, and aspirations for power," or, alternately, "the social sphere, comprehending the psychological, political, and economic fields" ("PFIL," 269, 283). Not only should a realistic study of international law take heed of the basic moral ideals motivating international law, but it also had to highlight the complex ways in which law as a system of norms interacted with a constantly changing environment constituted by antagonistic interests. Only this approach, Morgenthau deduced, could explain the actual workings of international law and help guide reform.

The result was Morgenthau's embrace of what we might describe as *a normatively minded critical sociology of international law*. This standpoint maintained the characteristically neo-Kantian tension between *Sein* ("is") and *Sollen* ("ought"), but, in some contrast to strict neo-Kantians like Kelsen, refused to hypostasize that tension. By doing so, Morgenthau hoped, his theory could successfully stress the normative core of international law without reducing legal science to the pursuit of pie-in-the-sky utopian schemes. It also might avoid the opposite danger of integrating an awareness of the harsh social realities of international political life at the price of interpreting law – along the lines of crude Marxism or reductive versions of legal sociology – as a mere superstructural plaything of the dominant political and social forces.

The *AJIL* article again highlighted the fundamentally sociological or social-scientific character of this approach. International legal practice and science remained underdeveloped because they analyzed legal reality in isolation from the social conditions of international political life:

> The precepts of international law need not only to be interpreted in the light of the ideals . . . which are their basis. They need also to be seen within the sociological context of economic interests, social tensions, and aspirations for power, which are the motivating force in the international field, and which give rise to the factual situations forming the raw material for regulation by international law. ("PFIL," 269)

While "[n]obody would ever endeavor to grasp the legal meaning of economic legislation without making economic interests and conflicts part of their reasoning," international lawyers consistently obfuscated the decisive role of social power relations at the global level. To be sure, even at the domestic level, one still encountered remnants of a "decadent [positivist] legal science" occluding legal reality by ignoring the ways in which "new economic and social needs" altered the functions played by seemingly unchanged legal rules ("PFIL," 270). This decadence was both pervasive and potentially more destructive at the international level, however. At the domestic level, the state "has developed not only an overwhelming power apparatus, but also highly refined mechanisms of legislative and judicial readjustment, which lead the social forces into certain channels without disrupting the legal and social continuity" ("PFIL," 275). Under optimal conditions, national law achieved a "temporarily stabilized society where there was approximately no tension between law and sociological context" ("PFIL," 272). Because the international arena still lacked a system of common overarching sovereignty, however, it remained unable either to calibrate law in accordance with social life, or, alternately, to funnel social change into existing legal channels. When struggles between rising states and beneficiaries of the legal status quo took place, the lack of a common sovereign meant that too often a ruthless and potentially violent "competitive contest for power will determine the victorious social force, and the change of the existing legal order will be decided, not through a legal procedure . . . but through a conflagration of conflicting social forces which challenge the legal order as a whole" ("PFIL," 275–6).

Even when conflict occurred *within* the confines of an unchanged legal order, legal positivism misconstrued this process because its exclusion of social factors from the proper domain of legal science kept it from grasping how apparently constant forms of law experienced far-reaching "modifications as a result of factual sociological changes." Changing social and political conditions led even seemingly clear norms to take on evolving and potentially competing functions. The *AJIL* essay concluded with a call for international lawyers to reconsider their fidelity to conventional notions of legal interpretation. At least in the international arena, traditional modes of interpretation were poorly equipped to deal with "the peculiar relationship between social forces and rules of international law" since they ignored how an unmodified legal norm could easily perform a diversity of changing political and social functions ("PFIL," 282). To be sure, the same dilemma could arise in the domestic arena. Nonetheless, jurists there for the most part might ignore it without violating the integrity of the legal order: the existence of a sovereign state typically mitigated extreme disjunctures between legal and social reality. In the international realm, however, where no single sovereign exists and the free interplay of political and social power determines the authoritative meaning of legal material, rules underwent dramatic functional changes even within a relatively short period of time. Traditional interpretive devices were likely to founder because the real meaning of an international treaty was obscured by its language: "it is only from the social context that the treaty will receive its meaning" ("PFIL," 282).

Two attributes of Morgenthau's *AJIL* article deserve closer scrutiny. In contrast to more recent versions of legal sociology or socio-legal studies, his approach took law's underlying moral and normative aspirations seriously; its normative starting point remained modern international law's *own* underlying quest to minimize violent conflict. The young Morgenthau offered an immanent critique of modern international law which aimed to preserve its valuable normative aspirations while insisting that they could only be realized in novel ways.[41] Recall as well that Morgenthau called for the investigation of "the sociological context of economic interests, social tensions, and aspirations for power," or, in a related formulation, "the social sphere, comprehending the psychological, political, and economic fields." His comments here are revealing because they point to a deep ambiguity at the core of his initial interpretation of the realistic or sociological approach to international law: *which* social facts were most important for understanding power and inequality in the international arena? Morgenthau's answer to this question tended to be imprecise: it included economic interests *as well as* political, social, and even – as we will see – especially psychological forces. In sharp contrast to his left-wing Weimar friends, Morgenthau typically neglected economic forces as a causal factor. In principle, however, the earliest rendition of Morgenthau's Realism implied the necessity of a *broad* range of empirical analyses of power and inequality at the international level. Their shared goal would have been to provide a rigorous analysis of those social facts shaping international law, with an eye, at least in Morgenthau's early writings, towards modifying them for the sake of reform.

Justin Rosenberg's recent claim that Realism founders because it perceives "that the modern state seeks to mobilize the economy, but not that the economy is also part of a transnational whole which produces important *political* effects independently of the agency of the state"[42] is thus only partially applicable in the case of the young Morgenthau. To be sure, Morgenthau never managed to offer a systematic analysis of the operations of the global political economy and its wide-ranging implications for international law. Yet his prewar writings inferred the necessity of a systematic analysis of every form of social power shaping the operations of international law. Moreover, the crucial subtext of his early writings was that *legal, political, and social reform at the global level must go hand-in-hand.* The lack of a common sovereign constituted the most obvious source of many of the irrationalities of the existing international order. Pathologies resulting from its decentralized enforcement were aggrandized by vast inequalities which made a mockery of even modest forms of international law. Amid power inequalities, the potentially equalizing and protective functions of law risked taking a backseat to its exploitation by the great powers. Consequently, international law too often operated as an additional instrument for the powerful rather than as a meaningful check on them. For this reason, the young Morgenthau's animus by the late 1930s was chiefly directed, as noted, against positivists like Kelsen who, despite their own socially reformist impulses, supposedly allowed legal analysts to ignore the concrete political and social conditions undermining international law's operations. For Morgenthau, positivism blinded legal scholarship and reform-minded lawyers to power inequalities that worked to convert normatively attractive modes of general law into weapons of the handful of great powers who typically interpreted and enforced them.

Morgenthau's hostility to positivism, however, should not be taken as evidence that by 1940 he had already endorsed an institutionally conservative vision foreclosed to the possibility of fundamental reforms to the international order. As he had initially theorized in 1929, only a system of international law could provide, as domestic systems of law had, elastic legal mechanisms suited to the exigencies of social change. His principled commitment to a critical sociological theory of international law still held open the possibility of major reforms to the international order. To be sure, Morgenthau was already badly scarred by the political cataclysms of the 1930s. By 1940 he seemed somewhat more skeptical of the reformist legal ideas he had absorbed in Weimar-era Frankfurt: his polemical tone suggests a heightened impatience with reform models insensitive to the realities of power relations in the international arena. When *Scientific Man Vs. Power Politics* (1946) subsequently mocked the legalistic liberal faith "that man is able to legislate at will, that is, to realize through the means of law whatever aims he pursues," adding that this illusion was "shared even by contemporary Marxian practice," Morgenthau was probably engaging in self-criticism to a greater extent than was apparent to English-speaking readers unfamiliar with his earlier writings (*SM,*

116–17). Although Morgenthau had always criticized positivist visions of international reform, like his left-wing colleagues in Sinzheimer's law office, he had previously hoped for constructive legal reforms that might better funnel social change.

The terrible events of the 1930s and 1940s surely played a crucial role in Morgenthau's heightened skepticism. Yet immanent theoretical sources can be identified as well.

The concept of the political and the embrace of philosophical anthropology

Although committed to a sociologically minded analysis of international law shaped by left-wing Weimar legal thought, the young Morgenthau turned early on to the work of the right-wing authoritarian thinker Carl Schmitt in order to develop his realistic or sociological approach.[43] Morgenthau's precocious fascination with Schmitt, though at first glance surprising, is by no means difficult to fathom. Other members of the Sinzheimer School – including Ernst Fraenkel and Franz Neumann – similarly pursued a close and at times surprisingly sympathetic examination of Schmitt's work during the 1930s. Like Morgenthau, they vociferously criticized his extreme right-wing political preferences while acknowledging that Schmitt offered the outlines of a realistic (i.e., power-oriented) vision of politics too often missing from mainstream jurisprudence and legal positivism. Morgenthau's early writings highlighted deep flaws in Schmitt's thinking, not only denouncing his political choices but ultimately describing his theory as fundamentally unsound. Yet he credited Schmitt with acknowledging the need for precisely that realistic account of power relations in the international arena which legal orthodoxy had failed to deliver. Like Morgenthau, Schmitt had long been skeptical of mainstream international law, which he analogously interpreted as veiling the brutal realities of inequality at the international level. Morgenthau initially appears to have identified Schmitt's theory, despite its weaknesses and troublesome political orientation, as a potentially useful source of insights for his own alternative theory of international law.[44]

Morgenthau's first mention of Schmitt occurs in the 1929 Stresemann essay, where he praised Schmitt for having accurately diagnosed the failure of mainstream international law to appreciate the necessity of a dynamic legal order able to adjust to changing social conditions.[45] His *Die internationale Rechtspflege, ihr Wesen und ihre*

Grenzen offered a critical response to a widely read 1927 essay by Schmitt in which the right-wing theorist had defined the political as constituting a fundamentally distinct and independent sphere of activity, existing alongside alternative modes of human activity. In Schmitt's initial formulation, morality concerned the problem of good and bad, aesthetics was occupied with the distinction between beautiful and ugly, economics was preoccupied with profitability and unprofitability, whereas only politics concerned the contrast between what Schmitt famously described as friend and foe.[46] The young Morgenthau astutely diagnosed the Achilles' heel of this position: Schmitt's exposition misleadingly implied that political activity was limited to a pre-given set of objects or concerns, thereby obscuring the possibility that *any* conceivable sphere of activity could take on political qualities. In its stead, Morgenthau proposed that politics be described as "a characteristic, quality, or coloration which any substance can take on" (*IRWG*, 67). The distinctive attribute of political activity was captured best by focusing on the *degree of intensity* of the conflict at hand. Although drawing their substantive concerns from any of a host of (moral, aesthetic, and economic) arenas of human activity, identifiably political concerns were those in which a high degree of intensity of conflict had surfaced (*IRWG*, 69). Even though he admitted the difficulty of determining at what specific juncture a particular conflict had become intense and thus authentically political, Morgenthau insisted that his alternative model of intensity offered a superior way of capturing the distinctive traits of political life. In his view, politics was never an either/or state of affairs, but always a matter of degree, necessarily depending on *how* intense – and *potentially* violent – a conflict had become.

Schmitt apparently agreed. As Morgenthau noted in his 1978 autobiographical reflections, Schmitt subsequently "changed the second [1932] edition of the *Concept of the Political* in the light of the new propositions of my thesis without lifting the veil of anonymity from their author."[47] In fact, Schmitt's 1932 study dropped the misleading imagery of politics as a distinct or separate sphere, instead following Morgenthau's conceptualization of politics as concerning conflicts characterized by intense enmity.[48] Yet Schmitt never bothered to acknowledge his debts to the young left-leaning Jewish Morgenthau. For a politically upwardly mobile right-wing thinker busy cultivating influence with Germany's rising authoritarian political groupings, such an admission would have been inconvenient. In his 1978 comments, Morgenthau went so far as to accuse Schmitt of having engaged in mean-spirited plagiarism. He recounted a humiliating 1929 meeting with Schmitt in which Morgenthau hoped to discuss their shared interest in the political, only to encounter a calculating, mean-spirited careerist: "when I walked down the stairs from Schmitt's apartment, I stopped on the landing between his and the next floor and said to myself: 'Now I have met the most evil man alive.'"[49] Schmitt's subsequent kowtowing to the Nazis apparently did not take Morgenthau by surprise.[50]

Despite serious disagreements as well as deep personal animosity, Morgenthau's early exchange with Schmitt nonetheless helped bequeath to him a deeply conflictual or agonistic model of politics, in which the zenith of political action was ultimately identified with intense and potentially violent conflict. In this account, conflict – and thus politics – was a pervasive facet of human existence. Interstate conflict remained exceptional chiefly because it typically constituted a particularly intense – and thus explosive – form of antagonism. It was there that we most commonly encounter what Schmitt had described as potentially violent conflicts between friend and foe. But politics, as Morgenthau frequently noted, manifested itself in other arenas, including the workplace or family. Schmitt may have gone awry in formulating his concept of the political, but, from Morgenthau's perspective, Schmitt remained a formidable opponent precisely because his reflections astutely captured important features of political reality.

Exhibiting an unwieldy mix of fascination and revulsion, Morgenthau's published and unpublished writings from the early 1930s include many additional comments about Schmitt. In his inaugural lecture at the University of Geneva in 1932, Morgenthau again praised the realistic starting point of Schmitt's jurisprudence, contrasting it in some respects positively to Kelsen's legal positivism, before ultimately accusing Schmitt of theoretical eclecticism. Schmitt, Morgenthau concluded, had pursued a much-needed *recherche de la réalité*, but had still not succeeded in generating more than a hodge-podge of aphoristic anti-liberal and anti-parliamentary insights. This failure ultimately stemmed from Schmitt's subjectivism: Schmitt's deeply anti-normative orientation meant that he had irresponsibly given up on the traditional quest for an objectively valid science of law. His widely noted political opportunism – Morgenthau alluded to competing neo-Kantian, reactionary Catholic, decisionist, and irrationalist strands in his thinking – thus derived from deeper theoretical flaws.[51] A 1933 French-language volume subsequently elaborated on Morgenthau's earlier analytic criticisms of Schmitt's concept of the political.

Morgenthau, revealingly, did so without discarding the agonistic account of political life which he shared with Schmitt. Although Morgenthau worried that Schmitt's theory neglected the sociological as well as psychological bases of friend–foe politics, he seemed most agitated by the fact that Schmitt could provide no firm normative foundations for responsible moral or political action. Schmitt justified an irresponsible embrace of unmitigated politics – pure power politics – in which meaningful normative restraints on it had been discarded.[52]

Not surprisingly perhaps, Morgenthau soon turned his attention to the intellectual origins of Schmitt's subjectivism. An impressive unpublished 1935 manuscript on moral philosophy from Kant to Nietzsche chronicled the decline of ambitious universalistic moral philosophy and its replacement by competing brands of moral subjectivism which, Morgenthau pessimistically insisted, went hand-in-hand with the increasingly nihilistic character of western modernity.[53] Schmitt's subjectivism and nihilism, it turned out, epitomized a more general crisis in western civilization. If humankind were successfully to combat the dangers of "pure politics," power politics untamed by moral strictures, it would need to find sturdy normative foundations for opposing them. Nonetheless, the general developmental course of modern moral philosophy, which appeared to culminate in relativism, seemed to deny humanity the possibility of doing so.

For our purposes, Morgenthau's engagement with Schmitt is illuminating for two reasons. First, it explains a striking tendency even in his early writings to pursue a surprisingly truncated interpretation of his own realistic or sociological method. Second, the dialogue with Schmitt deepened an anti-utopian and perhaps even anti-reformist strand in Morgenthau's theory. While Morgenthau's embrace of a sociological approach to international law not only held open, but in fact endorsed, the possibility of far-reaching global reform, the dialogue with Schmitt likely strengthened an opposing tendency to discount it. Schmitt, of course, was always deeply skeptical of ambitious liberal models of international law. Some of that skepticism may have rubbed off on Morgenthau. In the aftermath of the Second World War, his harsh criticisms of international law and of many proposals for global reform occasionally echoed Schmitt's.

As we have seen, Morgenthau's early sociological method implied the virtues of a systematic analysis of a broad range of social power relations on the global scene. The young Morgenthau always described himself as a practitioner of legal sociology: when citing some of his own works even as late as 1940, he classified them as part of this genre. However, those studies which Morgenthau himself placed under this rubric tend to reproduce a revealing but problematic line of inquiry.[54] After espousing the virtues of an approach to international law grounded in the changing dynamics of social reality, Morgenthau typically jumped to a second step: he repeatedly argued that the realistic or sociological method requires a careful investigation of the immanent dynamics of political conflict, and thus sustained reflections about what he described as the concept of the political, by means of which he hoped to integrate the rational kernel of Schmitt's theory. Unfortunately, the inadvertent result of this move was a tendency to reduce, even in his most creative prewar writings, a potentially wide-ranging critical and normatively sensitive sociology of international law to a philosophically minded analysis of the historically unchanging dynamics of politics.

To be sure, there may have been good reasons why Morgenthau believed that a realistic theory of international law required clear ideas about the fundamental nature of political experience. Yet this otherwise potentially sensible intuition tended to short-circuit the broader project of developing an empirically minded critical analysis of power relations at the global level in favor of an analysis of the (for Morgenthau) historically constant contours of political conflict. A realistic sociology of law became, in effect, a somewhat one-sided political theory centered on an agonistic model of politics.

As Morgenthau later bluntly stated in his most influential postwar book, *Politics Among Nations*, politics "is governed by objective laws" which have "not changed since the classical philosophies of China, India, and Greece" (*PAN*, 2nd edn., 4). But even in his prewar writings, Morgenthau implicitly associated his theory with the effort to identify *historically unchanging* patterns of political experience interpreted as the real (i.e., more fundamental) basis for the pathologies of international law. A "Realist" approach of this type referred not primarily to an analysis of real (i.e., existing but alterable) social and historical facts influencing the operations of international law, but instead to trans-historical characteristics of political life conceived as the underlying basis for the ever-changing facticity of social experience. Morgenthau's repeated recourse to the concept of the political inevitably shaped his reflections in a subtle but significant manner: a realistic account of international law highlighted historical continuities and constants rather than serving primarily as a justification for fundamental reform.

Typically, a second analytic jump then followed. Having analyzed or at least alluded to the unchanging dynamics of conflict-laden politics, Morgenthau insisted that we locate the roots of political life in human nature and psychology since they best illuminated the real or primordial roots of political action. Social reality was thereby reduced to psychology and human nature: "Social forces are the product of human nature in action" (*PAN*, 1st edn., 4). Reminiscent of the conservative German theorist Helmuth Plessner, author of an influential 1931 book on politics and human nature, Morgenthau argued that an agonistic model of politics required a deeper grounding in psychology and philosophical anthropology.[55] Not only did a realistic or sociological approach demand recourse to the laws of politics, but basic political laws derived from fundamental features of human nature.

Even in his first book in 1929, Morgenthau implied the necessity of grounding a theory of international politics in basic psychological drives. But that point at least initially remained peripheral to the overall argument (*IRWG*, 4). In subsequent writings from the early 1930s, Morgenthau deepened this at first superficial interest in developing a theory of international politics rooted in philosophical anthropology and psychology. He briefly toyed with the prospect of a Freudian theory of international politics, writing a lengthy and ultimately unpublished manuscript, before abandoning the project.[56] When Morgenthau first employed arguments about human nature and psychology during the Weimar period, he typically underscored their historical and social *malleability*. In an unpublished 1931 manuscript on pacifism, for example, he attributed a crude psychological determinism to the right-wing authoritarian author Ernst Jünger, accusing him of misleadingly justifying the worst horrors of modern warfare by crudely deducing them from primary human instincts. What Jünger and others ignored, Morgenthau countered in both a Freudian and legally reformist vein, was the possibility of successfully *sublimating* our potentially destructive basic instincts so they might find socially constructive outlets. The likelihood of warfare might be reduced, Morgenthau suggested, but only if humankind could figure out how to develop new channels for mobilizing our most disturbing instincts and impulses in a pacific direction.[57] In accordance with his early faith in the possibility of fundamental legal reform, the young Morgenthau in 1931 still deemed this achievable.

Even after Freud faded from the scene, however, Morgenthau typically drew a close analytic link between a realistic or sociological account of international law and psychology and human nature.[58] Once again, this move initially appears tenable: a persuasive realistic theory might plausibly make use of psychology or philosophical anthropology. No a priori reason excludes the possibility of a plausible reform-minded sociology of international law rooted in psychology or philosophical anthropology. Nonetheless, this conceptual link ultimately reinforced a troublesome tendency to discard an otherwise rich set of analytic and explanatory possibilities: Morgenthau jettisoned a multifaceted analysis of power at the international level in favor of an underdeveloped political psychology and philosophical anthropology. In turn, this move refurbished the subterranean tendency to associate his theory with an account of *historically unchanging* elements of political experience deriving from the real (i.e., primordial) basis of human nature. Politics was not simply governed by objective laws, but those laws had "their roots in human nature" conceived as fundamentally constant (*PAN*, 2nd edn., 4).

This conceptual strand, which had no immediate parallels in Sinzheimer's theory or in the ideas of his left-wing disciples, helped prepare the ground for Morgenthau's postwar reflections. In his most famous postwar US publications, Morgenthau would repeatedly highlight the importance of a sound view of human nature as a starting point for international relations theory. For many plausible reasons, however, both friends and foes of Realist theory have worried about this attempt to build on the shaky foundations of a dreary version of philosophical anthropology.[59] One immediate result of this intellectual move was that many of the most familiar dilemmas of international politics might be seen as rooted in transhistorical attributes of human nature. Even though Morgenthau's *Politics Among Nations* bluntly asserted that "nothing in the realist position militates against the assumption that the present division of the political world . . . will be replaced by larger units of a quite different character," and despite the fact that he defended a world state in which the horrors of interstate violence had finally been eliminated, Morgenthau soon became associated with far-reaching skepticism about the prospects of international reform (*PAN*, 2nd edn., 9). Even if his postwar reputation as a rather conservative defender of the international status quo was undeserved, his repeated assertions about the psychological roots of international politics opened the door to easy misinterpretations of his views. They also likely strengthened a certain tendency in his thinking to exaggerate the impediments to reform.

For readers familiar with Schmitt's writings on international law, this result is hardly surprising. In the 1932 version of *The Concept of the Political*, rewritten with Morgenthau's conceptual innovations in mind, Schmitt famously commented:

> A world in which the possibility of war is utterly eliminated, a completely pacified globe, would be a world without the distinction of friend and enemy and hence a world without politics. It is conceivable that such a world might contain many interesting antitheses and contrasts, competitions and intrigues of every kind, but there would not be a meaningful antithesis whereby men could be required to sacrifice life, authorized to shed blood, and kill other human beings . . . The phenomenon of the political can be understood only in the context of the ever present possibility of the friend-and-enemy grouping.[60]

"[R]ejecting the illusory security of a status quo of comfort and ease," while "holding in low esteem a world of mere entertainment and the mere capacity to be interesting," Schmitt vehemently attacked ambitious proposals for global political and legal reform.[61] A world without intense conflicts, lacking in meaningful possibilities for physical conflict with political enemies, would devalue and potentially trivialize human existence. Ambitious models of global governance rebelled against human nature: Schmitt directly linked his concept of political to a pessimistic version of philosophical anthropology.

By similarly welding his own agonistic vision of politics directly to the fundaments of human nature, Morgenthau inadvertently found himself traversing contiguous intellectual terrain. As we will see, the mature Morgenthau, in striking contrast to Schmitt, repeatedly emphasized the desirability of a world state. Yet his endorsement of the world state was always qualified by deep reservations about even relatively modest attempts (e.g. the League of Nations or United Nations) to begin building it. Like Schmitt, Morgenthau occasionally seemed to presuppose that *interstate* conflicts – characterized by what Schmitt had dubbed the "real possibility of killing" the enemy – represented the most authentic expression of the political. Notwithstanding Morgenthau's refreshingly forthright insistence on the desirability of an alternative to the international status quo, his exchange with Schmitt probably intensified his deep hostility to what he would soon regularly excoriate as "idealist" visions of reform.

2

Morality, power, and tragedy

Morgenthau exploded onto the North American intellectual scene with the 1946 publication of *Scientific Man Vs. Power Politics,* a book which quickly garnered him a reputation as a brilliant young émigré scholar of international politics and political theory.[1] It also helped secure Morgenthau a desirable tenured professorship at one of North America's most prestigious universities, the University of Chicago, from which he immediately began to shape the emerging discipline of international politics. Blunt in its attack not simply on mainstream international law but also on liberalism and western modernity, the thin but densely argued volume provoked heated responses from prominent intellectuals like Jerome Frank, Sidney Hook, Ernest Nagel, and Michael Oakeshott.[2] Notwithstanding the wide reception enjoyed by the book, as well as the fact that it soon became required reading for young disciples of the emerging Realist school of international politics, *Scientific Man* has often been misunderstood. Although helping to pioneer the increasingly influential Realist approach to international politics, Morgenthau went out of his way to criticize *Realpolitik* and the amoral pursuit of power politics by nation states. As Richard Ned Lebow has aptly pointed out, "[c]ritics misread his insistence on the enduring and central importance of power in all political relationships as an endorsement of European-style *Realpolitik* and its axiom that might makes right."[3] Not only did Morgenthau criticize proto-realists like Machiavelli and Hobbes, but he also endorsed a vision of political ethics which underscored a series of severe moral tests which responsible political actors had to pass. *Scientific Man* may have paved the way for the acceptance of Realist international theory, yet its author remained at best an uneasy Realist, so uncomfortable with the label that he resisted using it to describe his own intellectual efforts. An offspring of the Weimar left, Morgenthau struggled to outline a theoretical approach attuned to the harsh realities of power on the international scene while still arguing that the deepest moral impulses of the western tradition required that we transcend political brutality and violence. Morgenthau's political ethics, in short, suggests a more complex and appealing international political theory than typically described by those who pigeonhole him as a dogmatic defender of *Realpolitik*, hostile to any attempt to transcend the existing state system, and supposedly blind to the moral roots of responsible political action.

Against the repudiation of politics

Scientific Man's early critics focused on its frontal assault on what Morgenthau polemically dubbed the "scientistic" faith that the social world can be understood in accordance with the methods of natural science, and thus that the natural sciences can serve as "an instrument for social salvation" able to resolve even the most difficult political and social dilemmas (*SM*, 4). For Hook, Nagel, and other early critics, Morgenthau had drawn a crudely unsympathetic portrait of modern science, exaggerating the extent to which it promised easy solutions to difficult technical and practical problems. For Morgenthau, however, a naïve faith in natural science led too many of its admirers to advance simplistic answers to deeply rooted political and social dilemmas for which we can only hope to find unavoidably fragile and provisional answers. The invention of the air-cooled engine, "when it was solved, it was solved unequivocably and definitely," for example, and humankind could then proceed to "forget about it, cherishing the solution as one of its imperishable possessions." Yet the pressing challenge of world peace, Morgenthau noted, cannot be easily and definitively resolved by any mechanically applied doctrinal or scientific formula, but instead "must be solved every day anew." The postwar rush to spin out ambitious models of international reform, allegedly realizable if only enough virtuous right-minded people took up the cause, reproduced the scientistic illusion that if we simply came up with the correct invention or discovery – hitherto supposedly ignored by an unenlightened humanity – world peace could be established once and for all.[4] For a skeptical-minded Morgenthau, more books had been written on world peace in the last hundred years than in the previous thousands of recorded history, but we remained no closer to a "solution today than ... when it first presented itself to the human mind" (*SM*, 215–16).

Scientism was faulted for distorting "the problem of ethics, especially in the political field," since it implied that ethical quagmires could be more or less conclusively resolved by application of the scientific method. The morally right decision, scientism implied, was determined by the universal laws of science, and thus only ignorance or irrationality prevented individuals from acting ethically. Education and social reform, it naïvely concluded, necessarily generated moral enlightenment. Scientism also missed what human nature was about, obfuscating the reality of our basic impulses and "the lust for power which is common to all men" (*SM*, 5, 9). Once again, Morgenthau directly linked his agonistic conception of politics to philosophical anthropology: "Politics is a struggle for power over men, and whatever its ultimate aim may be, power is its immediate goal, and the modes of acquiring, maintaining, and demonstrating it determine the technique of political action" (*SM*, 195). Since conflict is ubiquitous in social life, politics was universal as well. What we generally describe as "politics proper" refers to scenarios where conflict is most intense: there the struggle for power represents "the very essence of the intention, the very life-blood of the action," in contrast to other settings where power conflicts were "blended with dominant aims of a very different kind" (*SM*, 195). Echoing his writings from the early 1930s, *Scientific Man* praised Freud for having "rediscovered the autonomy of the dark and evil forces which, as manifestations of the unconscious, determine the fate of man," before attacking neo-Freudians like Alfred Adler and Karen Horney for succumbing to the scientistic faith that the Freudian unconscious "will be overcome with relative ease by the standard devices of the age, such as education and individual and social reform" (*SM*, 205).

Their Weimar background unfamiliar to most readers, Morgenthau's blunt comments about the tight nexus between human nature and political antagonism understandably struck many reviewers as conceptually underdeveloped; critics were probably justified in underscoring the vulnerability of Morgenthau's appeal to philosophical anthropology. From Morgenthau's perspective, however, the reality of agonistic politics based in human nature served as a useful weapon with which to pillory scientism. The harsh fact that our "inner and outer life bears the marks of constant conflict and strife" vividly contradicted its naïve rationalism and correspondingly childish political agenda (*SM*, 8). The struggle to gain power over others not only represented a built-in facet of human nature, but it put to rest harmonistic models of politics and society.

In hindsight, the tendency for reviewers to focus on the incongruities of Morgenthau's assault on scientism probably missed the forest for the trees. In our post-positivist age, some of Morgenthau's concerns seem remarkably prescient, even if he tended to overstate scientism's commitment to absolute certainty: his assertion that answers to pressing political questions were necessarily incomplete, for example, actually meshed with the fallibilistic orientation commonplace among defenders of the quantitative social sciences. Whatever their specific flaws, Morgenthau was undoubtedly onto something when he worried that social and political analysis was becoming overly enamored of the natural sciences: the less-than-stellar history of mainstream cold war US social science readily corroborates this suspicion. Although missed by both admirers and critics, Morgenthau's critique of scientism by no means culminated in a frontal assault on the scientific enterprise per se, let alone, as some crudely asserted, irrationalism.[5] Even though his own polemical tone sometimes got in the way of articulating the point properly, Morgenthau appreciated that the social sciences could play a constructive role when they "indicate certain [social] trends and [try] to state the possible conditions under which one of those trends is likely to materialize in the future." The social sciences properly operated in the realm of "statistical averages and probability," not absolute certainty and airtight predictions as some social analysts seemed to promise (*SM*, 137–8). The observation that political science should pay proper attention to the irrational forces in human nature, as Morgenthau's own recourse to Freud should have reminded his critics, hardly entailed abandoning systematic intellectual inquiry.

Reminiscent of Max Weber, Morgenthau worried that overly self-confident social scientists looking uncritically to the natural sciences ignored their craft's unavoidable limits. Most important perhaps, the social sciences necessarily provided only partial guidance in the face of "ultimate decisions" about how we were to live our lives (*SM*, 165). Fundamental questions about the meaning of human existence were necessarily left unanswered. Modern science helped to disenchant both the natural and social worlds, thereby "destroying the confidence of the human mind in the answers that art, religion, and metaphysics" had tried to provide for untold eons. Despite his anxieties, Morgenthau resisted traditionalistic quests to re-enchant the world, regularly rejecting backwards-looking attempts to salvage religion or natural law.[6] Scientism not only rested on the myth that modern science could resolve the great questions of human existence, but, when it inevitably failed to do so, the fundamental questions at hand were excluded from the confines of systematic intellectual inquiry: scientism "left man the poorer and has made the burden of life harder to bear." Not surprisingly, people increasingly sought refuge in "astrology, prophecy, belief in miracles, occultism, political religions, sectarianism, all kinds of superstitions, and all the lower types of entertainment" (*SM*, 125).

Most creatively perhaps, Morgenthau asserted that the social sciences depended on a model of the natural sciences that had already been abandoned by its best practitioners. The neatly law-governed, Enlightenment-based vision of a predictable and calculable natural universe, Morgenthau noted, had been jettisoned for a more complex account in which unpredictability and contingency loomed large. But modern social scientists continued to model their own inquiries on an account of natural science which owed more to Galileo and Newton than Einstein or Heisenberg. Unlike some critics of the social sciences, Morgenthau's criticisms of them did not rely chiefly on underlining differences between natural and social reality, though he did identify a number of them. On the contrary, he blurred the divide between the natural and social sciences, but chiefly in order to show that social scientists lagged behind in understanding the severe limitations of a rigid nomological model of scientific inquiry that emphasized the establishment of universal laws.

Most of the critics who focused on Morgenthau's criticisms of scientism also downplayed the import of his provocative discovery of a "general decay in the political thinking of the Western world" (*SM*, vi). From the perspective of contemporary debates in political theory, however, this claim seems no less perceptive than Morgenthau's worries about the tendency among postwar social analysts to borrow uncritically from the natural sciences. Much political theory in recent decades has been motored by anxieties, reminiscent of Morgenthau's in *Scientific Man*, that western modernity has allowed the distinctive attributes of "the political" to be swallowed up or at least submerged by competing modes of economic or administrative action. The intense fascination with the writings of both Hannah Arendt and Jürgen Habermas can be described as motivated in part by a quest to defend the special attributes of political action and public engagement against inappropriate inroads from other modes of activity.[7] Perhaps the single most influential book in postwar US political theory, Sheldon Wolin's landmark *Politics and Vision: Continuity and Innovation in Western Political Thought* (1960), analogously attacked the mainstream of modern western political thought for threatening to reduce politics to the economic, social, and organizational.[8] Like Morgenthau, Wolin placed much of the blame for the anti-political contours of modern thought and practice at the doorstep of modern liberalism. Similarly, the ongoing renaissance of interest in Carl Schmitt has been motivated at least in part by an attempt to develop an agonistic model of the political as a corrective to the purportedly rationalistic and legalistic excesses of contemporary liberalism.[9]

This intellectual trend would likely have cheered Morgenthau.[10] At the very least, *Scientific Man* not only anticipated the recent preoccupation with determining the special attributes of politics, but also astutely pointed to some of its potential perils. Fascism, Morgenthau believed, could be plausibly interpreted as a direct real-life embodiment of pure power politics, *la politique pour la politique*, in which political action disastrously freed itself from any normative bearings, and humanity's built-in lust for power was placed on a pedestal: Hitler and Mussolini delighted in "the will to power and the struggle for power as elemental social facts," and thus should be interpreted as providing a clear warning of the dangers of "pure politics" unrestrained by any moral signposts (*PAN*, 2nd edn., 206).[11] Fascism failed, Morgenthau observed in *Scientific Man*, because "it did not understand the nature of man, who is not only an object of political manipulation but also a moral person endowed with resources which do not yield to manipulation" (*SM*, 8–9). For Morgenthau, a "man who was nothing but a 'political man' would be a beast, for he would be completely lacking in moral restraints," and fascism correspondingly constituted nothing less than a terrifying practical experiment in which men and women were given free rein to act as brutal and power-hungry creatures (*PAN*, 2nd edn., 12). Accordingly, the motivating idea behind National Socialist international law was "the lust for power which knows no limits nor values beside or above it."[12]

When the young Morgenthau had previously attacked Schmitt's ideas about politics in the late 1920s and early 1930s, he did so in part because he believed that Schmitt had devised a disturbing model of pure politics where the pursuit of power was unrestrained by minimal normative rules. In his initial reflections on politics, Schmitt had depicted politics as referring to a distinct sphere of activity, cleanly removed from the competing spheres of morality, economics, and aesthetics. Morgenthau criticized this position for misleadingly implying that human existence could be neatly carved into competing political, moral, and economic realms, each preoccupied with distinct objects. In contrast, he tried to capture the specificity of politics *without* endorsing Schmitt's peculiar claim that human experience could be broken up into separate political, moral, economic, and aesthetic objects. As noted in chapter 1, Morgenthau instead opted to describe politics as a pervasive characteristic of social existence. Although conflict and antagonism are well-nigh universal, those conflicts which take on especially explosive attributes – for example, interstate affairs between hostile powers – constituted the realm of politics proper. In response to Morgenthau's early criticisms, Schmitt substantially modified his initial conceptual formulations. Nonetheless, Schmitt would always continue to insist that politics should be seen as clearly distinct from morality: "normative illusions" are inappropriate to authentic politics, as he categorically declared even in the revised 1932 version of *Concept of the Political*. In Morgenthau's reading, Schmitt's vision of politics as a distinct value sphere fundamentally unrelated to morality, like fascism's brand of brutal power politics in which the central moral preoccupations of western thought were systematically discarded, provided a crystal-clear warning of the dangers of any attempt to salvage the autonomy of the political at the risk of abandoning necessary normative limitations on political action. Morgenthau was convinced that he had to do better, and the political ethics outlined in *Scientific Man* represented his attempt to do so.

Not surprisingly, key components of *Scientific Man* can be read as a critical dialogue with Schmitt. Even though Schmitt was never mentioned, its basic argument paralleled an essay published by Schmitt in 1929, "The Age of Neutralizations and Depoliticizations," which was subsequently included in the 1932 edition of *Concept of the Political*.[13] We know that Morgenthau was familiar with this version of Schmitt's argument: he believed that Schmitt had stolen some of his main ideas when preparing it. Morgenthau seems to have returned the favor at least to some degree by borrowing from Schmitt's reflections on the anti-political contours of western modernity.

According to Schmitt's essay, western modernity had always pursued a doomed quest to locate "a neutral sphere" in which conflict could be superseded and common agreement achieved by peaceful means. Stated in the simplest terms, western civilization fled the deadly disputes of theology in the seventeenth century to embrace a seemingly neutral sphere of metaphysics, before advancing humanitarian ethics (in the eighteenth century) and finally economics (in the nineteenth century) in order to neutralize and depoliticize social conflict. The twentieth century, Schmitt posited, was moving towards an "age of technicity" in which faith in science and technological development was widely thought capable of superseding intense conflict and antagonism. In this highly speculative interpretation of western modernity, social actors have repeatedly sought but inevitably failed to escape intense conflict and unavoidable disagreement, incessantly pursuing what was taken to be a new basis for harmony and universal consensus before that basis soon inevitably revealed itself to be as unstable and conflict-ridden as previous ones. Both nineteenth-century liberals and socialists, for example, hoped naïvely that they could rely on economic mechanisms to dissolve intense forms of political conflict. Liberals advanced visions of the free market at least in part as a mechanism for "neutralizing and depoliticizing" social existence, while Marx and his followers fantasized about the demise of politics via a rationally planned economy. In Schmitt's account, each stage in this process represented nothing more than a doomed quest to circumvent the harsh realities of a world in which intense antagonism – in Schmitt's language, constellations of existentially distinct friends and foes – remained irrepressible.

Western modernity, in short, has been predicated on a misconceived struggle to escape or at least suppress the political, according to Schmitt. Both modern liberalism and socialism are complicit in the attack on the political; both are destined to fail. Notwithstanding the dreams of both liberals and socialists of achieving a harmonious economic order able to minimize conflict, "religious wars evolved into the still cultural yet already economically determined national wars of the nineteenth century and finally into economic wars."[14] Economics offered no sturdy basis for harmony. The faith in scientific progress and technological development shared by both contemporary liberals and left-wingers, Schmitt presciently predicted, would prove no more effective at fleeing the harsh realities of politics.

Scientific Man's main story line reproduced Schmitt's reflections. The dominant intellectual currents of western modernity conspired systematically in favor, as Morgenthau titled chapter 3, of "The

Repudiation of Politics." In the twentieth century, both the White House and Kremlin "share[d] the belief that if not now, at least ultimately, politics can be replaced by science, however differently defined" (*SM*, 4). The contemporary faith in the neutralizing and depoliticizing force of science rested on deeper roots in western modernity, however. Scientism was only the latest instantiation of a naïve rationalistic current in modern thought which hides the harsh realities of human nature and our congenital "lust for power" from view. *Scientific Man* bemoaned the fact that the West "developed a political philosophy without a positive conception of politics" (*SM*, 87). For much of the modern western tradition, politics – when conceptualized in terms of intense conflict or power struggle – represented an embarrassment, an atavistic vestige from which humankind should cleanse itself in favor of a more harmonistic model of political and social order. Morgenthau, like Schmitt, directed much of his ire at mainstream liberalism; Marxism was criticized because it reproduced too much of liberalism's anti-political Achilles' heel. Liberalism sought to tame deep political conflicts rooted in human nature by naïve and overly ambitious models of the rule of law, or via an economistic faith in the essentially pacific force of free markets. Morgenthau discounted the latter strategy, though he admitted that the former had some real basis in the concrete experiences of eighteenth- and nineteenth-century liberals at the domestic level, where the rule of law helped ward off the perils of European Absolutism. But liberals conveniently ignored the fact that the lack of a common system of sovereignty at the international level meant that law there necessarily functioned differently from its domestic corollary; contemporary liberal models of international law too often operated as little more than a misguided escape from the harsh realities of international politics. Alternately, liberals embraced technological utopias in which technologies were naïvely envisioned as unifying and potentially harmonizing forces.

Reminiscent of Schmitt as well, *Scientific Man* formulated a devastating critique of modern liberal international law: when read *selectively*, it offered easy pickings for those eager to read Morgenthau as an up-and-coming Realist. Because the history of modern international thought embodied the worst facets of modern western political thinking, its anti-political tendencies were especially pronounced. Contemporary liberals depended on simplistic but grandiose institutional cure-alls for deep and complex political enigmas, blind to the many ways in which their proposals disfigured the distinctive attributes of politics at the international level.

Given the lack of shared sovereignty, "even where legal relations hide relations of power, power is to be understood [in international politics] in terms of violence, actual and potential; and potential violence tends here always to turn into actual warfare" (*SM*, 50). In Schmitt's original language, "the real possibility of killing" was manifest at the international level, and thus politics was most authentic there. In international affairs, Morgenthau noted, "power is pitted against power for survival and supremacy," and thus what should weigh in the mind of every policy maker was the straightforward question of whether a particular policy improves the power situation of his or her country, or not. Since "the power of the individual nations serves here only the national interests which are ready to clash with those of other nations," wise statesmen should accordingly free themselves from exaggerated illusions about the efficacy of international law: no "rational system of legal rules for the satisfaction of economic needs and the prevention of arbitrariness and violence" has been established there (*SM*, 85). What was needed were not well-trained lawyers but farsighted statesmen, schooled in the art of politics, who understood that not the judicial process but instead "the balance of power is the essence and stabilizing factor of international relations" (*SM*, 103). At stake in most international legal conflicts

> is not who is right and who is wrong but what ought to be done in order to combine the particular interests of individual nations with the general interest in peace and order. The question to be answered is not what the law is but what it ought to be, and this question cannot be answered by the lawyers but by the statesman. The choice is not between legality and illegality but between political wisdom and political stupidity. (*SM*, 120)

In his early writings, Morgenthau had made the same point that international lawyers unavoidably stumbled when they faced the question of what "ought to be done": existing international law was static and underdeveloped, poorly attuned to the ever-changing exigencies of social and political experience, and thus vulnerable to manipulation and potentially violent upheaval, since it deals haphazardly with dynamic political and social realities. Imperative was a new mode of international legislation capable of effectively confronting the exigencies of social and political change, not a rigid legal system that misleadingly pretended that lawyers and traditional legal methods could effectively undertake the deeply political task of updating law in response to altered conditions. As discussed in chapter 1, Morgenthau in the 1930s had considered the possibility that a reformed system of international law could mitigate the dilemmas facing international lawyers. In a dynamic system of international law, ascertaining "what the law is" would perform a fruitful function on the international scene, as on the domestic, since law would typically prove well adapted to changing political and social realities.

On occasion *Scientific Man* forcefully reiterated Morgenthau's previous arguments about the pathologies of static international law. But his answer to the quagmires he had earlier diagnosed was no longer to describe those who *resisted* far-reaching reform as "metaphysical" and ahistorical, but instead to tar advocates of international reform with similar criticisms. As he wrote amid the devastation of the Second World War, most varieties of legalistic international reformism now apparently struck Morgenthau as excessively naïve. As he noted in a parallel 1946 *Yale Law Journal* article, "the legalistic approach to essentially political problems is but an aberration from the true laws of politics," and those laws required nothing less than that political leaders "return to the traditional principles of diplomacy which, truly understood, reflect the nature of man, the nature of politics, and the conditions for successful political action."[15] The ills of international law cried out for wise statesmen who fully grasped its limitations and embraced the tried and tested methods of traditional diplomacy. Only classical diplomacy, Morgenthau asserted, rested on a sufficient appreciation of human nature and the deep political antagonisms built on it. While pushing for a revitalization of diplomacy, Morgenthau found himself referring appreciatively to thinkers like Alexis de Tocqueville, whose views about modern democracy were at best ambivalent.[16] Especially in the late 1940s and 1950s, they loomed large in his pantheon of intellectual giants. The quest for sage statesmen who understood the fundamental laws of politics – Winston Churchill soon served as an examplar[17] – tended to overshadow the earlier commitment to international legal reform inspired by Weimar Social Democracy.

Despite this subtle shift in Morgenthau's thinking, it remains inaccurate to describe his views in the 1940s as Realist in the conventional sense. In order to see why, we must turn to his political ethics. In the process, we can also see more clearly how *Scientific Man*, despite its parallels to Schmitt's ideas, constituted a firm rejection of Carl Schmitt.

Morgenthau the moralist

The misleading cliché that "Morgenthau finds moral considerations unfit for the necessities that characterize politics, particularly international politics," continues to dominate the secondary literature.[18] In fact, the final chapters of *Scientific Man*, where Morgenthau developed a sophisticated political ethics, systematically attacked the view that politics operates in distinction from morality. Morgenthau undertook this assault in part because he hoped to distinguish his reflections from Schmitt's, in which exactly such a strict division had been drawn. To the extent that Realism has been associated with a tendency to minimize the proper role of moral considerations in international politics, it is unclear that Morgenthau's political ethics, at least as formulated in *Scientific Man*, can be associated with it. In fact, he clearly rejected the term "Realism" when describing his own position.

Scientific Man declared that "[m]an is a political animal by nature" and "a moralist because he is a man" (*SM*, 168). We are political by nature, first, because of the scarcity of "food, shelter, security, and the means by which they are obtained, such as money, jobs, marriage, and the like" (*SM*, 193). Inevitably, conflict ensues: "what the one wants for himself, the other already possesses or wants, too" (*SM*, 192). We may seek to be unselfish, but the demands of scarcity necessarily force us to undertake selfish and ultimately conflictual action. When *Scientific Man* occasionally referred to the *biological* sources of political conflict, Morgenthau meant that our basic biologically rooted – though socially variable – needs for food, shelter, and security represent an elementary source of social conflict. Second, the *animus dominandi*, or lust for power, constitutes an additional feature of human nature. We not only seek the satisfaction of our basic needs, but are necessarily preoccupied with our relative position in relation to others even after our survival has been guaranteed: "This lust for power manifests itself as the desire to maintain the range of one's own person with regard to others, to increase it, or to demonstrate it" (*SM*, 192). When *Scientific Man* mentioned the *psychological* roots of conflict, this is presumably what Morgenthau had in mind. While our basic biological needs can be satisfied and thus in principle are limited, our psychologically rooted lust or "will to power" has no such limits: it can only be satisfied "if the last man became an object of his domination, there being nobody above or beside him, that is, if he became God" (*SM*, 193). The "resting point" of our quest for position and status in relation to others "is reached only in the imagination but never in reality" (*SM*, 194).

Readers will search in vain here, as in Morgenthau's earlier German and French writings, for an adequate justification for this by now familiar attempt to draw a close conceptual link between human psychology and conflict. While he previously had drawn on Freud to justify this standpoint, *Scientific Man* merely alluded to Freud, instead marshaling a panoply of literary and historical examples: Cecil Rhodes, William Blake, Don Juan, and Faust were all mentioned as illustrations of the thesis that a fundamentally unlimited "lust for power" incessantly forces us "to maintain the range of one's own person" in relation to our peers (*SM*, 192–4). As Morgenthau would similarly remark in his monumental *Politics Among Nations* just two years later, "power is a psychological relation between those who exercise it and those over whom it is exercised. It gives the former control over certain actions of the latter through the influence which the former exert over the latter's mind" (*PAN*, 1st edn., 14). We necessarily seek to assert ourselves in relation to others because only by doing so can we gain the social recognition or social distinction for which we strive (*PAN*, 1st edn., 50). What better way to do so than by gaining power and control over them? The need for self-assertion can never be fully satisfied, in part because others simultaneously make similar impositions on us, but also because the possible objects by which self-assertion is pursued are both diverse and limitless: "the love of Don Juan, Faust's thirst for knowledge," as well as Alexander the Great's and even Hitler's military expansionism, represent just a handful of its innumerable possible manifestations. In short, conflict – and thus politics, which for Morgenthau referred to intense and potentially violent conflict – plagues social interaction because of our naturally given, albeit socially and historically diverse, quest to satisfy our basic needs, as well as a no less fundamental imperative by means of which we seek to assert ourselves and impose ourselves on others. The process by which we struggle to gain recognition from others is inevitably tension-ridden and agonistic. Conflict can be tamed and civilized by means of

> social pressure which is capable of containing the evil tendencies of human nature within socially tolerable bounds; conditions of life, manifesting themselves in a social equilibrium which tends to minimize the psychological causes of social conflict, such as insecurity, fear, and aggressiveness; and finally, the moral climate which allows

man to expect at least an approximation to justice here and now, and thus eliminates the incentive to seek justice through strife.[19]

Yet any suggestion that conflict or struggle might be jettisoned for a perfectly harmonious society remained implausible.

Nothing about this view conflicts fundamentally with either Schmitt's views or conventional accounts of Morgenthau as a Realist hostile to the place of moral considerations in politics. The second part of our story dramatically complicates matters, however.

"Man is a political animal by nature," but our shared humanity means that each one of us strives simultaneously to act morally: "he is a moralist because he is a man." By linking nature to politics, Morgenthau did not intend to deprecate political action. Nonetheless, the quest for power partakes of "mere" nature to the extent that it remains directly based in biological and psychological propensities. In contrast, the "problem of justifying and limiting the power which man has over man" arises from "the discord between man's desire [for power] and his actual condition," in which he typically finds himself dominated and even "a slave to the power of others" (*SM*, 168). We assert ourselves and seek to control others, yet instead we regularly find ourselves objects of their power. Since power relations contravene our deepest desires, we necessarily seek some explanation and justification: why must I obey my parents? Why must I send my children to risk their lives in a distant war? Why must I pay taxes when I prefer to spend my money on something else? Essential to the human condition, in short, is a need to make sense of, as well as somehow justify, the exercise of power: we seek moral knowledge in part because the realities of power consistently conflict with our own built-in desire for power. To be sure, the moral answers provided "are mumbled, ambiguous, and distorted," but the quest for moral insight is just as indispensable to humankind as the struggle to gain power. Moreover, since the moral answers provided often demand of us that we *restrain* our own biological and psychological needs, and that we subject our own pursuit of power to strict limits, morality can be said to *transcend* our most basic natural proclivities: the quest for moral knowledge is what alone makes us fully human, since it helps ward off a potentially barbaric situation in which the quest for power would be untamed and violent. Our capacity for moral reasoning forces us beyond our biological and psychological drives, even if we often fail to follow moral strictures partly because our most deeply rooted drives persistently campaign against them.

Scientific Man consequently referred to the "curious dialectic of ethics and politics, which prevents the latter, in spite of itself, from escaping the former's judgment and normative direction" (*SM*, 177). We seek recognition from others and power over them, but since we repeatedly find our own "back[s] . . . bent under the political yoke," we are driven to raise moral and ethical questions about power; hence the perennial intellectual preoccupation in human history with delineating legitimate from illegitimate power. Inevitably, political judgments are inextricably intertwined with normative and moral ideas, since the harsh realities of power themselves engender moral reflection. *Pace* Schmitt, who tended to view morality and politics as distinct spheres, Morgenthau held that "[m]orality is not just another branch of human activity, coordinate to the substantive branches, such as politics or economics. Quite to the contrary, it is superimposed upon them, limiting the choice of ends and means and delineating the legitimate sphere of a particular branch of action altogether."[20]

For this reason, the human condition is thus deeply tragic. Since we are *both* political *and* moral creatures, we are forced to seek power while *simultaneously* justifying and ultimately limiting its exercise. We aspire to dominate others, while typically acknowledging the legitimacy of some limits on our desires. Without such limits, human coexistence itself would probably be impossible or at least unbearable. While seeking power, we realize as moral beings that the quest for unlimited power is destructive and illegitimate. Our tragic destiny means that we must act both politically *and* morally, despite the fact that power and morality make competing and even contradictory demands on us: "In the combination of political wisdom, moral courage, and moral judgment, man reconciles his political nature with his moral destiny" (*SM*, 203). But this reconciliation tends unavoidably to take the frustrating form of a "*modus vivendi*, uneasy, precarious, and even paradoxical" since the dictates of politics clash with the voice of conscience. The pursuit of power regularly contradicts moral strictures on its necessary limits: "For man's aspiration for power over other men, which is the very essence of politics, implies the denial of what is the very core of the Judeo-Christian morality – respect for man as an end in himself."[21] No easy recipe can be found for mediating between the lust for power and morality. Successful as well as praiseworthy statesmen are neither *Realpolitiker* who sacrifice morality to the altar of power politics, nor simple-minded moralists who ignore the realities of power, but instead only those who simultaneously observe the competing dictates of both power and morality. We want neither "the political realist, the Machiavellian bargainer, who conceives of foreign policy exclusively in terms of power and for whom the end of power justifies all – or almost all – means employed," nor the "moralist, 'talking like a professor' – or should one rather say 'like a preacher'? – whose ability to bargain is strictly circumscribed, both in width and in depth, by his insistence upon principle."[22] Hammering away at the same point in his *Yale Law Journal* essay, Morgenthau observed that "whether they swear by Wilson or follow Machiavelli, they are always Utopians pursuing either nothing but power or nothing but justice, yet never pausing to search for the rules of the political art."[23]

Political actors must "choose among several [politically] expedient actions the least evil one," and even when doing so, they should remain uneasy about any moral compromises (*SM*, 203). The outstanding attribute of great political leaders is that they grasp this crucial point and have succeeded, especially when the stakes are highest, in both effectively pursuing power and respecting significant moral imperatives. Churchill, in this assessment, was a brilliant statesman because he fused an instinctive awareness of the realities of power with a deep moral sensibility, whereas Hitler and Stalin lacked minimal moral acumen even though they were ruthless *Realpolitiker*. Morgenthau's position is thus *not* that political actors should merely follow the demands of power accumulation, while, as a "moral thinker and a private citizen," we can be expected to respect moral demands.[24] This is precisely what Morgenthau, as we will see shortly, angrily dismissed as an irresponsible "dual standard." Instead, even those engaging in politics in the proper sense of the term – that is, actors forced to manage conflicts possessing a potentially life-or-death significance – must try to follow the voice of conscience. Political actors are obliged to acknowledge the harsh realities of power conflict in order effectively to pursue political goals while simultaneously pursuing "the least evil" of possible acts. Political action is not only *limited* by moral concerns, but moral reflection inevitably enters directly into the sphere of political judgment: successful political actors are both calculating power-oriented political animals *and* at the same time always committed moralists.

This is why Morgenthau could praise even Quaker pacifism as representing both a morally "moving" and "truly political" approach. Quakers aptly acknowledged the tragic "conflict between the demands of Christian ethics and the way man must live."[25]

Rather than disingenuously escape the conflict, they courageously sought

> action which is both politically relevant and morally tenable in the light of Christian teaching . . . [T]hey have endeavored to elevate the political sphere to the level of Christian ethics not by superimposing upon that sphere a rigid dogma but rather by penetrating it with a pragmatic goodness . . . The Quaker approach to foreign policy is not so much a doctrine as a disposition of the soul translated into action. It is truly political in its adaptability to circumstances; it approaches Christian moral excellence in being consistently informed by the pure demands of Christian ethics.[26]

Morgenthau ultimately conceded that Quaker pacifism was "doomed to ever renewed failure" given the realities of political life.[27] Yet it remains noteworthy that he described it as an admirable quest to suffuse political action with a deep moral sensibility.

No less striking in this context are Morgenthau's surprisingly harsh comments on the great British scholar of international relations and, like Morgenthau, major influence on modern Realist theory, E. H. Carr. To be sure, many argumentative parallels between Carr and Morgenthau exist; it is no accident that Morgenthau described Carr in a 1948 article as a great mind who had provided "a most lucid and brilliant exposure of the faults of contemporary political thought in the Western world." More revealing, however, was Morgenthau's simultaneous claim that Carr's work "exposes its own share" of the pathologies of contemporary thought.[28] Carr, in depressing harmony with those who advocated a pure politics or unvarnished power politics, simply missed the fact that "man is a moralist." Carr's conception of morality, Morgenthau claimed, was relativistic and instrumentalist, and, lacking a "transcendent standard of ethics," it surrendered to the blind worship of power.[29] In advocating *Realpolitik* but no rigorous morality, Morgenthau polemically observed, Carr succumbed to the same intellectual mistakes committed by Carl Schmitt. A superior theoretical inspiration for those hoping to develop a hard-headed as well as morally demanding political theory, Morgenthau noted, was the work of the Protestant theologian Reinhold Niebuhr, who had "seen more clearly and exposed with acute brilliance the essential defects of Western political thought."[30] Niebuhr grasped the harsh realities of power relations especially on the international scene, but, unlike Carr, he maintained a demanding model of moral action faithful to the highest aspirations of the western religious tradition.[31]

Morgenthau's praise for Niebuhr is revealing for another reason as well. In contrast to scientism and its naïve and overly harmonistic view that scientific method can resolve difficult moral and political dilemmas, *Scientific Man* asserted, major strands of premodern and especially Christian and Jewish thought were alert to the intrinsic quagmires of human action: they forthrightly recognized "the existence of two forces – God and the devil, life and death, light and darkness, good and evil, reason and passion – which struggle for dominance of the world" (*SM*, 205). The Judeo-Christian tradition aptly underscored the deep tensions between morally conscientious action and the struggle for power. Morgenthau worried that this underlying normative intuition had been lost. Modern thought glibly downplayed the tensions between the quest for power and morality, reducing politics to morality (e.g. a simple-minded "moralism") or, no less troubling, morality to politics (e.g. pure politics or *Realpolitik*). *Both* tendencies sought to overcome the antinomies of human existence, but they did so only at the cost of relegating fundamental attributes of the human condition to the sidelines. Both typically proved irresponsible. In contrast to its premodern forebears, Morgenthau claimed, even modern aesthetic experience was plagued by the tendency to ignore or at least downplay the tragic character of human action: "The lack of tragic art in our age is but another manifestation of the rationalistic unawareness of the tragic element in life" (*SM*, 207). The Greeks, Shakespeare, and even Goethe possessed an understanding of the fundamental antinomies of human action, and their great aesthetic achievements in part derived from their reflections about it. Modern literature, in synch with the harmonistic spirit of modern thought in general, disingenuously runs away from the conflicting moral and political imperatives under which humanity is necessarily forced to act.

For Morgenthau, "the test of a morally good action is the degree to which it is capable of treating others not as means to the actor's ends but as ends in themselves" (*SM*, 196). To be sure, Morgenthau was not first and foremost a moral philosopher; his moral reflections remain theoretically underdeveloped. Nonetheless, his interpretation of what constituted the core achievements of western moral and religious thought remains striking and provocative. He repeatedly praised Kant and even Marx for having "decried the use of man as a means to an end" (*SM*, 184),[32] while repeatedly appealing to the rigorous "nonutilitarian ethical standards of Western civilization" and their roots in the Judeo-Christian religious tradition (*SM*, 209). This legacy, it seems, is the most valuable achievement of the struggle to provide moral significance to an otherwise dreary universe characterized by seemingly meaningless struggles for power. With an undeniable whiff of nostalgia, he reported that: "The Decalogue is a code of ethical norms which cannot be derived from premises of rational utility. The concept of virtue as the sum of human qualities required by ethics bears no resemblance to the standard of utilitarian rationality" (*SM*, 209). Although by no means secure in contemporary times, at least on occasion "the ethical norms which men feel actually bound to follow . . . endeavor to satisfy nonutilitarian aspirations" (*SM*, 209). A demanding morality, in which our relations to others are noninstrumental and their interests cannot be legitimately sacrificed for the "greatest happiness," still possesses some basis in everyday moral consciousness.[33]

These strands in Morgenthau's reflections have encouraged some commentators to describe him as a covert theological thinker, perhaps a Jewish ally of Niebuhr and his brand of Christian Realism.[34] Even though this reading is to be commended for recalling, in stark contrast to the conventional view, Morgenthau's deep moral impulses, it risks overstating his commitment to conventional religious practice. To be sure, in a fascinating short review essay on Arnold Toynbee from 1955, Morgenthau conceded that "most of the failings of the modern age . . . stem from one single source: the lack of religiosity."[35] Irreligious self-glorification, for example, contributed to the proliferation of hubristic political ideologies which deny meaningful limits on human action. However, Morgenthau resisted the traditionalistic view that the only answer to these dangers was a return to traditional faith and organized religion. First, significant empirical evidence supported the view that the flowering of modern civilization, and not simply its dangers, presupposes the weakening of traditional religious faith. Second, it was naïve to believe that religious faith could be recaptured by a conscious act of will, as though the disenchanted structure of our moral universe might simply be rolled back by an organized campaign among intellectuals. By advancing precisely this agenda, Toynbee risked playing the role of a "kind of Billy Graham of the eggheads."[36] Missing from modern moral sensibility was indeed a sufficient awareness of the tragic character of human experience, as well as an appreciation of the mysteries which shroud the most profound questions of human existence. Nevertheless, it was misleading to believe that a consciously manufactured religious revival might recapture that sensibility.

Also lacking from our present-day moral sensibility, Morgenthau lamented in the Toynbee essay, was a sufficient sense of guilt. Our shared moral heritage demands of us that we seek to treat others non-instrumentally, as ends in themselves. Yet the tragic quality of human existence derives in part from the patent impossibility of doing so. Too often we prefer to ignore this harsh fact by circumventing the necessity of acknowledging that human action unavoidably generates harm; to accept this fate would require an acceptance of moral guilt. Even though our intentions may be innocent, "the human intellect is unable to calculate and to control completely the results of human action," and thus we generate evil when seeking the opposite (*SM*, 189). Even before we act, good intentions are corrupted or polluted, despite our best efforts to the contrary. We often face equally legitimate moral demands, but only one of them can be effectively satisfied. "While trying to render to Caesar what is Caesar's and to God what is God's, we will at best strike a precarious balance" (*SM*, 190). Any attempt to realize justice inevitably remains incomplete, even if our moral nature drives us to try to do so.[37] On a more trivial level, I seek to show my love for my two daughters, but time constraints mean that I devote myself to one and neglect the other, despite my best efforts to love both equally: "Whatever choice we make, we must do evil while we try to do good; for we must abandon one moral end in favor of another" (*SM*, 190). Tragedy inheres in all human action since it inevitably entails disservice and harm to someone, even when we merely aspire to advance good. Yet such immorality "is to a higher degree and more obviously present in political than in private action, owing to the particular conditions under which political action proceeds" (*SM*, 188). In the context of intense and potentially explosive conflict, the stakes are higher than when we fail to pay proper homage to religious tradition or neglect a loved one: in order to advance legitimate political goals, I may be forced to take up arms.

Echoing Max Weber, Morgenthau defended an "ethics [*sic*] of responsibility to which all action affecting others, and hence political action par excellence, is subject" (*SM*, 186).[38] Like Weber, Morgenthau expressed skepticism about an "ethics of conscience" according to which moral actions are to be judged primarily on the basis of an actor's intentions. Part of the tragic quality of the human condition for Morgenthau, as for Weber, was that even the best intentions sometimes produce disastrous and morally defective results. Despite this significant overlap, a noteworthy difference separates the two authors. Although critical commentators on

Morgenthau have described his political ethics as noncognitivist and anti-rationalist,[39] this is misleading, though it perhaps goes some way towards characterizing Weber's political ethics. To be sure, Morgenthau, like Weber, questioned whether modern science could provide a firm grounding for our moral and religious ideas. In Morgenthau's gloss, however, this chiefly suggested that modern scientism was insufficient; by no means did it demonstrate the irrelevance of our deepest moral and ethical intuitions. To be sure, Weber was also aware of the limitations of modern science. Yet his view of it was probably more affirmative than Morgenthau's. Correspondingly, the fact that science cannot ground fundamental moral preferences encouraged Weber to underscore their noncognitivist and perhaps even irrational character: western morality finds itself in crisis because it lacks a sufficiently scientific basis. In contrast, Morgenthau fervently endorsed the most demanding moral strands within the western tradition. Although Morgenthau, again like Weber, worried that these ideas may have surrendered their foundations in our increasingly disenchanted age, he doggedly held onto them, refusing to see in them nothing but the decadent vestiges of a premodern age. Morgenthau reproduced core elements of Weber's political ethics. Yet he stubbornly insisted, to a degree Weber arguably did not, that key moral and political accomplishments of the western moral tradition were still deserving of our loyalty.

Morgenthau's position is hardly lacking in internal tensions, particularly in light of the fact that, like Weber, he conceded that – especially modern – science undermines the most worthwhile moral insights of our historical predecessors, and that ours is increasingly a morally disenchanted universe haunted by the twin specters of relativism and skepticism. Yet his account of the proper place of moral considerations in political action was ultimately more demanding than Weber's. For Morgenthau, more clearly than for Weber, we need to preserve a demanding nonutilitarian ethic and the key idea of persons as ends in themselves, even if we can no longer ground such ideas by appeals to religion or natural law.

So much for the widespread assessment that Morgenthau's view of politics neglected the proper place of moral considerations. To be sure, Morgenthau repeatedly denounced the "moralism" of some views of politics, and his polemical tone might easily lead readers to misconstrue his ideas. Of course, many Realist authors – including, as Morgenthau himself argued, even those as supple as E. H. Carr – have undoubtedly tended to find "moral considerations unfit for the necessities that characterize politics, especially international politics." Those Realists – Henry Kissinger comes to mind – who have condoned systematic violations of the laws of war might also accurately be described in these terms. Yet this was not Morgenthau's position, at least as it was formulated in *Scientific Man*, his most important contribution to political ethics. Not surprisingly, Morgenthau himself refused to describe his endeavors as representing a variety of *Realpolitik* or even Realism in *Scientific Man*.

In chapter VII, appropriately titled "The Moral Blindness of Scientific Man," Morgenthau outlined a series of strategies by means of which contemporary thought systematically evades the tragic character of human action. The most commonplace strategy is what he described as "utilitarian realism," according to which "the attainment of the greatest amount of satisfaction" represents the aim of moral action (*SM*, 171). This position simply pretends that tough moral choices depend on anachronistic moral philosophy or mere misunderstandings: if the greatest satisfaction or happiness is achieved by what traditionally has been considered an immoral act (e.g. committing torture in order to ward off the possibility of terrorist violence), conventional moral scruples should be regarded as little more than an atavistic leftover or perhaps even a psychotic ailment. This was the moral position, Morgenthau claimed, taken by a group of Harvard undergraduates who reportedly argued that the protagonist of Conrad's *Lord Jim* should simply "get on with things" and not worry too much about the fact that he saved his own life by abandoning a ship filled with native passengers (*SM*, 170–1). Here the demanding nonutilitarian idea that we should treat others as ends in themselves is simply discarded. Tellingly, Morgenthau dismissed this form of "Realism," concluding that it represented a false escape from the tragic contours of human action.

More importantly, *Scientific Man* devoted considerable energy to criticizing the postulate of the "amorality of politics." In this view, the political sphere is cleanly separated from the private sphere; only in the latter do conventional moral concerns play a role. The most extreme version of this argument, according to which political action is exempt from ethical restraints, has been associated with Machiavelli and Hobbes and "known in the history of ideas as 'reason of state.' According to it, the state is subject to no rule of conduct but the one which is dictated by its own self-interest. *Salus publica suprema lex*" (*SM*, 176). Elsewhere in *Scientific Man*, Machiavelli is described as a "realist," and grouped unsympathetically alongside the "sophist" Thrasymachus (*SM*, 35).[40] Revealingly, many intellectual histories of Realism trace its origins to Machiavelli and Hobbes and early modern *Realpolitik* before typically locating Morgenthau in this tradition.[41] Rather than embrace this heritage, as one might expect given the conventional reading of his views, *Scientific Man* attacked it:

> The importance of this conception has been literary rather than practical. Mankind has at all times refused to forgo ethical evaluation of political action. Political philosophy from the Greeks to our time has started from the assumption that man in the political sphere is not allowed to act as he pleases and that his action must conform to a standard higher than . . . success. (*SM*, 176)

In opposition to Machiavelli, Hobbes, and *Realpolitik*, Morgenthau instead repeated his view that politics must always be subjected to stringent moral restraints. *Scientific Man* even accused Hobbes of totalitarianism, suggesting that both he and Machiavelli had succumbed to scientism – in Morgenthau's view, the main culprit in the pathologies of western modernity (*SM*, 169, 174). Whatever the value of his rather heavy-handed interpretive labels, Morgenthau's point was clear enough: *Realpolitik* and its intellectual predecessors downplayed the crucial fact that "man is a moralist," and Realism of this type consequently provides a poor starting point for grappling with the tragic character of the human condition. In the history of political thought, Machiavelli and Hobbes constituted "an accident without consequences, a sudden flash of lightning, illuminating the dark landscape of man's hidden motives but kindling no Promethean fire for a grateful posterity" (*SM*, 169). They shed light on the dynamics of power, but provide no real guidance for those, like Morgenthau, who believe that political life should also be concerned with the moral evaluation of power.

Having sternly criticized *Realpolitik* and its great intellectual progenitors, *Scientific Man* provided no evidence that Morgenthau himself sought to embrace the label "Realist" to describe what he was up to. In chapter 1, we saw that Morgenthau's own initial methodological approach took the form of a critical-minded sociology of law, in which the harsh realities of power at the international level were fruitfully contrasted to the operations of international law. Worried that the term "Realist" might prove badly misleading, he rejected it altogether in favor of "functionalism" in his first US publications. Perhaps we can now better understand the sources of this anxiety: if Realism is necessarily predicated on a commitment to *Realpolitik* and the embrace of an amoral conception of political action, Morgenthau was indeed no Realist.

In an eye-opening essay from 1945, "About Cynicism, Perfectionism, and Realism in International Affairs," Morgenthau addressed the vexing issue of how best to characterize his theoretical trajectory. He reported that some critics now labeled him, to his surprise, a moral perfectionist, chiefly because of his emphasis on the moral character of politics. In 1929, he also noted, his work had been labeled "cynical" for voicing skepticism about the Kellogg–Briand Pact and its attempt to illegalize war, and in 1938 it had been described as "Realist" for expressing doubts about the capacity of small European nations to avoid involvement in the Second World War: "Have I passed like a butterfly, through a number of metamorphoses, without knowing it? Or am I afflicted with a three-way split personality?"[42] His answer was a resounding "no." The only change was in the concrete historical and political situation. In a setting in which a naïve moralism (i.e. "Wilsonian utopianism") was neglected in favor of a no less one-sided embrace of power politics ("Machiavellian utopianism"), Morgenthau claimed that he was merely pointing out, as he supposed he always had, "that whereas international politics cannot be understood without taking into consideration the struggle for power, it cannot be understood by considerations of power alone." In this view, the world has changed, but not Morgenthau's theory, and all that had transpired was that so-called "cynics went to the left and are now called perfectionists, for they point out, as they always have done," that humanity is both a political and moral creature.[43]

Although probably downplaying some shifts in Morgenthau's thinking, this interpretation remains a useful starting point for understanding why his idiosyncratic international theory is so easily misunderstood. A viable political theory must start with the harsh facts of power politics as they exist, while simultaneously doing justice to the fact we are only fully human to the extent that, as moral creatures, we try to transcend them. In those historical conjunctures when power politics took center stage and humanity's moral impulses were neglected, Morgenthau apparently considered it his proper task to counter *Realpolitik* and dangerous "Machiavellian utopias." The moral and even perfectionist side of his thinking was then accentuated. When naïve moralistic and legalistic ideas dominated the stage, Morgenthau believed it his duty to stress the unavoidability of political conflict and the harshest attributes of

human nature in order to check moralism or "Wilsonian utopianism." What Morgenthau always shared with more conventional
versions of Realism was an awareness of the unavoidability of power
politics, as well as the special challenges it posed to every attempt to
extend the rule of law to international affairs. What separated his
theory from theirs was an abiding sense of the immorality of power
politics along with the necessity of taming it.

Read from this perspective, *Scientific Man* waged a two-front war.
Most obviously, it was directed against naïve models of international law and global reform, which for Morgenthau too often
engendered a simplistic moralism insufficiently attuned to the
harsh realities of power inequality. They also tended to rest on a
crude hyper-rationalism: "it is utopian to assume that a rational
system of thought by its own inner force can transform the conditions of man." But Morgenthau had another target in his aim as
well. While writing in the early 1940s, when power politics remained
alive and well in a Europe dominated by Hitler and Stalin, he also
considered it vital to remind his readers of the coeval perils of
"Machiavellian utopianism." Even when discussing the foundations of what would soon become the United Nations, Morgenthau
was haunted by the latter dangers at least as much as by the former.
In a 1945 essay commenting on the Dumbarton Oaks meetings,
he argued that the heroic but naïve "Wilsonian Utopia" which
had doomed the League of Nations "is being replaced by the
Utopia of Machiavelli," which mistakenly posited that "a stable,
peaceful society can be built on power alone."[44] Not surprisingly,
Morgenthau considered it his duty to highlight ways in which a
successful model of postwar international government would need
to rest on common moral standards, without which it could not
possibly thrive. At least initially, Morgenthau criticized the United
Nations *not* because it had suffered from an "idealistic" blindness
to the laws of politics, but instead because it uncritically *built on*
normatively deplorable attributes of a political universe in which a
shrinking number of great powers exercised hegemony.

Scientific Man also criticized what Morgenthau dubbed a "dual
standard," according to which politics and morality operate via
rival ethical codes: "there is one ethics for the public sphere and
another ethics for the private sphere" (*SM*, 179). Morgenthau was
alarmed by precisely what we would expect him to *embrace* if in fact
he devalued moral reflections in political life. Yet instead he criticized this position for allowing politicians to escape strict moral
imperatives, thereby evading the difficult task of doing justice

simultaneously to the necessities of power politics and of a strict moral code. Morgenthau also attacked the clichéd idea that the "end justifies the means," meaning that the goodness of an end justifies immoral acts, a notion which *Realpolitiker* from Machiavelli onwards have embraced in order to justify politically useful yet immoral action. Of course, Morgenthau, like Weber, was familiar with the paradox that immoral acts can produce positive political actions. Nonetheless, he rejected any attempt to transform this observation into a complete political theory. The basic weakness of this position is that the moral goodness sought for is typically, at best, itself partial and incomplete: we commit violence for the good of the community or state, for example, yet "the welfare of the group, for the sake of which the welfare of another group is sacrificed, is an end with a positive ethical quality only for the members of that group" (*SM*, 183). This idea also neglects the fact that every action is "at the same time means and end," meaning that in reality there is no point at which a chain of actions comes to a complete conclusion. We wage war in order to advance the "common good," for example, yet in the meantime our action becomes part of a complex set of interlinking (and oftentimes unpredictable) actions contributing to deep transformations in our understanding of what the "common good" entails. One danger here, Morgenthau observed, is that the fiction of an absolute and unalterable moral aim (e.g., the common good) potentially opens the door to the abandonment of moral standards altogether.

Against the nation state

Morgenthau's political ethics inevitably left a deep mark on his reflections about the modern state system. Although skeptical of the imminent prospects for reform at the international level, *Scientific Man* proffered a devastating critique of the modern nation state, arguing bluntly that the existing state system contributed decisively to the deterioration of fundamental moral standards. One of the paradoxes plaguing Morgenthau's theoretical reflections in the 1940s and early 1950s probably derived from the fact that his *own* political ethics pointed to the necessity of replacing the international status quo with a radical alternative to it: Morgenthau grasped that the modern nation state was complicit in many of the worst horrors of the contemporary era, and his own observations about its pathologies regularly cried out for a concerted effort to establish a humane alternative. Yet his own hard-headed political instincts simultaneously left him skeptical not only of woolly-headed talk of immediate global transformation, but at times even of the relatively modest aims of the newly formed United Nations.

As we will see, Morgenthau would struggle for many years to resolve this tension. In his view, humanity desperately needed to move beyond the Westphalian system, yet fundamental political mechanisms militated against the likelihood of successfully doing so. As he famously declared in *Politics Among Nations*, a "world state is unattainable in our world, yet indispensable for survival" in light of the terrors of modern interstate warfare (*PAN*, 1st edn., 419). Much of Morgenthau's thinking, especially in the 1940s and 1950s, can accordingly be interpreted as a series of attempts to find some *modus vivendi*, however "uneasy, precarious, and even paradoxical" the endeavor inevitably appeared, by means of which political actors might realistically circumvent the worst dangers of the Westphalian system and its core principle of national sovereignty, while somehow, despite the improbability of success, cautiously moving towards a superior world order.

In this respect as well, Morgenthau's position was always deeply at odds with what now passes for Realist theory. Contemporary Realists build on his skepticism about global reform, even to the point of consistently downplaying the novelty of post-national political innovations like the European Union. Yet they appear more at ease than he ever was with a state system in which infringements on national sovereignty remain the exception to the rule, and a substantial body of international law is subject to the whims of nationally based political actors. Of course, present-day Realists vividly describe the dangers of what they describe as interstate *anarchy*, and even occasionally admit that "Realism merely requires anarchy; it does not matter what kind of political units make up the system."[45] Nonetheless, it remains difficult to imagine Morgenthau announcing, as one prominent Realist recently declared in a surprisingly Pollyannaish tone, that the nation state has a "bright future," since "nationalism is probably the most powerful political ideology in the world, and it glorifies the state."[46] The tendency to associate Realism with an insufficiently critical view of the nation state accurately captures the views of many of Morgenthau's intellectual offspring. Yet it badly distorts his ideas.

Scientific Man boldly asserted that some of the most morally enigmatic attributes of political action are exacerbated "by the particular conditions under which political action proceeds in the modern nation state." At the level of domestic society, the lust for power is still hemmed in by "mores and laws of society" working to limit the worst excesses of humanity's built-in desire for power. Such restraints are vastly more fragile in international politics, however. The modern nation state "has become in the secular sphere the most exalted object of loyalty on the part of the individual and at the same time the most effective organization for the exercise of power over the individual." In our disenchanted universe, the state has indeed become a "mortal God": "for an age that believes no longer in an immortal God, the state becomes the only God there is" (*SM*, 197). Legal, moral, and customary checks on the *animus dominandi* operate with some effectiveness in the international sphere, but they typically prove far less efficacious than their domestic corollaries.

Even more fundamentally, "impulses which both ethics and the state do not allow the individual to satisfy for his own sake are directed by the state towards its own ends" (*SM*, 198–9). The nation state permits and indeed condones extreme forms of power egotism as long as they serve its goals. Recent history provides innumerable examples in which individual power impulses are destructively transferred to the nation: "What was egotism – and hence ignoble and immoral – there becomes patriotism and therefore noble and altruistic here" (*SM*, 198). Since selfish power impulses can be veiled and justified far more easily when actualized collectively, they are too often given free rein at the level of national politics. Morgenthau went so far as to speculate that those social groups "most thoroughly deprived of outlets for their own power drives or . . . most insecure in the possession of whatever power they may have within the national community" typically make up the core of rabid nationalistic movements because they are most in need of some outlet for their psychologically based power drives. Not surprisingly, the working and lower middle classes tend to "identify themselves completely with the national aspirations for power" (*PAN*, 1st edn., 75). Making a bad situation worse, messianic "political ideologies blunt the individual conscience," engendering a dangerous conflation of the pursuit of national power with morality itself. Political action undergoes "a complete reversal of ethical valuation": not only do political actors deny the tragic tensions between moral action and the struggle for power, but brutal *power politics* becomes an exemplar of moral action (*SM*, 199). We erect statues to political leaders who have decimated foreign foes, sing their praises on patriotic holidays, and teach our children to imitate their examples.

The existing state system debilitates our already fragile moral sensibilities, opening the door to both a deeply immoral *and* politically irresponsible *Realpolitik* in which a collectivized lust for power stands ready to be unleashed against those excluded from the nation state's highly particularistic identity. Although "the national state is to a higher degree than ever before the predominant source of the individual's moral and legal valuations," in the nuclear age its "very power and sovereignty . . . imperils the existence of civilization and, with it, of the national states themselves."[47] Modern nationalism may have had its origins in the admirable libertarian impulses of early liberal and democratic movements, but for Morgenthau it has long since regressed to the level of a potentially self-destructive "political religion," or "nationalistic universalism which identifies the standards and goals of a particular nation with the principles that govern the universe." Succumbing to the worst dangers of political hubris, modern nation states become the standard-bearers of narrow egotistical ideals for which they smugly claim universal validity. The present-day nation state is thus an even more dangerous institutional configuration than its nineteenth-century predecessor: it represents "the starting point of a universal mission whose ultimate goal reaches to the confines of the political world." Whereas nineteenth-century liberal nationalists sought "one nation in one state," their offspring are congenital rather than accidental imperialists because of the universalizing missions with which nation states – or at least those still having real power in the international order – are intimately associated.[48] In the contemporary international climate, "put at the service of the state, the individual's *animus dominandi* has not only in imagination but in actuality the world as its object" (*SM*, 198).

The nation state also risks decimating what remains of humanitarian international law and ethics. According to Morgenthau, we should resist the tendency to exaggerate the role of "transcendent ethical considerations" in international politics while avoiding the no less troubling tendency to ignore their achievements altogether. In stark opposition to those (including E. H. Carr) whom Morgenthau accused of succumbing to the latter error, the 1948 "Twilight of International Morality" pointedly noted that legal and moral norms have many times effectively tamed state power even during moments of violent conflict, precisely when one-sided *Realpolitiker* would have least expected this to occur: "the fact of the matter is that nations recognize a moral obligation to refrain from the infliction of death and suffering under certain conditions despite the possibility of justifying such conduct in the light of a higher purpose, such as the national interest."[49] Nonetheless, the horrors of modern total war demonstrate that traditional moral limitations on killing in warfare "have shown a tendency to weaken and disappear altogether."[50] The sources of this trend are manifold. Probably decisive, however, has been the ascent of the nation state, with the resulting political religions working recklessly to jettison universalistic and cosmopolitan international ethics – resting, in his account, on a shared western cultural and political heritage – for the predominance of "nationalistic ethics" in which national power consistently trumps moral considerations: "Instead of the universality of an ethics to which all nations adhere, we have in the end the particularity of national ethics which claims the right to, and aspires toward, universal recognition."[51]

More recent Realists and their *Realpolitiker* allies may continue to embrace the nation state and sing its institutional praises, whereas Morgenthau's supple political ethics admirably prevented him from doing so. Although skeptical of many proposals for global reform, he refused to decorate the harsh realities of the nation state and the existing state system with a moral apology. The fact that we remain mired in the Westphalian system was cause for alarm, and not, as it soon became for Morgenthau's Realist children, a source of moral and political complacency.

3

Defending the national interest

On August 29, 1949, the Soviet Union successfully tested its first atomic bomb, putting an abrupt end to the brief nuclear monopoly enjoyed by the United States. Although in reality deeply alarmed, American policy makers rushed to underplay the momentous character of the Russian atomic test. President Harry Truman publicly declared, his apparent self-confidence masking deep anxiety, "this probability has always been taken into account by us." In fact, his intelligence experts had badly overestimated US atomic superiority, and most had doubted that Stalin would acquire the bomb for many years to come. Worried about the likelihood of public panic, and eager to hide their own strategic miscalculations from critical scrutiny, Truman's disingenuous reaction was widely reproduced by military and foreign policy elites. The *New York Times* observed that "In no quarter was there any hint of dismay."[1]

In a flurry of polemical articles penned for liberal-minded journals like the *Bulletin of the Atomic Scientists*, *Commentary*, and the *Nation*, Hans J. Morgenthau offered a more forthright assessment of the Russian tests. Developing an argument he would repeat throughout the 1950s, Morgenthau described the Soviet acquisition of atomic weapons as an "event of the greatest importance," overshadowing all competing political events of the immediate postwar years.[2] Not only had the Soviet Union rapidly achieved rough military parity with the United States, but it raised the possibility of human extermination as never before in recorded history. In the nuclear era, war was no longer a viable foreign policy option since it risked destroying all those involved. Nonetheless, the specter of nuclear war now loomed large on the horizon. Morgenthau interpreted the deceptive reaction among US officials as evidence that both they and much of the American public were suffering from a "typical neurotic reaction to a reality unpleasant and full of surprises." Rather than face the hard facts of a postwar world haunted by Soviet military prowess and the looming specter of nuclear war, Truman and his fellow citizens had "succeeded in withdrawing completely from reality as it actually was, substituting for it the reality of his delusion."[3] Failing to encourage the American public to deal rationally with the political realities of the new world, political leaders irresponsibly exacerbated the worst delusional tendencies of popular discourse. They pursued this path, Morgenthau posited, because too many of them embraced smug and increasingly reckless illusions about intrinsic US military, as well as political and moral, superiority. Like Truman, who greeted initial news of the Russian test with deep skepticism, they preferred to hide their heads in the sand when faced with the novel exigencies of postwar political life.

Previous chapters have traced Morgenthau's complicated relationship to Realism. While Morgenthau's European period called for a "realistic" sociological analysis of the limits of mainstream international law and its chief theoretical proponents, his first major English-language publication, a 1940 *American Journal of International Law* article, rejected the term. Throughout the 1940s, Morgenthau distanced himself from the Realist label. Beginning in 1950, however, he fervently embraced it.[4] Our task in this chapter is not only to try to understand what Morgenthau meant by "Realism" during this influential period in his intellectual career, when he became America's most famous scholar of international politics, his views were widely reported in the press, and he regularly hobnobbed with elite foreign policy experts like George Kennan and Dean Acheson, but also to show why an "atomic flash somewhere in Asiatic Russia in 1949" played a decisive role in Morgenthau's mature reformulation of Realist international political theory.[5]

Stalin's bomb and the makings of cold war Realism

In a series of articles on the Soviet atomic test written in late 1949 and early 1950, Morgenthau opined that the only option available to the United States and its allies was to pursue a negotiated settlement with the Russians. Given the deep political divide between the USSR and the West, nuclear war now was a real possibility. The

United States no longer could restrain the Soviets by overwhelming force, since the Americans had lost their military advantages. The recourse to military power as the main instrument for taming the Russians was excluded for more fundamental reasons as well. With the ascent of nuclear weapons,

> [w]ar is no longer, as it once was, a rational instrument of foreign policy, the continuation of diplomacy with other means. In centuries past resort to war could be defended as a means to an end . . . The total war of our age has fundamentally altered this traditional relationship between political ends and military means. Today war has become an instrument of universal destruction, an instrument which destroys the victor with the vanquished.[6]

What then of the possibility of a continuation of "the twilight state between peace and war in which we have been drifting in recent years," in other words, what commentators were already describing as a "cold war," in which relations between the two sides remained minimal, and the issue of war and peace always hung uneasily in the balance?[7] In an edited volume put together by the editor of the *Nation*, Morgenthau questioned the viability of this option, at least for the long term:

> It must be said that this possibility is so extremely unlikely to materialize as to be no real possibility at all. Even if the United States had and the Soviet Union had the psychological and material resources necessary to withstand for decades the pressures of open hostility short of war, two factors would be bound sooner or later to put the cold war to an end. One is the threat of ever more potent weapons of mass destruction, which while it makes for extreme caution makes also for desperation. The other is the extreme instability in those regions . . . which are not firmly controlled by the other side . . . Under the conditions of the cold war only superhuman wisdom, foresight and self-restraint would be able to localize revolutions, civil wars and international wars likely to take place in those regions and to prevent them from igniting a general conflagration.[8]

A "cold war" ultimately offered no alternative to the real thing since it underplayed human fallibility and obscured the depth of potentially explosive political conflicts which might rapidly and unpredictably explode into a nuclear conflagration. In the *Bulletin of the Atomic Scientists*, Morgenthau unfashionably reminded its pacifist and anti-nuclear readers of the dangers of naïve models of disarmament oblivious to deep political tensions which generated arms races in the first place. Whenever previous attempts at disarmament failed to defuse underlying power conflicts, he categorically declared, they had failed miserably. Unless the USA and USSR openly negotiated over those political conflicts which propelled military competition, a nuclear arms race could not be realistically warded off. Disarmament, in short, only made sense in the context of a broader effort at mitigating deeply rooted Soviet–US political tensions. In response to the question of whether the United Sates should now pursue the development of the H-Bomb, he pessimistically noted: "the modern state can no more afford to be without all the weapons which modern technology puts at its disposal than a medieval knight afford to be without a sword." Yet Morgenthau simultaneously confessed that "peace through competitive armaments" – in other words, a nuclear arms race – was "indeed an illusion."[9] He reminded his readers that just such an arms race had preceded the First World War. He worried that its prospects aggrandized the now very real possibility that human civilization might culminate in universal destruction.

So how then might US officials at least minimize the nuclear peril? Since "there are only three ways by which international conflicts can be settled," and two of them had already been effectively eliminated, only one option remained: hard-headed but unemotional negotiations between the Americans and the Soviets.[10] As Morgenthau pointed out, Churchill, Arnold Toynbee, and even the Vatican had issued similar calls for diplomatic negotiations with the Soviets, in which both sides would agree to accept spheres of influence, while pragmatically reducing political conflicts posing an unmediated threat to peace. At least in principle, US Secretary of State Dean Acheson had analogously proposed "negotiation from strength." In fact, Morgenthau endorsed Acheson's view that the USA should increase military spending in order to match the immediate Soviet threat. However, he criticized Acheson for putting off negotiations until the United States had regained the military upper hand: even if the USA were to reverse its postwar cutbacks in military spending, the promise that the US position would be vastly superior to the Russians a few years down the road remained overly optimistic. To be sure, the Soviets had often violated previous agreements, and many plausible reasons for questioning Stalin's trustworthiness could be identified. According to Morgenthau, however, Stalin had behaved in a fashion analogous to previous Russian leaders who had just as aggressively defended their "natural" sphere of influence in Eastern Europe, as had the Americans in their Latin and South American "backyard" despite frequent shifts in the political climate. Soviet talk of world revolution was now chiefly an ideological instrument of traditional Russian imperialism, and even if Russia tomorrow were somehow miraculously to take a non-communist form, its leaders would likely pursue many policies similar to Stalin's.[11] For that matter, throughout history, statesmen had discarded international legal agreements, as Stalin did after the Second World War, when they conflicted with the pursuit of their country's basic power interests; those opposed to sitting down with the Soviets and hammering out a *modus vivendi* for the postwar world could not convincingly appeal to the fact of Stalin's betrayals of postwar agreements as an effective counterargument. In the final analysis,

> [i]f we cannot settle the political conflicts which threaten to involve us in war with the Soviet Union . . . we must face, as we must threaten, destruction with the latest technological means of destruction available to men. If the United States and Soviet Union can settle these conflicts peacefully by safeguarding their vital interests and compromising on secondary issues, the technological progress of mankind will, by that very fact, have lost its threat. They can then afford to agree upon limitation of their armaments.[12]

Morgenthau conceded that there was no guarantee that the two sides might recognize their opponent's vital interests, let alone determine which issues were of secondary or even peripheral significance and thus might be reasonably compromised. But what deeply alarmed him was that, despite Soviet overtures, the US government and public opinion for the most part seemed incapable of even seriously considering the possibility of negotiations, instead demonizing the Russians as the source of all evil in the world. Having fled one totalitarian regime, Morgenthau had few illusions about the horrors of its Soviet variant, vividly acknowledging them in many postwar publications. Despite his own left-leaning political sympathies and consistent support for domestic social reform, he criticized postwar Democrats who had yet to come to terms with the disturbing realities of Soviet political and military might.[13] No less than the right-wingers who overestimated US power and hoped to defeat the Russians by overwhelming force, left-wingers suffered from their own delusional fantasies, oblivious to political novelty and the unavoidable fact that the Soviet–US wartime alliance was now necessarily a closed chapter.

Notwithstanding his growing scholarly and popular acclaim, Morgenthau still saw himself as something of a lonely voice in a political culture which refused to think about the Soviet threat in eminently *political* terms, rather than predominantly moralistic or legalistic ones. For many in his adopted country, and especially those on the right, nothing less than a full-fledged battle between "good and evil" was at stake. Their peers on the left rejected this simplistic and hubristic assessment of the East–West conflict. Yet they succumbed to the equally naïve legalistic fantasy that discovering the "right" legal agreement or proper constitutional design alone would ensure international harmony. By no means hostile to the idea of a world state, Morgenthau considered its realization premature, and he vociferously criticized those on the left who, he felt, were repeating the disastrous errors of interwar legal positivism and liberal international law (*PAN*, 1st edn., 391–418). Once again, liberals and progressives were placing undue faith in the pacifying potential of international legal reform, ignoring differences between domestic and international society. They closed their eyes to the harsh realities of power on the international scene, which continued to subvert otherwise well-meaning legal and constitutional attempts to funnel and tame political conflict. From this perspective, President Truman was merely a typical representative of a deeply neurotic political culture which refused to "face the problem of a negotiated settlement on realistic [i.e. *political*] terms."[14]

The anti-political character of US political thinking manifested itself in two widespread misunderstandings about the demand for a negotiated settlement. First, its critics misleadingly equated negotiations with moral approbation of the opponent and his interests. By crudely interpreting political conflicts about the distribution of power as a battle pitting good against evil, those preoccupied with the evils of the Soviet system simply excluded the politically significant possibility that the great powers might reach an uneasy but workable political *modus vivendi*. The categorical nature of their hostility to negotiations represented a self-destructive and inconsistent moral position because it smugly closed its eyes to the possibility that negotiations might prevent an even greater evil than Soviet totalitarianism, namely full-scale atomic war. If "the struggle between east and west is not primarily a struggle for power, but a crusade of good against evil," there "can be no accommodation," and it was only a matter of time before a third world war occurred.[15]

Second, critics delighted in linking the defense of a negotiated settlement to the sad history of 1930s appeasement, when Neville Chamberlain effectively agreed to German domination of Eastern and southeastern Europe in exchange for what proved to be an illusory and short-lived peace. Morgenthau bluntly rejected the analogy. For him, appeasement represented a "politically unwise negotiation that misjudges the interests and power involved" (*IDNI*, 136). The widespread tendency to associate negotiations per se with appeasement simply confirmed his belief that Americans had lost any capacity to distinguish between wise political judgments which preserve national power and unwise judgments which unnecessarily sacrifice it. Tough bargaining with the Soviets might be able to gain some meaningful concessions in relation to China or Yugoslavia, for example, which had not yet been fully integrated into the Soviet bloc.[16] Spheres of influence should only be worked out subsequent to a process of give-and-take, where both sides might be obliged to bargain away some matters of secondary strategic value in order to strengthen primary strategic interests.

Morgenthau forcefully opposed the criticism that acceding to the possibility of a Soviet sphere of influence meant, for example, handing over control of not only all of Eastern Europe but also much of Asia to the Russians. Asian communism was a fundamentally different creature from its distant Soviet cousin: the former sought national liberation and social revolution, whereas the latter had in some crucial respects become a relatively conservative force internationally.[17] It would be a mistake to treat all communist movements equally, let alone assume that they were being uniformly steered by Moscow. Morgenthau even went so far as to suggest that a tough anti-communist stance in Eastern Europe might be effectively complemented by the United States breaking its ties with the forces of economic privilege and counterrevolution in the developing world: when it served vital interests, the USA could effectively work alongside revolutionary movements.[18] Consequently, he criticized the Truman Doctrine, arguing that Truman had begun transforming a sound quest to contain Soviet expansion in Eastern Europe into a moralistic worldwide anti-communist crusade which the USA could not possibly win.

Through the 1950s, Morgenthau would mechanically repeat his defense of negotiated settlements, only wavering in the aftermath of Khrushchev's ascent to power, when he worried that deliberations with the dynamic new Soviet leader would likely boomerang against the United States in light of the ineptness, as he saw it, of

Dwight Eisenhower's Republican Administration in Washington.[19] Not surprisingly, Morgenthau's defense of negotiated settlement was widely criticized. With some justification, A. J. P. Taylor pointed out that Morgenthau's belief that the Russians and Americans might sit down and sensibly hammer out their differences in an unemotional and even rational manner was probably at least as "idealistic" as the views Morgenthau repeatedly attacked.[20] After all, Morgenthau's *own* analysis repeatedly highlighted the manner in which both American liberals and Soviet communists had succumbed to increasingly irrational messianic political religions, according to which more-or-less narrow values and ideals were seen as possessing universal validity. Why then expect their representatives to overcome these congenital flaws of contemporary political life? As Raymond Aron also noted, the Soviets and Americans in fact did soon carve much of the world up into competing spheres of influence.[21] How else to explain American inaction in the face of Soviet aggression in Eastern Europe? In the aftermath of US passivity in the face of the 1956 Hungarian Revolution, Morgenthau was ready to concede this point. Yet he countered that the disingenuous way in which the Eisenhower Administration accepted Russian domination of Eastern Europe – after all, official policy still was to pursue its *liberation* – was "tantamount to a unilateral recognition of a Russian sphere of influence wherein the United States concedes, without receiving any concessions in return, what she consistently refused to concede since Yalta, and what Winston Churchill urged us to concede only in the give and take of a negotiated settlement."[22] The United States should at least have gotten something valuable in return before relinquishing de facto control of Eastern Europe to the Russians.

Most importantly, for our purposes, Morgenthau's postwar restatement of Realism can be interpreted as a theoretical corollary to his advocacy of superpower negotiations. His major conceptual amendments from this period are directly linked to his deeply rooted anxieties about the possibility of a nuclear war and the closely related belief that only a negotiated settlement provided a sensible way out. No concept is more fundamental to his postwar reconstruction of Realism than the "national interest." Although the term occasionally had appeared in his previous writings, only in 1949 and 1950 did it begin to occupy center stage. Writing on US foreign policy in 1951, he declared that "the fate of the United States and of all the western world may well depend" on the regeneration of "realistic statecraft."[23] Indeed, there could "be no successful foreign policy which cannot be justified by the national interest."[24] The revival of realistic statecraft, Morgenthau declared in *In Defense of the National Interest* (1951), commanded that it rigorously pursue "but one guiding star, one standard for thought, one rule for action: THE NATIONAL INTEREST" (*IDNI*, 242). Morgenthau capitalized the term for an obvious reason: he wanted his readers to understand that it was now the central category of his theory.

The national interest

For better or worse, the concept of the "national interest" is probably Morgenthau's most influential contribution to major strands of contemporary international relations thinking. A prominent US-based Realist journal still calls itself the *National Interest*, political organizations devoted to various foreign policy causes integrate the term into their names, and scholars, politicians, and media pundits delight in bandying it about, typically employing it so as to stress the hard-headed content of their policy preferences. Echoing Morgenthau's reflections from the 1950s, the concept serves as a convenient device for establishing a stark contrast to "idealistic" foreign policy positions allegedly inconsistent with the realities of power politics. It functions as a useful battering ram against "moralists" (for example, those who argue that foreign policy should give priority to the defense of human rights) as well as "utopians" and "legalists" who seek a dramatically strengthened system of global governance. Although contemporary appropriations can be partly explained by its original internal ambiguities, they rest on a truncated interpretation of Morgenthau's version of a complex and multifaceted idea.

Its underlying political inspiration was neither amoral nor anti-legal. Only a foreign policy dedicated to pursuing the national interest held out the possibility of preserving the peace: a negotiated settlement could ensue only if the superpowers pursued Realist statecraft based on the national interest. Policy makers should focus on defending those *vital* and relatively *constant* interests indispensable to the political entities whose protection was their duty: "The idea of interest is indeed of the essence of politics."[25] In an era in which nation states remained the most important form of political organization, the most significant political interests – i.e., those concerning the fundamental question of life or death – were directly related to it. Diplomats should distinguish effectively between primary and secondary power interests. They could not be permitted to sacrifice the former, as Chamberlain's appeasement policies disastrously had, whereas concessions concerning the latter might prove appropriate as a way to preserve peace. The focus on indispensable or fundamental national interests encouraged a "restrictive and rational foreign policy," Morgenthau hoped, in which enemies might potentially find a common basis for meaningful give-and-take.[26] It induced diplomats and politicians to cut through counterproductive ideological divides that obfuscated potential points of agreement. What better antidote to the hubristic and delusional political religions dominating contemporary political discourse?

In turn, the resulting settlement "would give us time," as Morgenthau loved to quote Toynbee, "to try gradually to build these two spheres together and eventually to unite them in a co-operative world government" (cited in *IDNI*, 156). In this unabashedly evolutionary model, a negotiated peace could potentially crack open the door for new forms of cooperation between East and West. It might help prepare the groundwork for the end of national sovereignty, which Morgenthau repeatedly identified as a main source of the evils of modern war. The only answer to the terrors of atomic warfare, he argued forcefully in *Politics Among Nations*, was ultimately a world state. The problem, however, was that no international society had developed yet on the basis of which a world state could effectively operate. The multifaceted presuppositions of effective state sovereignty functioned at the domestic but hardly at the global level. Morgenthau was by no means in principle opposed to establishing global government. However, he derided its creation by means of what he dubbed "constitutional fiat," insisting that its realization rested on an arduous long-term process in which the endlessly complex presuppositions of statehood were slowly and cautiously established beyond the level of the nation state.[27] At the present time, he asserted with obvious plausibility during the darkest days of the cold war, they were lacking. Clear evidence for this lacuna was the disturbing reality of a globe dominated by two deeply antagonistic political and social systems, both armed to the teeth and ready to launch a nuclear war at a moment's notice. Only if the two superpowers tackled negotiations in a sober and even objective manner, ready to compromise on secondary matters whose genuine political significance was widely exaggerated by political ideology and public opinion, might they gain humankind the time it desperately needed to progress towards less destructive political forms.

Unfortunately, Morgenthau's own preference for polemically opposing the "realistic" pursuit of the national interest to the idealistic "utopian" and "sentimentalist" embrace of moralism and legalism meant that its underlying moral and legal impulses sometimes faded into the background. According to the influential *In Defense of the National Interest*, his most important book from the early 1950s, the great failing of US foreign policy was that it had sacrificed its early sober realistic orientation, embodied most clearly in the figure of Alexander Hamilton and his clear-eyed pursuit of US national security, for the pursuit of abstract moral or legal principle; the latter was pictured as having disastrously determined the course of US foreign policy since William McKinley and Woodrow Wilson. Morgenthau defined moralism as an abstract universal principle "divorced from political reality" (*IDNI*, 22); legalism was a similarly naïve belief in the rule of law divorced from political exigencies. Both induced US leaders to overextend political resources, pick the wrong fights, and, even when choosing the right ones, to do so in counterproductive and self-destructive ways. If the United States were now to negotiate successfully with the Soviets, it would finally need to free itself from childish moralistic and legalistic illusions, instead identifying achievable political goals, and start exhibiting a long overdue ability to shed ideological shibboleths and compromise on matters of peripheral strategic value. Despite his occasionally overheated rhetoric, Morgenthau's critique was not directed against morality or legality per se, but instead against political actors who pursued universal moral principles or models of international law oblivious to the many ways in which the "lust for power" and realities of political conflict necessarily subverted them.

Who could possibly deny the seemingly self-evident verity that every nation state possessed some relatively stable interests of greater strategic value than others, or that great political leaders – Morgenthau's favorite example from this period was Churchill – seemed to have an almost instinctive capacity to protect them? At times, Morgenthau wrote and spoke about the national interest as though its meaning were somehow self-evident. His only book-length treatment of the subject, *In Defense of the National Interest*, offered surprisingly limited conceptual illumination. Only when prodded by critics was he forced to sketch out his ideas, doing so most clearly in a major 1952 *American Political Science Review* (*APSR*) article, "Another 'Great Debate': The National Interest of the United States." Revealingly, the most succinct early definition of the "national interest" probably came from one of his students, Kenneth Thompson, who noted that Morgenthau:

> postulates that every nation by virtue of its geographic position, historic objectives, and relationship to other power centers possesses a clustering of strategic interests each more or less vital to its security. At any point in time, a rational foreign policy must attend to the safeguarding of these claims. The national interest stands above and absorbs the limited and parochial claims of sub-national groups, even though such groups seek to interpret the national interest in their own terms. Interests are the permanent part of the political landscape . . . It so happens that the present era in international relations compels statesmen to put first the interests of the territorial nation-state.[28]

But even this useful attempt at clarification could not hide significant ambiguities.

Most immediately, the idea that politicians should be expected to pursue vital and relatively unchanging national interests meshed uneasily with Morgenthau's own avowal of the increasingly anachronistic character of the modern nation state. On the one hand, he characterized the pursuit of the national interest as nothing less than a *universal* empirical and even scientific verity, ignored only by irresponsible political actors at the risk of political suicide. A politician who failed to heed the exigencies of the national interest acted no less inanely than a natural scientist who prescribed that we violate the laws of gravity or relativity: Woodrow Wilson was nothing less than a crackpot political astrologer. On the other hand, he openly conceded in the 1952 *APSR* article, the nation state was "destined to yield in time to different modes of political organization . . . When the national state will have been replaced by another mode of organization, foreign policy must then protect the interest in survival of that new organization."[29] Yet, he asserted, new supranational organizations could only realistically emerge and survive on the basis of individual countries recognizing that their national interests overlapped. The national interest by no means necessarily implied narrow-minded national *egoism*: the national interests of the US and west European liberal democracies, for example, intermeshed in their opposition to Soviet communism; this overlap allowed for potentially significant forms of international cooperation. In this version of the argument, the present national orientation of a great deal of political conflict and struggle was historically transitory, fated to be jettisoned in favor of supranational institutions. The only truly universal attribute of the idea of national interest was the inevitability of power politics or, as Morgenthau now described it, the pursuit of power or political interests: despite changing "circumstances of time and place," this pursuit constituted a permanent feature of political existence.[30]

Of course, this was a relatively uncontroversial observation, far less jolting in nature than Morgenthau's bold and sometimes dogmatic assertions about the primacy of the national interest. Not surprisingly perhaps, he tended to emphasize the more provocative theses about the ubiquity of nationally based power politics and the pursuit of the national interest. Yet he did so at the cost of downplaying what in his better moments he always conceded:[31] the national interest was itself a deeply *historical* concept, integrally related to the particularities of an international system subject to profound change and evolution. In an era in which the nation state remained dominant, political leaders were obliged to pursue its interests. In a different global climate, however, relatively distinct forms of political conflict and interest mediation might emerge. The "lust for power" represented, as Morgenthau tirelessly repeated, a universal aspect of human nature. But he always admitted that it was capable of manifold expressions.

Morgenthau was predisposed to suggesting that the national interest referred to some set of vital matters or issues, of varying significance, but nonetheless all of strategic value. When pressed to explain this idea, however, the story typically became more complicated. In the 1952 *APSR* article, for example, he admitted that in crucial respects the term was similar to what jurists had long described as the "great generalities" of the US Constitution: it contained a core or primary meaning, but beyond that core one could legitimately point to a variety of secondary competing but plausible interpretations and practical policies: "The concept of the national interest, then, contains two elements, one that is logically required and in that sense necessary, and one that is varied and determined by circumstances."[32]

The first or "necessary" element referred to those interests which constituted an irreducible minimum essential to national survival, which Morgenthau interpreted in surprisingly broad terms. The integrity of a country's territory was its most familiar element, but it also included maintenance of basic political and cultural traits: "all nations do what they cannot help but do: protect their physical, political, and cultural identity against encroachments by other nations."[33] Defense of the American national interest thus not only called for maintenance of the territorial integrity of the United States, but also preservation of what he elsewhere described as "the integrity of the American experiment," including, first and foremost, US political values.[34] Although he tended to criticize other analysts for exaggerating the extent to which competing ideological and political orientations decisively shaped foreign policy, his *own* definition in fact took political and cultural factors *directly* into consideration. By implication, the pursuit of the national interest of the United States operated differently from that of Stalinist Russia because the basic definition of what "survival" meant for the competing systems necessarily varied due to deep differences in their respective political and cultural identities. Morgenthau's stock claim from the 1950s that *every* country was destined to pursue the national interest masked his own implicit acknowledgment that fundamental political and ideological differences contributed to meaningful and potentially dramatic differences in real-life foreign policies.[35]

Morgenthau also repeatedly spoke of the primacy of national *survival* as constitutive of the national interest. Yet this was potentially misleading, since sometimes he apparently had more in mind than the Hobbesian view according to which the fundamental goal of political life was the preservation of physical *life* or *existence*. Pursuit of the US national interest required protecting not only the *physical* or *biological* existence of US citizens, but a particular normatively defined "way of life" having distinctive political and cultural traits. If Truman had decided to avoid the horrors of atomic war by simply surrendering to the Soviets, for example, American lives would have been preserved, but the American way of life – and thus, in Morgenthau's terms, US national interests – would have been violated. Despite the occasional Hobbesian undertones, Morgenthau's emphasis on the centrality of survival and self-preservation was anything but Hobbesian. At least implicitly, he grasped that a goal as seemingly uncontroversial as survival was necessarily value-laden since it always directly raised questions about the political and cultural identity of the particular political community at hand. Unfortunately, his analysis of the national interest was not always consistent in its acknowledgment of the far-reaching implications of this view. Preoccupied with contrasting it favorably to competing accounts of foreign policy which stressed the ideological and philosophical source of conflict, Morgenthau tended to downplay the fact that his account referred directly to ideological and philosophical questions about political and cultural identity.

What then of the "variable" or secondary aspects of the national interest? "While the interests which a nation may pursue in its relations with other nations are of infinite variety and magnitude," no political unit has the power resources available to advance its power interests everywhere and at all times.[36] However desirable, the advance of certain policies in some contexts was ill advised, for the familiar reason that national power is necessarily limited, and some matters more essential to national well-being than others. One of the most demanding tasks of policy making was thus to delineate between constant and variable elements of the national interest, in part for the familiar reason that defenders even of peripheral foreign policy goals always dressed up their political preferences to make them seem indispensable. Subnational political and economic constituencies often possessed an obvious interest in advancing a narrow set of foreign policies which "may well fall short of what would be rationally required by the overall interests."[37] As a result, "[t]he necessary elements of the national interest have a tendency to swallow up the variable elements so that in the end all kinds of objectives, actual or potential, are justified in terms of national survival."[38]

For example, Morgenthau argued in *In Defense of the National Interest*, the core national interests of the United States had remained consistent over time; even the most moralistic and legalistic of US political leaders at least intuitively acknowledged their primacy. In order to flourish, the American project required US preponderance in Latin and South America, as well as a rough balance of power in both Asia and Europe: domination of either continent by a single foreign power would necessarily imperil US liberal democracy. The United States had effectively pursued its national interest in the Second World War, for example, by warding off German domination of Europe and Japanese hegemony in Asia. By the same token, the USA after the Second World War possessed a fundamental national interest in preventing Soviet control of Europe. Some policies, Morgenthau believed, clearly served these goals, while others did not. For example, the widespread assessment that "the rearmament of West Germany and the defense of Formosa [Taiwan]" constituted nothing less than life-or-death preferences, Morgenthau opined, was ideologically and perhaps even morally satisfying, but hardly self-evident from the perspective of a sober analysis of the East–West distribution of power.[39] Such policies represented "variable" facets of the national interest to the extent that they remained deeply controversial, and thus deservedly subject to careful critical scrutiny.

The point was not that they were necessarily misbegotten, but instead that it was rationally conceivable that their pursuit might overextend power resources better deployed elsewhere. It might make sense to trade away the prospect of German rearmament or the defense of Taiwan in negotiations with the Soviets or Chinese in exchange for more valuable political goals. The same, however, could not be said about other aspects of contemporary US policy – those undergirding US preponderance in Latin and South America, for example – which represented core elements of the national interest.

Yet even when examined in the most sympathetic light, the call for policy makers to discriminate effectively between the permanent and variable attributes of the national interest inexorably raised an obvious question: who could be expected to pull this off? Notwithstanding his own tendency to underline the ways in which "the yardstick of the national interest" provided relatively practical "hands-on" guidance to real-life policy makers, Morgenthau's examples instead generally worked to remind the reader that his yardstick in fact called for impressive and perhaps superhuman political acumen.[40] No wonder that his postwar writings were filled with deep anxieties about the insufficient professionalism of the contemporary foreign service, along with unabashedly nostalgic longings for the golden age of nineteenth-century "high politics" and elite diplomacy. Given the terrifyingly explosive character of nuclear-age global politics, as well as the irrational attributes of most political thinking, relatively traditional forms of diplomacy were more needed than they ever were before. Yet they were more difficult to cultivate than previously as well.[41] Despite Morgenthau's claims to the contrary, any determination of the national interest inevitably required complex and unavoidably controversial normative *interpretative* – indeed, ideological – claims: understanding the primary interests of the United States, for example, required taking a position on complicated and necessarily controversial norms and ideals concerning political and cultural identity. A libertarian and a democratic socialist, for example, would likely endorse widely varying views of the national interest. As Michael Smith has aptly noted, "[h]ow one defines the national interest depends on the values he espouses and the way he ranks them."[42] Nonetheless, Morgenthau repeatedly criticized the "sentimental illusion" that in East–West rivalry, for example, what was really at stake was "a struggle between virtue and vice, morality and immorality, or two ways of life."[43] Although justified in his anxieties about the sense of smug superiority plaguing contemporary political religions,

Morgenthau's idea of the national interest could not possibly free political actors from making difficult normative and ideological choices.

Morgenthau also frequently declared that the national interest provided "rational" and even potentially "objective" guidance to policy makers, and was capable of offering systematic direction to statesmen and diplomats in a manner which competing approaches simply could not match.[44] Those who grasped its centrality immunized themselves against the unavoidable irrationalities and pathologies of contemporary political thinking better than their peers. Pursuit of the national interest encouraged an objective analysis not only of one's own power position, but also of an opponent's, and thus helped protect political actors from delusional fantasies. In part by demanding of policy makers that they distinguish between its constant and variable elements, it induced them to pursue a clear-headed analysis of real-life power relations, guarding them from ideological rationalizations and intoxications. At times, a faint echo of Morgenthau's early Freudian preoccupations resurfaced in these deliberations: because of our congenital but deeply unsettling "lust for power," political actors inevitably deceived themselves about their real aims and capacities, and especially in the international arena, where the quest for power was insufficiently harnessed, such illusions were at their worst. Just as successful Freudian therapy alerted patients to the illusions under which they had been laboring, enlightening them about the irrational forces to which they had been unduly subjected in order to ensure heightened autonomy, so too might politicians fruitfully pay heed to Morgenthau's call for a Realist theory in which, first and foremost, the national interest served as the "guiding star, one standard for thought, one rule for action."

Whatever its intellectual genesis, Morgenthau's insistence on the rational and objective character of the national interest still badly disfigured the unavoidably controversial core of *any* definition of the national interest. Not surprisingly perhaps, whenever he "faced strong disagreement with his approach and recommendations, Morgenthau called his opponents prisoners of sentiment or moralistic illusions," conveniently ignoring the ways in which his own definition of the national interest raised controversial questions about competing values and ideals.[45] Even its core intuition, namely the idea that national survival or self-preservation constituted a fundamental political goal, unavoidably posed tough questions about political and cultural identity. In the original early modern rendition of this argument, Hobbes could argue with some consistency that his approach was objective and rigorously scientific, in part because he thought that all rational persons could accept the fundamental goal of self-preservation. Yet, somewhat differently, Morgenthau occasionally conceded that even the hard core of the national interest referred to basic questions of political and cultural identity. He may have wanted to hold onto the appealing Hobbesian quest for methodological objectivity, but he could not consistently do so while at least implicitly conceding that basic matters of self-preservation and survival were always deeply normative and inevitably contestable.

Not surprisingly, Morgenthau's own attempt to distinguish between the constant or permanent aspects of US national interest and its variable elements now hardly seems uncontroversial: why, for example, presuppose that the American experiment necessarily required permanent US hegemony in Latin and South America, especially since it clearly contributed to a terrible record of exploitation and political oppression? To the extent that the American political experiment included, in Morgenthau's *own* interpretation, praiseworthy political and economic aspirations for political freedom and equal economic opportunity, his apparent disinterest in the sad and sometimes disastrous record of US intervention in the Americas raises eyebrows.[46] On the one hand, he admitted that the national interest included political and cultural factors inevitably transcending narrow military ones. On the other hand, condoning a history of US intervention in Latin and South America in which liberal and democratic ideals were repeatedly sacrificed, his interpretation at times discounted political and cultural factors in favor of narrowly strategic and military ones.

The moral dignity of the national interest

Morgenthau postulated that the concept of the national interest was a useful tool for empirical social science since it explained how political actors in fact typically acted. Yet the yardstick of the national interest was also intended as a normatively minded contribution to political ethics. As we have seen, he frequently accented its intrinsic capacity to rationalize foreign policy, claiming that it immunized policy makers from political illusions and encouraged responsible decision making. Focusing on the national interest, political actors were outfitted with a powerful corrective to ideologically induced political hubris and moralistic self-congratulatory delusions. Only statesmen committed first and foremost to the pursuit of the national interest, Morgenthau declared, possessed a healthy sense of humility and might even be able to interpret the political world from the enemy's perspective. In this view, pursuit of the national interest generated a political style resting on the old-fashioned virtues of humility, moderation, and prudence: it demanded a careful weighing of options, rigorous examination of their potential consequences, an appreciation for the familiar paradox that even the best intentions produce evil consequences, as well as a hard-headed consideration of the inevitable limits of one's actions. Political catastrophe occurred not when leaders methodically pursued the national interest, but instead when they abandoned it in favor of overreaching and unrealizable ideological goals. Hitler, for example, should obviously be criticized for violating fundamental moral principles. However, Germany also could be condemned on eminently political grounds for pursuing ideological objectives that "had no relation to either the power available to her or the power of the resistance to be overcome."[47] In contrast to Churchill and other praiseworthy political leaders, Hitler's actions lacked both humility and prudence, and as a result he plunged his country into a self-destructive war. By reproducing at least something of Hitler's hubris, and similarly failing to follow the rational and objective yardstick of the national interest (Morgenthau ominously warned his American readers in the pages of the liberal *Commentary* in 1952), they now risked engaging in no less self-destructive policies.

The general contours of this argument are consistent with what Morgenthau had written earlier in *Scientific Man*. Nonetheless, his 1950s writings introduced significant modifications. These changes made Morgenthau's contributions to an identifiably Realist theory vulnerable to the accusation that he lacked a sufficiently robust political ethics.

Recall that *Scientific Man* formulated an extraordinarily demanding political ethics, according to which political actors were obliged to pursue political power while simultaneously maintaining fidelity to a rigorous universal moral code. The ideal statesman, Morgenthau suggested, was both attuned to the harsh realities of power politics *and* necessarily obliged to maintain loyalty to uncompromising moral standards, based in the highest achievements of western culture, which typically condemned the "lust for power" and the political struggles engendered by it. The tragedy of the human condition derived from the fact that human nature drives us to dominate others, while the quest to tame the lust for power by strict moral mechanisms remained no less constitutive of the human condition. Although no simple recipe could be identified, great political leaders managed both to pursue power and to respect fundamental moral imperatives, typically by achieving an "uneasy, precarious, and even paradoxical" *modus vivendi* between the competing dictates of power and morality.

As in the work of Reinhold Niebuhr, who exercised an enormous influence on Morgenthau's political ethics and especially *Scientific Man*, this position suffered from a difficult if not impossible to overcome *dualism*: morality and politics were pictured as placing dueling but equally trying demands on us, and it became difficult to fathom, as Morgenthau himself occasionally intimated in *Scientific Man*, how anyone possibly could do justice to both.[48] By definition, a consistently moral actor seemed destined to founder in a political universe in which lying, deceit, and violence seemed unavoidable; effective political actors were similarly fated to violate fundamental moral imperatives. Morgenthau, in short, proffered an account of morality and politics in which the very idea of a coherent political morality was arguably impossible. On close examination, bringing morality and politics together appeared akin to synthesizing water and oil, two materials that simply cannot be effectively merged. Any attempt to fuse them, in fact, seemed similarly destined to produce inferior materials: we end up with a moralized but ineffective politics or, alternately, a politicized but watered-down morality. Of course, this was Morgenthau's point: our situation is tragic precisely because we are riveted unavoidably by the competing dictates of morality and politics, and we can never achieve a successful reconciliation of them.

When introducing the concept of the national interest, Morgenthau hoped that it might at least mitigate the severity of this dualism. Stressing the tragic contours of human existence was fine as far as abstract political and moral philosophy was concerned, but it did not provide political actors with serviceable advice. What precisely should the *modus vivendi* between morality and politics look like? How exactly might political actors respect political as well as moral imperatives? Worried about a prospective nuclear war, and implicitly cognizant of the fact that his earlier formulations provided little concrete advice to would-be political actors, Morgenthau now tried to construct a more practical and even hands-on political ethics, better able to guide them. Not coincidentally, Morgenthau himself was now involved with actual policy making, serving between 1949 and 1951 as a consultant to George Kennan's famous Policy Planning Department of the US State Department. Although US policy, even during this period, by no means dovetailed with his advice, Morgenthau briefly had the ear of those officials struggling to come up with a plausible response to the Russian atomic explosion, the division of Germany, and the Chinese Revolution. Like Kennan, whom he admired deeply despite some disagreements, he tended to view Russia as a great power with relatively traditional foreign policy interests, he worried about the political perils of a US moral crusade against communism, and he was more than willing to consider practical alternatives to the emerging cold war status quo in Europe and elsewhere.[49] Kennan's own famous Realist tract, *American Diplomacy: 1900–1950*, was based on a series of prestigious lectures which Morgenthau arranged for Kennan to give at the University of Chicago.

The idea of the national interest quickly became the key puzzle piece of a modified political ethics. Unfortunately, it suffered from precisely that Achilles' heel about which Morgenthau had so eloquently warned readers of *Scientific Man*: aspiring to overcome or at least minimize the tragic contours of human action, a political ethics centered on the idea of the national interest inadvertently did disservice to fundamental moral aspirations.

In the pivotal but forgotten "Moral Dilemma in Foreign Policy" (1951), Morgenthau accused continental European political thought of having always remained mired in the unproductive conceptual dichotomy of "reason of state" *versus* moral principles, *Realpolitik in opposition to* morality, Machiavellians *against* anti-Machiavellians. This was no mere scholarly point, Morgenthau added, because contemporary debates, in which purportedly amoral Realists faced off against Idealists and Utopians, mirrored the traditional dichotomy. In contrast to the abstract philosophical reflections about reason of state pursued by continental writers, he claimed, only in the English-language world did political writers and actors tackle the difficult issue of the proper nexus between politics and morality with an apt emphasis on "the practical merit of limited concrete issues." The famously practical and case-oriented character of Anglo-American political life had proven superior at synthesizing morality and the pursuit of power. In effect, it had gone much further in solving the riddles of international political ethics. Its contributions had been neglected by intellectuals, in part because it "never purported to offer an abstract proposition settling the issues once and for all."[50] Nevertheless, one could fruitfully turn to the political experience and practical wisdom of the Anglo-American world in order to figure out how politics and morality might be synthesized and, by implication, the dualism of Morgenthau's own earlier reflections superseded.

The remainder of the essay was then devoted to a selective retelling of debates between Hamilton and Madison on post-revolutionary US foreign policy, as well as Disraeli's and Gladstone's 1870s parliamentary debate on the Ottoman Empire's ruthless suppression of Bulgarian nationalism. Pursuing the same didactic aim, other publications from the early 1950s recounted parliamentary debates among Burke, Pitt, and Fox about the proper English political reaction to revolutionary France (*IDNI*, 70–8). Seeing clear parallels not only between revolutionary France and communist Russia, but also in the respective Anglo-American reactions, Morgenthau's central point was clear enough: those politicians – he sided with the "Realists" Hamilton, Disraeli, and Pitt – who rigorously pursued the national interest not only achieved political success, but also pointed successfully towards overcoming the false opposition of reason of state to morality. Hamilton, Disraeli, and Pitt focused on fundamental questions of basic security, rightly bracketing the overheated ideological preoccupations of their political rivals. Here potentially was the basis of a *new* form of reason of state no longer functioning in opposition to morality. A proper understanding of the crucial category of the national interest exhibited how morality could be "derived" from the laws of political action,[51] rather than seen as fundamentally opposed or external to it: the national interest possessed an intrinsic moral core, and politicians who made it their guiding star could be expected to act in a morally acceptable fashion. In short, pursuit of the national interest might minimize and perhaps even overcome the tragic contours of political action as diagnosed in *Scientific Man*.

But how then was morality somehow *intrinsic* to the pursuit of the national interest? Attempting to answer this question was a central intellectual preoccupation in the early and mid-1950s, as Morgenthau struggled to render "The Moral Dignity of the National Interest" – as he famously entitled a crucial section of *In Defense of the National Interest* – intellectually plausible. After all, the idea was by no means self-evident, especially in light of Morgenthau's own worries about modern nationalism and its tendency to deaden our moral senses.[52] Yet now, it seemed, politicians could follow the national interest and, in doing so, somehow conveniently pay homage to fundamental moral ideals.

In explicating the idea of the "moral dignity of the national inter-est," Morgenthau's starting point was typically a dramatic juxtapo-sition, in fact reminiscent of the dichotomy between morality and *Realpolitik* which he claimed to have superseded: *either* political actors based their foreign policy preferences on abstract moral prin-ciples, *or* they followed the national interest. As he noted in the 1952 *APSR* article:

> [t]he contest between utopianism and realism is not tantamount to a contest between principle and expediency, morality and immorality, although some spokesmen for the former would like to have it that way. The contest is rather between one type of political morality and another type of political morality, one taking as its standard universal moral principles abstractly formulated, the other weighing these principles against the moral requirements of concrete political action, their relative merits to be decided by a prudent evaluation of the political consequences to which they are likely to lead.[53]

Upon a closer look, the commitment to abstract moral principle was essentially what Max Weber had famously described and similarly discarded as an "ethic of conscience" or "pure intentions."[54] In Morgenthau's gloss, as in Weber's, this ethic was both universal and categorical, meaning that it obtained regardless of circumstances, and those committed to pursuing it were obliged to do so rigorously despite any potentially negative or counterproductive consequences: "All objectives are equal before the moral law. If universal democ-racy is the standard of political action, Korea is as important as Mexico, China is as worthy an objective as Canada, and there is no difference between Poland and Panama."[55] Democracy must be pursued everywhere with equal fervor, even though it was more vital and achievable, Morgenthau believed, for the United States to do so in some regions than others. The most basic weakness of an ethic of abstract moral principle was that it ignored the point that "a moral decision always implies a choice among different moral principles, one of which is given precedence over others."[56] It over-looked the fact that moral imperatives clashed, and that no moral actor could realistically hope to respect every moral law on all occa-sions. Compromises and tough choices had to be made. However, the ethic of abstract moral principle provided no real guidance for those facing competing moral principles.

Morgenthau followed Weber in highlighting the intrinsic irre-sponsibility of an ethic of abstract moral principle, similarly noting that it was a recipe for political disaster and moral evil: a principled moral commitment to realizing democracy in Soviet-dominated Eastern Europe, for example, was morally praiseworthy. Yet its unmediated categorical pursuit, blind to concrete political exigencies, could generate another world war and unprecedented violence. "A foreign policy based upon a moral principle . . . is of necessity a policy of national suicide," because it forgets that even the most powerful political actors operate with limited energies and resources and cannot possibly achieve moral aims universally without discrimination.[57]

Taking the argument a step further, Morgenthau added that such dilemmas were exacerbated at the international level by the relative fragility and poverty of international morality. The ethic of principled morality neglected the fact that appeals to moral principle are more controversial and easily manipulated by privileged power interests there than at the domestic level. Within the confines of the nation state, one could typically discern some rough working consensus about basic moral and political values: "What justice means in America I can say; for interests and convictions, experiences of life and institutionalized traditions, have in large measure created a consensus which tells me what justice means under the conditions of American society." Of course, even then moral and political consensus was subject to challenge and political renegotiation, and during extreme situations fundamental questions of political and moral identity might be dramatically reshuffled. Yet on the global scale, the exceptional situation was closer to the normal state of affairs: the meaning even of those values or norms universally endorsed could be up for grabs. Supranational norms were more controversial than their domestic corollaries, and moral appeals more likely to constitute ideological veils for privileged power interests eager to mask their particularistic pursuits in universalistic language. In an age in which most individuals identified uncritically with national goals, many purportedly supranational standards were inevitably little more than a "projection of national moral standards onto the international scene." At the present time, "supranational moral principles concrete enough to give guidance to the political actions of individual nations" were rare indeed, and "there is also no agency on the international scene to protect and promote the interests of individual nations . . . except the individual nations themselves."[58] In the case of conflicting legal interpretations, for example, at the global level powerful states often determined the meaning of legal clauses, whereas at least on the domestic level longstanding institutional mechanisms operated to reduce the advantages enjoyed by the powerful.

Morgenthau's point here was *not* that universal moral principles were necessarily chimerical. As we have seen, he repeatedly argued to the contrary, heralding throughout his career a universalistic non-utilitarian ethic whose roots he saw in the most demanding expressions of western religious and moral thought. In addition, he opposed the extreme view according to which international morality was non-existent, a sort of empty vessel into which powerful actors simply poured whatever content they wanted. Modern norms of civilized warfare, after all, had generally been respected by powerful as well as weak states. Nonetheless, appeals to universal moral principle remained more vulnerable to arbitrary employment and manipulation in the international than in the national sphere. They were more likely to serve as morally hypocritical political weapons of the most powerful political players than as genuine principled expressions of universal morality. The ethic of abstract moral principles blinked at the unsettling fact that what appeared as an incontrovertible universal principle at the domestic level might look quite different to actors having distinct political experiences and national backgrounds. It occluded some of the most politically significant consequences of moral, political, and cultural pluralism at the global level. In Morgenthau's own language, foreign policy based on an ethic of abstract moral principle undermined the need for "tolerance of other political systems and policies based on different moral principles," in fact typically undermining the fundamental "precondition of a number of nations living side by side in mutual respect and peace."[59]

Having disposed of the ethic of abstract moral principle, Morgenthau's argumentation then moved rapidly to demonstrate the purported superiority of a political morality based on the national interest. Only an ethic of the national interest, in short, could overcome the failings of abstract principled morality.

This conceptual move suffered from a clear weakness, however. Morgenthau followed Weber in expounding what was effectively a reworked version of the "ethic of responsibility." In contrast to the ethic of principled morality, we should demand of moral and political actors that they grapple with potentially counterproductive consequences, carefully weighing alternative possible courses of action with "their relative merits to be decided by a prudent evaluation of the political consequences to which they are likely to lead."[60] Ethical responsibility charged us with openly acknowledging the fundamental paradox that apparently moral acts based on good intentions may produce unexpected evils, and seemingly evil acts sometimes moral goods. This fundamental paradox plagued *every* form of action, but especially in the political sphere, where the stakes are typically highest, only by grappling seriously with it could we avert terrible violence. Only a consequentialist ethic permitted the complicated prudential considerations by means of which political agents might mediate intelligently among and between competing moral principles when faced with difficult ethical and political quagmires. It might be morally desirable to pursue a global crusade for liberty, for example, but in contradistinction to the ethic of principled morality, an ethic of responsibility aptly showed how doing so might prove counterproductive and even self-destructive in some settings and at some times.

Unfortunately, Morgenthau does not seem to have recognized that his restatement of Weber's ethic of responsibility by no means logically *required* what he frequently dubbed the "primacy of national interest." The reason for this conceptual slippage is clear enough: many aspects of the Realist preoccupation with the national interest, as interpreted by Morgenthau, in fact meshed conveniently with the fundamental contours of an ethic of responsibility. Morgenthau regularly focused on the overlap between the two: both served as useful correctives to hubristic moral overreaching, encouraged actors to engage in complicated prudential reflections, and forced them to grapple with the complicated ways in which all human action produced unforeseen and oftentimes undesirable consequences.

Yet Morgenthau was probably mistaken in assuming that the ethic of responsibility was necessarily tied to the pursuit of national interest. It might be logically consistent with a principled commitment to advancing universal human rights or even universal democratization, for example, as long as political agents who pursued them faced, as both Weber and Morgenthau appropriately commanded, the paradoxical contours of political action. A human rights-oriented foreign policy, for example, deeply skeptical of those means (for example, military intervention) likely to prove counterproductive, sensitive to the complex dilemmas generated by international political and economic inequality, and which forthrightly recognizes that universal human rights can be subject to distinct cultural interpretations, might prove congruent with an ethic of responsibility. In some settings, such policies might indeed *also* prove consistent with the national interest, especially if the political

identity of the country pursuing them rested on principled commitments to democracy and human rights. But if, instead, its power
and prestige depended on their suppression, their pursuit might
unsettle or even undermine its national interest, at least as hitherto
understood. Morgenthau was too quick to preclude the possibility
that policies he might decry as unrealistic or "idealistic" might be
effectively advanced in accordance with the sober consequentialist
ethic of which he was so enamored.

Like Weber before him, Morgenthau presupposed that the ethic
of responsibility went hand-in-hand with a brand of Realism in
which political actors and those who made foreign policy must
accept the "primacy of national interest." But this logical connection
only obtained if an additional set of arguments could be
defended.

In Weber's own writings on German foreign policy, international
politics generally was depicted as a harsh battle for self-assertion
among competing political and cultural entities, in which those
nation states which failed to exert effective power internationally
were threatened with destruction or at least irrelevance. Consistently expressing deep anxiety about Germany's position in relation
to the great powers, Weber worried that its fate might reproduce
that of small or extinct political communities which had been effectively swallowed up during the course of history: "We do not have
peace and human happiness to hand down to our descendants, but
rather the *eternal struggle* to preserve and raise the quality of our
national species."[61] The decline of German power was unacceptable,
he asserted, not simply because Germans had a rightful interest in
their own self-preservation, but also because German cultural and
political achievements were both distinct and valuable. Although
such evaluations unavoidably took us into the deepest realm of
controversial value-laden assessments, he admitted, in his mind
there could be no doubt that Germany's achievements rivaled those
of the French, British, Americans, or Russians. Germany's leaders
were obliged to advance its power interests abroad not only because
of an abstract right of self-preservation, but because humankind
would have lost something considerable if Germany and its way of
life were extinguished from the globe. Mixing a Hobbesian depic-
tion of the state of nature with a nationalism inspired by Social
Darwinism, Weber defended Germany's right to expand its influence abroad – if necessary, by military force.

Absent the German nationalism of the original, Morgenthau's
defense of the "moral dignity of the national interest" sometimes

echoed Weber as well. In a 1952 essay written for the prestigious *Annals of the American Academy of Political and Social Science*, Morgenthau reiterated that the "prime duty of all nations" remained the task of taking care of its own national interest, adding that the "moral justification for this prime duty of *all* nations – for it is not only a moral right but an obligation – arises from the fact that if this particular nation does not take care of its own interests, nobody else will [emphasis added]."[62] Who else could effectively do so given the lack of a world state and the underdeveloped character of existing international institutions? In an agonistic international climate, rival political entities must pursue their fundamental interests in order maintain themselves; it is unfathomable that others will consistently do so for them. At the national level, individuals can be expected to act altruistically because an immensely complex set of norms and institutions protects them from harsh negative repercussions. Yet, Morgenthau observed in a 1950 *APSR* article, "as the international society is at present constituted, the consistent neglect of the national interest can only lead to national suicide." In this view, "[s]elf preservation for the individual as well as for societies is not only a biological and psychological necessity," but "a moral duty as well."[63] Because no one else could be realistically expected to advance the national interest, that duty necessitated that all nationally based political leaders rigorously heed its call in order to ensure national survival.

Conveniently missing from this claim was a reminder that for Morgenthau himself every conception of the national interest, as noted above, necessarily referred to fundamental matters of shared political and cultural identity. Political entities were not in fact biological creatures which fight instinctively for self-preservation, but instead normatively constituted political and legal collectivities resting on specific political and cultural ideals. Is there then any reason to assume a "moral duty," as Morgenthau seemed to imply, to preserve *every* form of political and cultural identity? Despite his own skeptical remarks about the applicability of universal moral principles in international politics, Morgenthau in fact seemed here to advocate a rather controversial universal "duty" or principle. To be sure, *all* nation states may in fact seek to pursue their vital interests. Given the vast range of identities which constitute them, however, can we be quite so sure that we can speak of some fundamental *moral obligation* to do so? Nazi Germany and Stalinist Russia pursued their national interests; on an empirical level, Morgenthau's claim seems impeccable. Yet as soon as the postulate turns prescriptive, matters immediately look more complicated. As Morgenthau himself was well aware, there are many good reasons why some political systems and their identities should be condemned and ultimately replaced. Indeed, their survival may very well conflict with the imperatives of *biological* self-preservation: Nazism and Stalinism massacred large segments of their own populations as well as millions elsewhere. As an empirical matter, a political system based on cannibalism is likely to seek to preserve and perhaps extend its way of life. Whether or not it *should* do so, however, remains another matter. By transforming the idea of the national interest into a moral duty, Morgenthau obfuscated the difficult normative questions raised by the existence of deeply unappealing and potentially intolerable cultural and political practices.

Weber's original rendition of the argument was able to elide this difficulty because he was disturbingly unconcerned about the demise of small and – in his view – backwards political communities. For him, the real task at hand was preserving *German* influence, which was justified, at least in part, because of controversial presumptions concerning cultural and political superiority. Despite its nationalistic tones, Weber at least implicitly recognized that any defense of the national interest required a *substantive* evaluation of the particular nation state and the underlying political identity to which it was integrally related. For him, *not every national interest was created equal.* Of course, Morgenthau himself always discriminated between and among distinct political regimes, eloquently criticizing totalitarian systems like Nazi Germany which had rendered him stateless and murdered some friends and family. Yet the quest to transform the national interest into the keystone of a normatively minded political ethics, as well as the basis for empirical analysis, inexorably functioned to downplay the central conceptual status of such distinctions. Perhaps Morgenthau would have done better to assert that *certain* national communities committed to some set of *broadly acceptable* political and cultural values were morally obliged to advance their interests. But the same certainly cannot be said, as he implied, for *all* political communities, including those violent monstrosities predicated on systematic violations of deeply rooted universal moral laws. Indeed, depending on one's evaluation of the normative character even of less extreme cases, the moral dictate that leaders should focus on pursuing the national interest was likely to be true only to a *greater or lesser degree*: the extent to which a particular political entity possessed normatively admirable political and cultural attributes, and consistently pursued responsible policies based on them, determined the degree to which the pursuit of the national interest was morally praiseworthy.

The same dilemma plagued another stock argument regularly made in defense of the "moral dignity of the national interest." As he commented in *In Defense of the National Interest* and in countless other writings from the 1950s:

> [t]here is a profound and neglected truth hidden in Hobbes's extreme dictum that the state creates morality as well as law and that there is neither morality nor law outside the state. Universal moral principles, such as justice or equality, are capable of guiding political action only to the extent that they have been given concrete content and have been related to political situations by society. (*IDNI*, 34)

In this view, the nation state remained the primary site in which morality and legality flourish. For anyone committed to preserving universal morality, as well as a functioning system of legality or justice, preservation of the nation state and its vital interests necessarily took on an overriding moral significance. Alongside this Hobbesian point, Morgenthau also *hinted* at the Hegelian insight that only at the level of the nation state was morality concretely realized in accord with the exigencies of particular historically situated political communities.[64] Principled universal morality needed to be complemented by what Hegel described as *Sittlichkeit* ("ethical life"), where morality was embodied in a concrete set of normative practices and institutions with which individuals might identify in relatively direct ways. Whereas the imperatives of universal morality often seemed external and alien, concrete ethical practices – objectified in society's main institutions, which fleshed out fundamental normative aspirations – offered a set of everyday normative parameters by means of which individuals could fundamentally orient and guide themselves. Like Hegel, Morgenthau suggested that the nation state remained the primary site for concretizing morality. The quest for justice, for example, was universal, yet only at the national level did we find particular norms and institutions concretizing unavoidably abstract general ideals of justice. In this manner, they offered a "concrete content" with which particular nationally situated individuals could identify to an extent that had yet to be achieved at the supranational level.

Yet this otherwise suggestive set of arguments produced as many enigmas as they were intended to resolve. Even if Morgenthau was right to assert that only at the level of the nation state could we locate concrete expressions of universal moral ideals, it was by no means self-evident that *all* nation states concretized universal moral ideas to the same extent. Some national communities, in fact, systematically violate universal moral ideals and prevent even a bare modicum of justice as a matter of course, while many, if not most, allow for their concretization only in limited and arguably problematic ways. Once again, Morgenthau's argument implicitly called out difficult *substantive* normative considerations of the political and cultural ideals on which the national interest of any given polity was based. His suggestion that preserving the national interest remained something akin to a general moral *duty* begged the question of whether some nation states do a particularly good job of realizing morality and justice, and, if not, whether advancing their national interests can be said to represent anything more than a morally deplorable form of national egoism. The yardstick of the national interest, in short, was vastly more complex than Morgenthau wanted to admit. Any evaluation of it necessarily depended on deep reflections on controversial matters of political and cultural identity. Whether political actors should accept the primacy of national interest depended, in the final analysis, on whether the political and cultural ideals at its basis were deserving of their fidelity. Speaking primarily to his US audience, Morgenthau could perhaps avert his eyes from these questions by presupposing a morally sound basis for the national interest. Like other liberal democracies, the United States could perhaps make a plausible claim to advance its vital interests because they gave expression to political and cultural ideals more attractive than those of its cold war rivals. But the "moral duty" Morgenthau spoke of derived from a substantive and by no means uncontroversial evaluation of those ideals, not the idea of the national interest per se.[65]

Scientific Man had warned that any attempt to mitigate the tragic character of political life risked doing an injustice to fundamental moral ideals. Morgenthau's claim that the national interest could provide political as well as moral guidance ultimately distorted the proper place of moral considerations in foreign policy. Morgenthau was right to remind his academic, as well as a growing public, audience that political action required a commitment to the ethic of responsibility. Yet he was wrong to equate that ethic with the pursuit of the national interest.

4

Politics among nations and beyond

The evolution of Morgenthau's most famous book, the massive *Politics Among Nations: The Struggle for Power and Peace*, corroborates my interpretive claim that a subtle but decisive shift took place in Morgenthau's thinking between the 1940s and early 1950s. In accord with *Scientific Man*, in the first 1948 edition Morgenthau nowhere characterized his theoretical undertaking as identifiably Realist. He again firmly rejected the intellectual legacy of Machiavelli and Hobbes, describing their theories as having appropriately "met with the disapproval of prevailing opinions" for having "accepted rather than condemned and restrained" the ubiquity of power drives (*PAN*, 1st edn., 169; also 397). Characterized as conflicting with the "Western tradition which seeks, if not to eliminate, at least to regulate and restrain the power drives which otherwise would either tear society apart or else deliver the life and happiness of the weak to the arbitrary will of those in power," Nietzsche's glorification of the will to power was again associated with the horrors of fascism and Nazism (*PAN*, 1st edn., 197). The 1948 edition of *Politics Among Nations* also challenged the Hobbesian view that interstate relations in the modern system could be captured by the metaphor of the state of nature, criticizing it for underestimating the significant role that ethics, mores, and law played in restraining state action even in the absence of world government (*PAN*, 1st edn., 169).

An unusual publishing success given its demanding 500 pages, *Politics Among Nations* was immediately adopted as a textbook, primarily for large introductory courses, at Columbia, Harvard,

Princeton, and Yale, as well as ninety additional colleges and universities in the United States by April 1949. By October 1953, Morgenthau's book was apparently used by more North American university-level instructors than all competing texts in international politics combined.[1] The textbook ultimately went into seven editions, with the later ones periodically updated by Kenneth Thompson, and it remains in print, even if its use in university courses has declined in recent decades. It would only be a slight exaggeration to claim that *Politics Among Nations* singlehandedly initiated many generations of US international relations students into the field.

Nonetheless, the book's reception has been disappointingly one-sided. Whereas Morgenthau continued to fuse empirical and normative concerns, US political scientists increasingly tended to draw a sharp line between the two. The result was that those political scientists most attracted to Morgenthau's Realism mined his work for scientifically testable empirical hypotheses, while unfortunately downplaying the work's normative preoccupations and, in particular, its concern with the "struggle for power *and* peace" (emphasis added). Morgenthau was quickly interpreted in a rather one-sided fashion as an advocate of power politics whose main weakness, as neo-Realists like Kenneth Waltz quickly argued, was precisely his failure to develop a sufficiently value-free and scientific vision of international politics.[2] Morgenthau's Realist offspring would soon follow Waltz in systematically driving normative issues from the proper confines of Realist inquiry. For their part, normative political theorists tended implicitly to accept this truncated reading of *Politics Among Nations* or simply to ignore the work altogether. Predictably, Morgenthau was soon the unhappy founding father of an influential but normatively numb Realist research paradigm. No wonder that he wrote angry jeremiads about the direction the discipline was taking: despite his enormous influence, Morgenthau was badly misunderstood.[3] Of course, his own proclivity for making sweeping empirical claims invited one-sided interpretations of his thinking.

Not surprisingly in light of its impressive sales figures, the book's illustrious publisher, Alfred Knopf of New York, asked Morgenthau periodically to update the text in accord with new developments in international politics. Even though much of the text remained fundamentally unaltered, Morgenthau's revisions offer illuminating perspectives on his own intellectual and political path between 1948 and the 1970s. The most dramatic changes occurred early on in the second 1954 edition, however, in which Morgenthau included a new introductory chapter laying out what he described as the "six principles of political realism," to which he now forthrightly subscribed.

Six principles of political realism

Some of the principles simply restated ideas Morgenthau had previously endorsed without having consistently described them as Realist. The first consisted of the familiar attempt to wed philosophical anthropology to an agonistic model of politics: not only was human nature historically unchanging, but the "laws of politics" had their roots in it. Its most basic law, Morgenthau noted, was that politics was unavoidably a struggle for power, in which competing forces sought to gain control over their rivals. Although the threat of violence often played a decisive role, especially in power struggles in the international sphere, even there power should not be conflated with force or violence. At its core, political power was "a psychological relation between those who exercise it and those over whom it is exercised," and such influence could be achieved by a variety of devices, including "orders, threats, persuasion," and even, Morgenthau added in the 1960 edition, charisma (*PAN*, 3rd edn., 29–30).[4] Thus, we might speak cogently of "the political power of an industrialist, labor leader, or lobbyist in so far as his preferences influence the actions of other men," even though such power-holders typically lacked any recourse to organized violence. In fact, when a political tension exploded into unmitigated violence, it no longer made sense to talk of political power in the proper sense of the term. Then "[t]he exercise of physical violence substitutes for the psychological relation between two minds, which is of the essence of political power, the physical relation between two bodies, one of which is strong enough to dominate the other's movements" (*PAN*, 2nd edn., 27).

When Morgenthau subsequently described the core elements of *national power*, he thus quite consistently emphasized that military force represented *one* necessary but insufficient source, accusing those who exaggerated its real-life worth as succumbing to *militarism*. In fact, "of all the factors that make for the power of a nation, the most important ... is the quality of diplomacy" since only diplomacy combined power's raw materials – for Morgenthau, geography, natural resources, industrial capacity, military preparedness, population, national character, and quality of government –

"into an integrated whole," thereby giving them the right direction and appropriate weight (*PAN*, 2nd edn., 128–9). This analytic point was by no means purely academic: Morgenthau worried that US policy makers regularly overestimated the political utility of military power. Like others throughout history, they falsely assumed that military muscle was the most vital instrument by means of which complex international problems could be resolved. Just as interwar France foolishly relied on the Maginot line while neglecting the cultivation of alternative power resources, so too did postwar US policy makers wrongly believe that US military muscle, and especially an unsurpassed nuclear arsenal, guaranteed their predominance in a rapidly changing world.

Albeit in a roundabout way, the second principle offered an abstract restatement of Morgenthau's recent conceptual innovations from *In Defense of the National Interest*: "the concept of interest defined in terms of power" took center stage in allowing Realism to "find its way through the landscape of international politics." Working from the admittedly counterfactual assumption that politicians tended to advance the national interest, Morgenthau suggested, offered significant methodological advantages. It allowed observers of foreign affairs to gain intellectual discipline and much-needed objectivity: by focusing on how the statesman advanced "interest defined in terms of power," analysts could successfully "look over his shoulder" and "retrace and anticipate, as it were, the steps a statesman – past, present, or future – has taken or will take on the political scene." By thinking in terms of the pursuit of the national interest, one might "understand his thoughts and actions perhaps better than he, the actor on the political scene, does himself" (*PAN*, 2nd edn., 5). Just as political actors who opted systematically to pursue the national interest could counteract the perils of both self-congratulatory political ideology and moral self-delusion, so too might the practitioner of Realist theory successfully ward off the tendency to exaggerate the role of ideology and morality in foreign affairs. After all, *both* practitioners and students of international politics risked succumbing to ideological and moral illusions. Ideology often obfuscated the character of political undertakings; motives were hard to discern, and their good or bad character was unrelated to the moral consequences generated by them. Though politically disastrous, "Neville Chamberlain's policies of appeasement were, as far as we can judge, inspired by good motives" (*PAN*, 2nd edn., 6). By the same token, ideology and morality too often got in the way of a scholarly assessment of foreign affairs.

As the negative example of Chamberlain recalled, however, not all political actors rigorously pursued the national interest. This, of course, was Morgenthau's main gripe with most twentieth-century US foreign-policy makers. But by using the national interest not simply as a yardstick for policy itself, but also as a *scientific* measure by means of which we could properly *understand* political action, Realism permitted its scholarly disciples to distinguish between foreign policies that "followed so rational, objective, and unemotional a course" and those that did not. In Morgenthau's view, the pursuit of the national interest was not only both the politically and morally right thing to do, but it alone was rational and objective as well, and thus the key instrument in any scholarly tool kit purporting to offer an objective and scientific – i.e. free of self-satisfying ideological and moral illusions – view of international politics (*PAN*, 2nd edn., 7). *Scientific Man* had earlier vehemently criticized the dangers of crudely extending an out-of-date version of the natural sciences to social inquiry. But *scientism* was different from *science*: Morgenthau always remained a defender of a systemic analysis of international politics, even if he worried about the intellectual provincialism of what soon passed for mainstream US political science. For him, the keystone to scientific inquiry relied substantially, as it had for Max Weber, on *ideal types* which could not possibly "show everything that can be seen by the naked eye," but nonetheless, when effectively constructed, shed light on the essential or indispensable attributes of the social phenomenon under consideration (*PAN*, 2nd edn., 7). The national interest represented a useful ideal type with which scholarly observers could impartially interpret political action.[5]

The third principle simply reiterated the view that "interest defined as power" was necessarily determined by historical circumstances: "the kind of interest determining political action in a particular period of history depends upon the political and cultural context within which foreign policy is formulated" (*PAN*, 2nd edn., 8). Only under the historically transitory conditions of the modern nation state was "interest defined as power" *integrally* linked to the nation state: "the contemporary connection between interest and the national state is a product of history, and is therefore bound to disappear in the course of history." As *Politics Among Nations* proceeded to show, the obsolescence of the sovereign national state was indisputable since it no longer provided lasting security in a political universe haunted by the possibility of nuclear war (*PAN*, 2nd edn., vii).[6] In short, "nothing in the realist position militates against the assumption that the present division of the political world into nation-states will be replaced by larger units of a quite different character, more in keeping with the technical circumstances and moral requirements of the contemporary world" (*PAN*, 2nd edn., 9). Not only did Morgenthau point hopefully to the basic fundaments of what has since become the European Union, but a paramount feature of *Politics Among Nations* was his defense of the world state.

The fourth and fifth principles simply summarized Morgenthau's political ethics, emphasizing the affinities between Realism and moral prudence as well as the dangers of hubris: "All nations are tempted – and few have been able to resist the temptation for long – to clothe their own particular aspirations and actions in the moral purposes of the universe." Moral laws are universal and actors are obliged to respect them. Yet "to pretend to know with certainty what is good and what is evil" in a particular political situation, let alone endorse "the blasphemous conviction that God is always on one's side" in the political and especially international realms, was a recipe for political irresponsibility (*PAN*, 2nd edn., 10). Despite widespread claims to the contrary, Realism was well "aware of the moral significance of political action" (*PAN*, 2nd edn., 9). Yet it was more attuned than its intellectual rivals, Morgenthau insisted, to the paradoxes and complexities of action in an agonistic and violent political universe in which simple-minded moralism too often produced terrible violence.

Only Morgenthau's sixth and final principle evinced the internal tensions plaguing his mature Realist political ethics. The sixth principle posited that the Realist "maintains the autonomy of the political sphere, as the economist, the lawyer, the moralist maintain theirs" (*PAN*, 2nd edn., 10). Moreover, "the political realist is not unaware of the existence and relevance of standards of thought other than the political one. As political realist, he cannot but subordinate these standards of thought to the political one" (*PAN*, 2nd edn., 11). No wonder that generations of students read Morgenthau as advocating the subjection of moral standards to political expediency, despite the immediate qualification that anyone "who was nothing but 'political man' would be a beast, because he would be completely lacking in moral restraints" (*PAN*, 2nd edn., 11). His emphasis in the sixth principle on the autonomy of politics sat at best uneasily alongside the fourth and fifth principles and their emphasis on Realism's moral preoccupations. How could Realism be "aware of the moral significance of political action" *and* simultaneously respect the strict autonomy of politics *as distinguished from morality*?

In his Weimar-era critique of Schmitt's *Concept of the Political*, Morgenthau had rejected the idea that politics should be represented as a sphere of action fundamentally distinct from economics, aesthetics, or morality. Unfortunately, Schmitt's confused conceptual imagery now resurfaced. Why its reappearance? *In Defense of the National Interest* had tried to establish that, merely by following the eminently *political* yardstick of the national interest, statesmen could not only successfully pursue sound foreign policy, but also minimize moral harm. Sound morality or ethics was *latent* in the laws of politics. Respect for the autonomy of the political sphere by no means conflicted with responsible and ethically sound moral action. From this perspective, the Realist defense of autonomous politics appeared to cohere nicely with Morgenthau's deep moral preoccupations, and there seemed nothing contradictory about proclaiming the autonomy of the political while drawing attention to Realism's moral credentials.

Perhaps rightly uneasy about this conceptual move, however, the 1954 *Politics Among Nations* sometimes reverted to his earlier dualistic political ethics, according to which the autonomy of politics entailed a morally reprehensible "lust for power" fundamentally in conflict with the highest ambitions of the western moral tradition. In this alternative view, a pure or unrestrained political creature was always a potentially dangerous beast who needed to be reined in by moral laws, or what Morgenthau described in the opening chapter of *Politics Among Nations* as the competing "moral sphere." How then might the moral sphere be brought to bear on politics? "Political realism is based upon a pluralistic conception of human nature," Morgenthau declared, and fortunately "real man is a composite of 'economic man,' 'political man,' 'moral man,' 'religious man,' etc." (*PAN*, 2nd edn., 12). Nonetheless, it ultimately remained unclear how this recourse to the idea of a pluralistic vision of the human condition coincided with the competing claim that the core difference between Realism and its intellectual competitors was the former's embrace of the *strict* autonomy of the political sphere (*PAN*, 2nd edn., 10).

These ambiguities probably derived in part from the conceptual dilemmas identified in the previous chapter. When defining the national interest, Morgenthau had occasionally noted that it included a nation's cultural and political identity. In part because of his preoccupation with contrasting Realism favorably with the pathologies of legalism and moralism, however, his analysis generally shied away from fully pursuing the intuition that any interpretation of the national interest inevitably touched on deep and invariably controversial normative and ideological questions about values and ideas. At times, morality and ideology were depicted as *external* to power politics and the national interest, when in fact they necessarily helped constitute it. The same basic conceptual tension reemerged here. On the one hand, *Politics Among Nations* underscored the moral and thus normative core of Realism and the central analytic place it accorded the concept of the national interest. At the same time, it portrayed political action, and with it the rational pursuit of "interest in terms of power," as somehow fundamentally *distinct* from morality and ideology. In fact, Morgenthau now sometimes depicted the latter as representing little more than a *superstructure* by means of which power-hungry actors shrouded their narrow interests in misleading moral and humanitarian language. Moral and political norms were at times *constitutive* of power politics and "interest defined as power"; at other junctures, they represented a mere veil or ideological superstructure. As Michael Smith has astutely pointed out:

> Morgenthau is unclear about whether ideologies can define "ultimate goals of political action" or whether they are mere "pretexts and false fronts" for the usual policies of power. He resolves the problem by dismissing ultimate goals [for example, the express intentions of political actors] as a concern of his theory – surely a problematic position – and asserting that power is *always* the intermediate, and usually the only important, goal of politics.[7]

Not only did this tendency in Morgenthau's thinking do a disservice to his otherwise thoughtful suggestion that questions of political and cultural identity were essential to the pursuit of power, but it also helped generate a sometimes reductionist interpretation of the role of norms and ideas in international politics. Correspondingly, a key chapter in *Politics Among Nations* was preoccupied with "unmasking the real purpose behind" political ideologies by tracing their origins to different versions of power politics.[8] Ideas and norms here primarily represented political weapons employed by fundamentally *preconstituted* political blocs, rather than themselves potentially offering a fertile terrain for constituting and potentially *reconstituting* political identity and relations of power.

Despite these conceptual tensions, *Politics Among Nations* offered a formidable and in some respects unsurpassed contribution to international political theory. Most surprisingly perhaps, Morgenthau formulated a powerful Realist defense of the world state and the moral imperative of superseding the existing system of states.

How to civilize politics among nations

Although revised over the course of three decades, the basic narrative of *Politics Among Nations* remained pretty much unchanged. That structure accurately captured the core theses of Morgenthau's mature international political theory.

The first third of the book (i.e. Parts One to Three) was devoted to analyzing the nature of power conflicts, their psychological roots, as well as their concrete manifestations in the international arena. Domestic and international politics were "but two different manifestations of the same phenomenon: the struggle for power," although the potentiality of organized violence loomed larger on the international than on the domestic scene. The differences between international and domestic politics were significant, even if they remained differences of degree rather than of kind, since the specter of political violence – e.g., civil war and revolution – also haunted domestic affairs (*PAN*, 2nd edn., 34). Politics at both levels could be neatly categorized into three basic types: some policies sought to keep or maintain power, others to increase it, and a third type aspired to show or demonstrate power. In the international sphere, three types of policy could be correspondingly grouped and captured by useful ideal types: *status quo* policies aimed to maintain an existing power constellation, *imperialism* referred to the attempt to acquire more power and unsettle the international status quo, and policies of *prestige* enjoined demonstrating or exhibiting power for its own sake or, more commonly, in support of either status quo or imperialist policies. Insisting on its eminently *political* characteristics by pointing out that even "during the entire period of mature capitalism, no war, with the exception of the Boer War, was waged by major powers exclusively or even predominantly for economic objectives," Morgenthau categorically rejected economic and Marxist conceptions of imperialism (*PAN*, 2nd edn., 46). Their error was to construct a universal theory on the basis of limited examples, and thus ignore an overwhelming body of evidence in support of the primacy of politics over economics in foreign policy (*PAN*, 2nd edn., 48). Morgenthau also noted that contemporary scholarship unfairly discounted policies of prestige in the international arena, misleadingly associating them with arcane political practices destined to be washed away by a rising liberal democratic tide. But this view failed to make sense of the staying power of diplomatic rituals and public displays of military muscle (e.g. May Day parades in the Soviet Union), let alone their psychological roots in the universal "desire for social recognition" (*PAN*, 2nd edn., 68).

Ideal-typical versions of international power politics were then related to specific ideologies. Status quo policies were often justified by appeals to peace and international law, whose fundamentally static attributes meshed well with the status quo powers' interest in preserving existing power relations. Imperialism employed a variety of ideological instruments; anti-imperialist rhetoric able to confound the observer "who cannot always be sure whether he is dealing with an ideology of imperialism or with the true expression of a policy of the status quo" (*PAN*, 2nd edn., 87) was particularly effective. How could nation states act effectively on the international stage? They needed *national power*, and *Politics Among Nations* proceeded to provide an analysis of its multiple sources. As in his ambivalent discussion of the national interest, Morgenthau clearly integrated normative elements into his definition, while at the same time lambasting competing interpretations of foreign policy for unduly highlighting moral and ideological attributes. A nation's power could be gauged by understanding not simply its geographical position, economic capacities, control over raw materials, or level of military preparedness, but also its national character, level of national morale, and even the quality of its government, which included a range of factors, among them the degree of "popular support for the foreign policies to be pursued" (*PAN*, 2nd edn., 132). Fatal to success in foreign policy was the "fallacy of the single factor" and its obfuscation of the unavoidably plural roots of power (*PAN*, 2nd edn., 146). Military muscle constituted *one* power factor; a rich variety of cultural and political factors could prove equally significant. The quality of a nation's diplomacy took on a special status, since diplomacy constituted "the brains of national power," and, without brains, even a muscle-bound giant would always stumble badly in a dangerous world. Without effective diplomacy, and "if its vision is blurred, its judgment defective, and its determination feeble, all the advantages of geographical location, of self-sufficiency in food, raw materials, and industrial production, of military preparedness, of size and quality of population will in the long run avail a nation little" (*PAN*, 2nd edn., 129). When describing this scenario, Morgenthau was obviously thinking of the postwar USA, whose vast power resources potentially overshadowed those of its competitors, but whose diplomacy he thought generally marked by incompetence.

Even during his mature Realist phase, Morgenthau refused to celebrate the untamed pursuit of power politics and the lust for power on which it rested. A crucial middle section (Part Four) consequently considered the possibility that *immanent* political mechanisms might function successfully to counteract the perils of interstate power rivalry. Here Morgenthau introduced the pivotal idea of the balance of power, according to which international political life contained decisive stabilizing factors even in the context of ruthless interstate competition. In contrast to those who argued that the balance of power was simply a historical vestige of an anachronistic system bound to decay along with the modern nation state, Morgenthau deemed it a universal feature of social life: "the balance of power in international affairs is only a particular manifestation of a general social principle to which all societies composed of a number of autonomous units owe the autonomy of their component parts" (*PAN*, 2nd edn., 155). In countless arenas of social life, a modicum of stability among autonomous units could only be established on the basis of a balance or equilibrium of social forces. In the state system, as in other arenas of social existence, whenever a balance or equilibrium was upset among independent units, "the system shows a tendency to re-establish either the original or new equilibrium" (*PAN*, 2nd edn., 156). Even at the domestic level the basic principle of the balance of power obtained: the US Federalists were right to construct a system of institutional checks and balances based on a realistic assessment of human nature as power-seeking and conflict-prone. Lord Bryce's description of the US polity as one in which "each branch of the government was to restrain the others, and maintain the equipoise of the whole," thereby ensuring both the autonomy of each of its constituent branches and the overall stability of the entire system, was taken as firm evidence for the theoretical impeccability of the balance of power (*PAN*, 2nd edn., 159).

Morgenthau thereby cleverly made his commitment to the balance of power look like a mere application to international affairs of the sound philosophical principles of the much-celebrated US framers. In international as in domestic political life, competition among and between antagonistic elements could only be stabilized by means of attempts to ensure a balance or equilibrium of forces while respecting the independence of each power unit (*PAN*, 2nd edn., 160). Consistent with this position, *Politics Among Nations* offered a detailed taxonomy, in which Morgenthau described in ideal-typical fashion various methods employed to secure a balance of power in international politics. Here again he fused empirical and normative perspectives: not only did the balance of power represent a universal empirical tendency in political and social life, but a proper understanding of it provided indispensable normative and policy advice to diplomats and political leaders smart enough to take it. Denying the virtues of the balance of power as a general operative principle in political affairs was akin to pretending that we could ignore fundamental laws of human existence. Nonetheless, too many politicians did just that, and a central aim of *Politics Among Nations* was to bring home to them the errors of their ways.

Even sympathetic readers have correctly noted that Morgenthau's analysis used "several definitions of the balance of power without effectively distinguishing among them."[9] But was his commitment to it intrinsically conservative, as many have insisted? In part a proper answer depended on the particulars of Morgenthau's own ever-changing employment of the concept. To the extent that Morgenthau believed that the balance of power had operated throughout history and a great deal could be learned from its successes, his position was indeed *intellectually* conservative. Yet he resisted the view that it required dogmatic fidelity to the existing Westphalian system of states: its status as a universal law of social action by no means conflicted with the possibility of alternatives as long as any prospective future global order respected the basic idea that security and stability were best guaranteed when power was made to check power. In theory, it might even be made to cohere with a world state since, as the US framers had shown, a balance of power could be institutionalized effectively within state borders.

Revealingly, Morgenthau ultimately zeroed in on the *limitations* of the balance of power as a method for preserving peace. Even in the best of circumstances, it was virtually impossible for countries to calculate accurately their power resources in comparison to those of their rivals. This "uncertainty of all power calculations" was masked by the mechanistic and rationalistic political thinking of the mainstream of modern political thought. Yet its congenital weaknesses were inarguable:

Since no nation can be sure that its calculation of the distribution of power at any particular moment in history is correct, it must at least make sure that, whatever errors it may commit, they will not put the nation at a disadvantage in the contest for power. In other words, the nation must try to have at least a margin of safety which will allow it to make erroneous calculations and still maintain the balance of power. To that effect, all nations actively engaged in the struggle for power must actually aim not at a balance . . . but at superiority of power on their own behalf. (*PAN*, 2nd edn., 189)

Proper fidelity to the idea of the balance of power had regularly warded off international violence. Yet it suffered from severe defects. The balance of power provided no final resolution to the "security dilemma."[10] Rather than the balance consistently taming political power, "the limitless aspiration for power, potentially always present . . . finds in the balance of power a mighty incentive to transform itself into an actuality" (*PAN*, 2nd edn., 189–90). When successful, the balance of power proved so in part because of an underlying moral and cultural consensus, prevailing from 1648 until the early twentieth century among members of a globally hegemonic European political and legal order (*PAN*, 2nd edn., 200). That moral and cultural consensus, Morgenthau believed, was now pretty much a thing of the past. With the ascent of hubristic political religions claiming universal validity, the balance of power was unlikely to preserve lasting peace.

In the context of a genuinely multipolar state system, as found in the classical state system, the effectiveness of the balance of power was facilitated by the large number of possible combinations among major political players. The relative flexibility and resulting unpredictability of foreign affairs "made it imperative for all players to be cautious in their moves on the chessboard of international politics" (*PAN*, 2nd edn., 325). Yet what could it possibly accomplish in a world order dominated by two nuclear great powers? In a bipolar system, Morgenthau noted, international flexibility was severely impaired. Neither the USSR nor the USA needed to look over its shoulder and worry too much about the defection of a major ally.[11] The possibility of major shifts in political alliances seemed minimal: "Thus the international system is reduced to the primitive spectacle of two giants eyeing each other with watchful suspicion. They bend every effort to increase their military potential to the utmost, since this is all they have to count on" (*PAN*, 2nd edn., 339). The USA and USSR faced one another like two hostile street fighters, ready to do battle at a moment's notice, in a dark and dangerous alley where no one else was strong enough to keep them from fighting, or even from joining arms with others, in order to prevent a fatal battle.

Despite his initial enthusiasm for the balance of power, Morgenthau's negative conclusion was unmistakable. In the final analysis, no *immanent* political devices could be identified by means of which we might rigorously civilize a state system in which increasingly terrible forms of violence remained the final means of conflict resolution. Parts Five and Six of *Politics Among Nations* thus turned to alternative candidates potentially capable of mitigating the perils of power politics: morality, mores, and law. Why bother taming power politics at all? Because the normative core of the western tradition, Morgenthau tirelessly repeated in each of the many editions of *Politics Among Nations*, correctly rejected the celebration of power politics:

> Superior power gives no right, either moral or legal, to do with that power all that it is physically capable of doing. Power is subject to limitations, in the interest of society as a whole and in the interests of its individual members, which are not the results of the mechanics of the struggle for power but are superimposed upon that struggle in the form of norms or rules of conduct by the will of the members of society themselves. (*PAN*, 2nd edn., 206)

Unfortunately, Morgenthau soon concluded, the record of such norms at mitigating violence on the international scene had been mixed.

Part Five reiterated Morgenthau's life-long position, contra cynical interpretations of international ethics, that international morality had successfully checked the worst dangers of the state system. Yet with the demise of an international order in which the most powerful European states shared far-reaching moral and cultural values, international ethics was becoming ever more fragile. Nationalistic universalism now flourished; the mechanical and technical imperatives of modern total war undermined the humanitarian laws of warfare; the intense emotional and psychological identification of most individuals with particular political communities disabled meaningful moral restraints on state action. From the seventeenth to the nineteenth centuries, international politics was exclusively the concern of "a relatively small, cohesive, and homogeneous group of aristocratic rulers" (*PAN*, 2nd edn., 221). Morgenthau nostalgically described how the social and political homogeneity of the traditional diplomatic corps served as the essential groundwork for a cohesive international society capable of blunting the sharpest edges of interstate conflict. Yet democratization and modern nationalism worked hand-in-hand to undermine moral and ethical checks on interstate relations. Married to increasingly retrograde forms of nationalism, modern popular political movements left us with a multiplicity of morally self-sufficient national units "which have ceased to operate within a common framework of moral precepts" (*PAN*, 2nd edn., 228).

In a similar vein, Part Six defended contemporary international law against extreme critics, while simultaneously reiterating Morgenthau's familiar arguments about its structural limits: "during the four hundred years of its existence international law has in most instances been scrupulously observed" (*PAN*, 2nd edn., 251). International law had always constituted much more than a crude strategic bludgeon employed, willy-nilly, by states in order to advance their power interests. States tended to follow their national interests, "but the way they define these is shaped by the rules prevailing in the society of states."[12] When faced with intense political conflicts, however, international law had proven somewhat less successful. To the most fundamental questions of international politics, its answers were too often unclear, ambiguous, and tentative. In the context of an international system in which nation states jealously guarded their sovereignty, its legislative, adjudicative, and enforcement functions remained fundamentally decentralized. Notwithstanding the notable achievements of modern international law, there was no "weaker system of law enforcement than this; for it delivers the enforcement of the law to the vicissitudes of the distribution of power between the violator of the law and the victim of the violation" (*PAN*, 2nd edn., 270).

Of course, lawyers and reformers had proposed a variety of panaceas for the ills of international politics, as Morgenthau dutifully noted in Part Eight. Some advocated far-reaching and perhaps even universal disarmament; Morgenthau again countered that disarmament only alleviated the prospects of war when successfully linked to a rigorous attempt to minimize underlying political conflicts. Unfortunately, its proponents typically closed their eyes to the deeper political divisions at hand. Others praised the virtues of collective security; Morgenthau conceded that its underlying logic was flawless, yet believed that past experience had demonstrated the improbability of collective security operating consistently and rigorously. For their part, enthusiasts for international arbitration and compulsory adjudication occluded the necessary limits of judicial and tribunal-like institutions in countering basic political tensions.

Still others turned hopefully to the prospects of an emerging world public opinion, which they hoped might be mobilized by international institutions in order to prevent war. Significantly, *Politics Among Nations* never denied a priori the possibility of a politically significant public opinion "that transcends national boundaries and that unites members of different nations in a consensus with regard to at least certain fundamental international issues" (*PAN*, 2nd edn., 236). In contrast to more recent communitarian and republican critics who suggest that the quests for a global public and cosmopolitan public opinion are inconsistent with the necessary preconditions of effective citizenship and self-government, Morgenthau's position was surprisingly open-minded.[13] He nonetheless remained skeptical of its contemporary prospects. It was naïve to assume that the ongoing technological and economic unification of the world necessarily engendered a psychological and political unification as well.[14] Despite the basic commonalities of human nature, modern social experiences remained disparate. Some starve; others seek expensive cures from obesity. Some enjoy a measure of political freedom; others suffer the horrors of tyranny. Even when humanity collectively endorsed a shared normative and legal goal (e.g. a prohibition of genocide or aggressive war), profound differences in social experience meant that it got interpreted in deeply antagonistic ways. Although the nation state was obsolescent, political identity remained highly particularized and nationalistic: "Even if the American, Russian, and Indian could speak to each other, they would speak with different tongues, and if they uttered the same words, those words would signify different objects, values, and aspirations to each of them" (*PAN*, 2nd edn., 240). This was inevitable given the national framework in which most political experience was still digested: the nation state continued to fill "the hearts and minds of men everywhere" with its "particular standards of political morality" (*PAN*, 2nd edn., 244). Technological and economic unification in fact *intensified* the sense of national and cultural differences since large numbers of people suddenly found themselves confronted with experiences of an alien and potentially alarming nature. At least under present conditions, Morgenthau concluded, a world public opinion capable of effectively restraining the foreign policies of national governments was unlikely to take form.

International government: the case of the United Nations

The most ambitious efforts to provide remedies for interstate conflict have consisted in novel experiments in international government in the footsteps of horrific military conflict. The Holy Alliance succeeded the Napoleonic Wars; the League of Nations, the First World War; and the United Nations (UN), the Second World War. From Morgenthau's perspective, international government represented an admirable yet ultimately insufficient quest to square the circle of international anarchy: "National sovereignty demands that the governments of individual countries decide for themselves the domestic and international issues that concern them. An international organization, in order to be effective, requires a transfer of that power of ultimate decision, at least in certain matters from the national to an international authority."[15] The paradox of every hitherto existing experiment in international government was that it tried to preserve national sovereignty while establishing a common global authority resting on a shared conception of justice and aspiring to preserve peace. Morgenthau simply doubted that one could achieve effective international rule while maintaining national sovereignty.

Both supportive and critical commentators have tended to highlight Morgenthau's skeptical comments about international government, pointing to his assertion that each of its most important modern varieties ultimately represented some permutation of the familiar attempt to place the central tasks of global government in the hands of the great powers. On this reading, Morgenthau serves as a convenient intellectual ally in the battle to discount both the normative aspirations and historical achievements of the United Nations. International government is at best a mirage and at worst a recipe for the political hegemony of those great powers able to mask their aspirations in humanitarian and universalistic legal norms.[16]

This view is more indebted to the cynical ideas of Carl Schmitt than to Morgenthau, however.[17] It does justice neither to Morgenthau's surprisingly complex claims about existing forms of international government, nor to the conclusions he draws from his criticisms. In contrast to those Realists who take the limits of existing international government as impeccable evidence for the flawed character of *any* far-reaching quest for government at the supranational level, Morgenthau instead insisted that the pathologies of the

United Nations implied that political actors would need to pursue substantially *more* ambitious alternatives. The failures of international government by no means proved the inevitability, let alone the attractiveness, of an international order based on competing sovereigns engaging in familiar forms of power politics, but instead indicated the necessity of a world state in which the main institutional source of modern warfare, national sovereignty, has been radically abrogated:

> What is needed in order to save the world from self-destruction is not the limitation of the exercise of national sovereignty through international obligations and institutions, but the transference of the sovereignties of the individual states to a world authority . . . What is needed, then, is a radical transformation of the existing society of sovereign nations into a supranational community of individuals. (*PAN*, 2nd edn., 470)

Morgenthau repeatedly revised especially his comments on the United Nations in Part Eight of *Politics Among Nations*. They reveal him to have been a keen observer of its evolution, fascinated by the ways in which its political dynamics could change dramatically (for example, with the admission of new members in the 1950s) despite an apparently unaltered constitutional and legal structure. He regularly applied the simple but fertile insight from his Weimar days that the functions of international law could change abruptly in response to altered relations of power. In his view, the Security Council indeed guaranteed that the United Nations, like the Holy Alliance, fundamentally represented the latest attempt to preserve "government by superpowers." Yet what separated the UN from its historical predecessors was a starker "contrast between pretense and actuality, between the democratic expectations roused by the words of the Charter and the autocratic performance envisaged by the actual distribution of functions which characterizes" its constitutional provisions and especially the privileged status awarded the permanent members of the Security Council. "The Security Council seems to be, as it were, the Holy Alliance of our time," yet that Holy Alliance existed in the context of the deeply democratic and humanitarian provisions of the UN Charter, as well as a General Assembly which aimed to provide meaningful representation to the entire planet (*PAN*, 2nd edn., 449).

Morgenthau did not pinpoint this tension, along the lines of Schmitt and those Realists who celebrate power politics, for the sake of discrediting the UN's normative pretensions. On the contrary, he showed how the tension between norm and reality could explain some of the institution's more surprising features. In a fascinating 1960 discussion of "the rise and decline of the General Assembly," for example, he vividly described how superpower paralysis in the Security Council had briefly allowed the General Assembly to take on a far more prominent role than its architects intended (*PAN*, 3rd edn., 484–93). The UN's institutional and normative contradictions had at least momentarily permitted the General Assembly to exercise far-reaching quasi-legislative functions.

More significantly, he noted early on that the UN system was in fact modifying the nature of diplomacy and conventional power politics. To be sure, he continued to polemicize against the view that the existing UN had radically transformed international politics. To a substantial degree the UN was simply another institutional vehicle by means of which traditional power politics could be waged: when describing the short-lived ascent of the General Assembly in the early 1950s, for example, he focused primarily on its political roots as part of an anti-Soviet alliance spearheaded by the United States. At the same time, the great powers could no longer rely exclusively on traditional power politics or diplomacy in order to get their way. The UN had opened the door to what Morgenthau cautiously described as a "new diplomacy," operating alongside its more traditional cousin. In traditional power politics, dominant states could "afford to disregard the preferences of small states whose power counts for nothing, making concessions only to those whose power counts" (*PAN*, 2nd edn., 463). Power and force were decisive, whereas the necessity for normative persuasion remained minimal. When even the weakest states were outfitted with equal votes, however, great powers were compelled to present their preferences in terms potentially acceptable to a significant number of states that they very well otherwise might have ignored. With the establishment of the UN, they were forced to engage in the art of political *persuasion*, whereas previously they "could afford not to care." Even the USA and USSR, if they were to make effective use of the UN (as Morgenthau assumed they must), were propelled to show how policies based in their respective national interests represented more than parochial concerns. "In an age dominated by two superpowers and threatened with atomic destruction," he commented in the *Foreign Policy Bulletin*, "a national policy has a chance to prevail only if it defines itself in terms transcending the [mere] national interest of a particular nation" and comprises the national interests of those countries whose support it seeks.[18] This tendency produced a subtle "linguistic transformation," by means of which the great powers tended to present their policies as palatable to a prospective working majority in the UN. Of course, ideological obfuscation typically resulted. Rather than discount this trend altogether, however, Morgenthau noted that the necessity of justifying policies in general, and even universal terms, could "exert a subtle influence upon the substance of the transactions themselves" (*PAN*, 2nd edn., 463). Policies that required supranational justification might potentially look quite different from their traditional predecessors: one could already observe a "blunting of the sharp edges of a national policy . . . and its reformulation and adaptation in the light of the supranational principles embodied in the language of the resolution" (*PAN*, 2nd edn., 463). In some contrast to the general tendency in *Politics Among Nations* to downplay the constitutive role of norms and ideas in power relations, his analysis of the UN attributed to them a meaningful capacity to reduce and even modify traditional power politics.

In short, the UN represented more than the tyrannical hegemony of the superpowers dressed up in moralistic humanitarian rhetoric. Morgenthau noted respectfully that it remained one of the few institutional sites during the cold war where "personal contacts between representatives of East and West" might be "used unobtrusively for the purpose of mitigating or settling conflicts" (*PAN*, 2nd edn., 465). Given the limited diplomatic contacts between East and West, this was no mean achievement on a planet haunted by the prospect of nuclear conflagration. On a number of significant occasions, he pointed out in a 1961 article for the *New York Times Sunday Magazine*, the UN had successfully limited the scope and duration of localized wars which might otherwise have exploded into global nuclear war.[19] As long as its universal and democratic aspirations possessed at least some institutional footing, the UN kept alive the noble vision of a world order capable of maintaining world peace, even if its own practices conflicted with those aims (*PAN*, 2nd edn., 465). Consistent with this assessment, Morgenthau showed significant sympathy for at least some proposed reforms to the UN: since it had performed indispensable positive functions, it made sense to pursue constructive change, rather than simply wish for its disappearance or lament its existence. In the pages of the *Review of Politics*, he thus argued in 1954 that the Charter should be revised not only in order to increase the number of permanent members of the Security Council, but also for the sake of periodically revising its membership: the dynamic character of world politics conflicted with the troublesome tendency to try to stabilize a specific set of historically transitory power relations, in this case by means of the "static permanent membership" of the Security Council.[20]

The same essay, revealingly, expressed deep skepticism about proposals to get rid of the veto enjoyed by members of the Security Council. Sacrificing the veto would entail a revolutionary transformation of the UN and not simply a reform to its basic structure, since "the veto is a mere reflection of the underlying structure of international society" and its use "a mere symptom of the underlying distribution of power" in the existing order.[21] The veto gave direct expression to the principle of national sovereignty, and its monopoly in the hands of Security Council members directly embodied the structural inequalities of an international order in which the great powers jealously guarded their national interests. The point, however, was not that either one of these attributes represented an unchanging ontological "fact" of international politics immune to modification. Instead, the appropriate remedy for them lay "in the transformation of these two underlying factors, not in the revision of the Charter" (*PAN*, 2nd edn., 19). Constitutional reform without corresponding shifts in the international relations of power was unlikely to succeed. Unless accompanied by alterations to the overall distribution of power at the global level, Morgenthau argued, legal reforms might simply play into the hands of the dominant global players. Premature constitutional reform put the cart before the horse: without the makings of a new international society, reforms would likely prove counterproductive.

For similar reasons, *Politics Among Nations* criticized proposals to develop a strengthened and relatively independent police force under the auspices of the UN.[22] As long as the nation state remained the dominant institutional vessel through which most political experience was filtered, it was unrealistic to expect the members of a UN police force to work neutrally and potentially against their own countries, as indeed might be required. At the domestic setting, the police could typically rely on a far-reaching moral consensus, and its coercive presence correspondingly reduced. Yet existing international society lacked a sufficiently far-reaching and determinate moral consensus. An international police force would inevitably be required to apply force when its domestic parallel could instead depend on custom or mores to ensure fidelity to the law. To an even greater degree than domestic settings plagued by relatively deep inequalities, the international order consisted of mammoth collectivities like the United States and Russia as well as pygmies like Luxembourg and Costa Rica. Consequently, "a giant in combination with one or two second-rate powers or a few small ones may easily exceed the strength of all the other nations combined." In this context, a police force "of truly gigantic dimensions" would be required in order to serve as an effective counterweight (*PAN*, 2nd edn., 399). The demand for an international police force implicitly pointed the way beyond the UN and its enshrinement of the principle of sovereignty: its realization would have to await the construction of a world state.

So why not simply rest satisfied with the existing UN? Morgenthau noted that many of the core principles (e.g. the idea of national sovereignty, or the prohibition on aggressive war) of the UN Charter were relatively undefined. This allowed every member of the national community to sign off on them, masking the fact that their concrete meaning, especially in the context of explosive conflicts, was rarely self-evident or self-explanatory. This failing was not simply a matter for improved legal or constitutional craftsmanship, however, since it directly resulted from the pluralistic character of political and social consciousness on a divided planet. Codification would fail here, as it had in many less explosive areas of international law, unless the underlying political tensions could somehow be healed or at least minimized. Even more immediately, the structure of the Security Council meant that the UN was ultimately disabled from consistently preserving world peace, its most important function. It simply had not been set up for the purpose of subjecting either the USA or USSR to international government against its will, despite the fact that a war between them threatened the entire planet. In the final analysis, the enigmatic quest to establish an effective common authority in the context of decentralized sovereignty and a principled commitment to national self-determination was badly equipped to pass the most important test of our time: the UN would likely prove impotent in the face of nuclear extermination.

World state

At this juncture, Morgenthau might easily have thrown his hands into the air, lamenting the limitations of conventional experiments in international government and leaving the story there. Indeed, his own tendency to underline the tragic contours of political existence could have led him to embrace the institutionally cautious position that, at best, a reformed UN might funnel and occasionally counteract the worst excesses of power politics, but that little more could be achieved. It speaks volumes about Morgenthau's deep moral impulses that he refused, in dramatic contradistinction to most of his Realist followers, to give up on the quest to develop more effective mechanisms to ensure world peace. Part Nine of *Politics Among Nations* thus bluntly asserted that the world state was "indispensable for the survival of the world," and, even if it was *presently* unattainable, it was "necessary to create the conditions under which it will not be impossible from the outset to establish" it (*PAN*, 2nd edn., 505). Modern weapons of mass destruction meant that humankind was "more in need of permanent peace and, hence, of a world state" than ever before (*PAN*, 2nd edn., 481).

At first glance, Morgenthau's stark conclusion may appear to represent a mere updated Hobbesianism, according to which peace can only be preserved under the auspices of an overarching system of shared global sovereignty. Skeptical that anything less than a sovereign world government could consistently preserve peace, Morgenthau did indeed build on Hobbes' "true message" that the state is indispensable for peace (*PAN*, 2nd edn., 476). Yet he also chastized Hobbes for believing that the state by itself can "maintain domestic peace . . . That the power of the state is essential, but not sufficient, to keep the peace of national societies is demonstrated by the historic experience of civil wars" (*PAN*, 1st edn., 397). If lasting peace were to be firmly secured, a world state would have to emerge. But it could only flourish on the basis of a highly developed international society capable of performing far-reaching integrative functions. Hobbes' fatal errors, in this gloss, were to overestimate the state's integrative capacities and miss the social and moral presuppositions of effective state action. Morgenthau worried that too many well-meaning proponents of global reform tended to commit the same mistake. They pushed hard for the more or less imminent realization of cosmopolitan government, conveniently downplaying the fact that many of its basic presuppositions were still missing. Since it was not only naïve but potentially counterproductive to push prematurely for its establishment, the world state should be seen as a *long-term* institutional aspiration. Nonetheless, decisive concrete steps could be taken right away in order to advance it.

Here again, Morgenthau sketched out a position very much at odds with more recent variations of Realism, which share his view that lasting world peace can only be secured by means of a world state, but then have little to say about how it might be built. These Realists may admit that a world state would be desirable; like Morgenthau, they also consider it presently unachievable. In stark contrast to him, however, they ignore objective tendencies in international affairs which at least cautiously suggest the possibility of novel forms of global government.[23] To his credit, Morgenthau never made this mistake, in part because his political ethics always helped remind him of the manifest normative ills of the existing state system.

But did not the biologically and psychologically rooted "lust for power" doom any attempt to construct a world state? Nowhere did Morgenthau assert that human nature or psychology *necessitates* political violence. At the level of domestic political and legal practices, stable societies successfully funneled the agonistic dynamics of human nature into peaceful forms of conflict, rivalry, and competition. For example, in the capitalist countries of the West, "the possession of money has become the outstanding symbol of the possession of power. Through the competition for the acquisition of money the power aspirations of the individual find a civilized outlet in harmony with the rules of conduct laid down by society" (*PAN*, 2nd edn., 209). To be sure, Morgenthau defined politics in terms of *intense* conflict where the *specter* of violence loomed large. Following Schmitt, his ideas about the political and its roots in philosophical anthropology made him exceedingly skeptical of many proposals for international reform. In contradistinction to Schmitt, however, he ultimately refused to reject the world state as necessarily entailing the supersession of the political and thereby human nature. The "lust for power" could manifest itself in a rich diversity of ways, as it generally did within the parameters of stable nation states where the rivalry for power took a peaceful form. In his overall theoretical framework, no a priori reason precluded the possibility that similar forms of peaceful conflict resolution might replace interstate war. The crucial intellectual task was to begin to figure out how analogous civilized outlets for the taming of potentially intense conflicts might emerge at the global level.

Like its domestic corollary, the world state would need to possess overwhelming power, in the form of a monopoly on organized force and the capacity to mobilize social pressure against recalcitrant actors (*PAN*, 2nd edn., 473–4). Yet even preponderant power would likely founder without a highly developed international society or "world community" capable of performing pacifying functions presently exercised by "domestic society as an integrated whole" in an efficient and seemingly matter-of-fact fashion (*PAN*, 2nd edn., 414, 486–502). At the present historical juncture, Morgenthau claimed, we merely have a "society of sovereign nations," in which a variety of norms and social practices (including international mores, ethics, and customs) provide a basis for coordinating *inter-state* affairs. A prospective world state, however, demanded a more intensive as well as extensive world or "supranational society" comprising all members of the human species and able to support global decision making in far-reaching ways (*PAN*, 2nd edn., 479).

Morgenthau never sufficiently defined his usage of terms like "international society" or "world community."[24] Yet what he had in mind seems clear enough from his detailed discussion of the normal operations of domestic political life. There, formal state institutions translated public opinion into policy and helped bring about social and political change. But they only represented "agents of society as a whole" (*PAN*, 2nd edn., 414). Unless propped up by public opinion and an underlying moral consensus, even the most impressive political and legal apparatus might fail when faced with the supreme test of effective government: "to change the distribution of power inside society without jeopardizing the orderly and peaceful processes upon which the welfare of society depends" (*PAN*, 2nd edn., 415). Fortunately, the interplay of social and political forces was typically responsible for altering public opinion in domestic society; shifts in public opinion manifested themselves in legislative and judicial innovations. The process as a whole only flourished, however, when every participant shared a basic commitment to the rules of the game. Consensus at the level of general principles, as well as a common faith that a measure of justice might be attained, with every social group enjoying "a chance to make themselves heard," were imperative (*PAN*, 2nd edn., 473). The employment of coercive power could be minimized because participants typically heeded even those laws with which they disagreed. Cross-cutting cleavages also played a decisive role in ensuring the stability of domestic society. A rival in one field of social experience might be a close ally in another. Since economic competitors could simultaneously turn out to be allies in the cultural or religious arena, for example, the potential explosiveness of group conflict was typically reduced. This "plural role of friend and opponent" imposed restraints on participants in the political struggle, impressing upon them "the relativity of their interests and loyalties" (*PAN*, 2nd edn., 471).

Parallels at the level of supranational or world society would have to emerge if a world state were to garner the requisite social and moral basis. Once again, a critical observer might retort that this standpoint remains intellectually conservative since it rigidly models the emergence of a world state as an extension of familiar trends at the level of the modern nation state. Why assume that political development at the global level should follow the developmental logic of modern national politics?[25] Revealingly, Morgenthau had little constructively to say, for example, about what form a moral consensus or public opinion could and should take at the global level. Though suggestive, his comments on supranational society remain incomplete.

Yet precisely this relative vagueness might represent a hidden theoretical strength. Even though the concrete details of any prospective supranational society will unavoidably look different from what we observe at the level of domestic society, Morgenthau might have responded, basic integrative functions will still need to be performed by global rather than domestic social mechanisms. A functioning supranational society indeed seems indispensable to supranational government. On this general point, at least, he was surely right. Interestingly, Morgenthau's ideas about the proper institutional structure for a world state were similarly unformed, in part because he considered it a long-term goal, and thus speculation about it unworthy of the hard-headed Realist method he advocated.[26] Yet here as well, his ambiguities are potentially fruitful. Although familiar with the complicated questions posed by the imperative of providing representation to a stunning diversity of peoples,[27] and correct to point out that the principle of majority rule posed special difficulties at the global level, he never described the dilemmas of global government – or, for that matter, his own preference for global liberal democracy – as a priori insurmountable (*PAN*, 2nd edn., 480). As in the history of the modern nation state, a complex and politically arduous process of institutional trial-and-error was in order. *Pace* more recent writers, however, Morgenthau would undoubtedly have insisted upon the necessity of far-reaching forms of relatively traditional *statehood* or government to any workable vision of global governance. "Global governance without government" might indeed serve positive functions,[28] yet ultimately only a world *state* resting on a supranational community – in which international anarchy and with it the terrible prospect of nuclear extermination had been dramatically reduced – could secure lasting peace.

In any event, it was simply wrong to posit that a world state could be established by world conquest: the necessary outcome would be a "totalitarian monster resting on feet of clay" (*PAN*, 2nd edn., 482). It was also inaccurate to insist that the world state was already or at least imminently achievable. *Pace* reformers who looked optimistically to federal models like the United States and Switzerland as possible models for global democracy, Morgenthau insisted on the historical idiosyncrasies of both cases as well as their limited relevance to the challenges at hand. Even at its founding, for example, the United States never consisted of thirteen fundamentally diverse sovereign states, but instead a relatively coherent political entity already resting on a shared identity and a common normative heritage (*PAN*, 2nd edn., 484). Appealing to John Stuart Mill's famous tests of support for any workable government from *Considerations on Representative Government*, Morgenthau considered it self-evident that humankind was not yet ready to perform the minimal requisite tasks. He did not celebrate the fact that the nation state remained "the recipient of man's highest earthly loyalties. Beyond it there are other nations, but no community for which man would be willing to act regardless of what he understands the interests of his own nation to be." Yet he considered it intellectually dishonest to ignore it. To be sure, recent history was filled with examples of generosity and humanitarianism across national borders. However, even international humanitarian action typically remained constrained by the tight corset of the national interest: "while international relief is regarded as compatible with the national interest, freedom of immigration is not" (*PAN*, 2nd edn., 479). When push came to shove, the vast majority of humankind would still clearly refuse to defend a prospective world government in opposition to its own nation states: how many Russians or Americans would employ arms against national compatriots to enforce the international laws of war? Unfortunately, little evidence suggested that humanity would soon shed its nationalistic corset for a new cosmopolitan one. Nationalistic universalism may have been reduced in some corners of the globe, but the enthusiastic zeal with which post-colonial societies were rushing to imitate the tragic historical trajectory of European nationalism put to rest the quaint fantasy that a novel cosmopolitan political identity was on the horizon.[29]

So what then was to be done? *Politics Among Nations* tried to provide two complementary answers to this question. Unfortunately, the answers were probably less consistent than Morgenthau recognized. The first looked back nostalgically to the eighteenth and nineteenth centuries; the second looked forward to Western Europe's novel experiment with the creation of a supranational polity.

Part Ten called for a revival of traditional diplomacy. Morgenthau's underlying justification for this conclusion was plausible enough: if humankind were to move towards the world state, it would need time to do so. Neither supranational society nor a world government could emerge overnight. How then to buy time and avoid a cataclysmic war? Imperative was a substantial "mitigation and minimization of those political conflicts" which in our era might rapidly lead to a horrific war (*PAN*, 2nd edn., 505). Only wise diplomacy could pull this off and thereby help create "peace through accommodation." If diplomacy were to succeed, however, it would have to follow a series of demanding strictures. Too often, recent excursions in diplomacy had aggrandized rather than minimized political tensions. Diplomacy should therefore be divested of moral smugness and the crusading spirit, conform to the national interest, learn to consider concrete conflicts from opposing political perspectives, and compromise on non-vital strategic matters (*PAN*, 2nd edn., 527–31). Some modern replacement for the aristocratic elite which had wisely managed interstate affairs in the heydays of the Westphalian system would have to be found. If only contemporary democracy could recapture the far-sighted wisdom of the predemocratic statesmen of the eighteenth and nineteenth centuries!

This argument ultimately took the form of a nostalgic "plea for the restoration of diplomacy to the eminence of its high days in old Europe, when its coolness of head and its clarity of sight prevailed over a public opinion not yet made unruly by mass ideologies."[30] Yet *Politics Among Nations* had also vividly recounted the far-reaching structural roots of traditional diplomacy's decline. Democracy's preoccupation with publicity and majority rule, popular disdain for elite-level foreign policy, as well as novel forms of communication and information technologies had all inexorably worked to impair traditional diplomacy and render its rituals quaint but anachronistic. Having established the roots of its decline, Morgenthau was able to offer little more than a desperate plea for the reestablishment of classical diplomacy, without being able to explain plausibly how it might thrive in a hostile political and social environment. He also conveniently downplayed the least appealing implications of his position: a return to traditional diplomacy might necessitate "the repeal of the nineteenth and twentieth centuries, which have witnessed the rise of popular sovereignty and ideology."[31]

Fortunately, Morgenthau also described a second strategy. His nostalgic remarks also included the important proviso that diplomacy "is the best means of preserving peace which a society of sovereign states has to offer, but, especially under the conditions of modern world politics and of modern war, *it is not good enough*" (*PAN*, 2nd edn., 534, emphasis added). Unlike later Realists who consigned the dream of a world state to the intellectual dustbin, the final pages of *Politics Among Nations* firmly reiterated the author's view that the political imperatives of our time demanded that we advance its cause.

Readers will typically look in vain in Morgenthau's writings for instances of unalloyed praise for other authors. One exception, as noted in chapter 3, was Reinhold Niebuhr, whom Morgenthau admired and from whom he drew some crucial insights. Another was David Mitrany, whose "functionalist" approach to international organization was warmly praised in *Politics Among Nations*, and whose *A Working Peace System: An Argument for the Functional Development of International Organization* (1946) Morgenthau borrowed heavily from as he tried to explain how political actors might contribute towards building the social preconditions of a world state.[32]

Like Morgenthau, Mitrany was a Jew from central Europe with a left-wing political background, having studied at the London School of Economics where he was close to G. D. H. Cole, Harold Laski, and others. A sustained research stay was spent in the 1930s in the USA, on the basis of which he came to consider Franklin Delano Roosevelt's New Deal an institutional inspiration for a functionalist model for both domestic and international reform, whose contours he sketched out in *A Working Peace System*.[33] Even a brief perusal of this short but provocative volume explains why Morgenthau was immediately attracted to Mitrany's ideas. Like Morgenthau, Mitrany was an advocate of gradualist reform as the best path to lasting peace. He worried about the tendency in the dominant discourse of international reform to downplay the continuing salience of national political identities. Alerted, with Morgenthau, to the static contours of traditional legal and constitutional devices, Mitrany was similarly unimpressed by contemporary proposals for a global federation of states. So-called "top-down" models of constitutional reform naïvely placed their faith in formal–legal devices. Unfortunately, such mechanisms too often misfired in the face of dynamic social and economic processes which easily escaped their confines. Neat constitutional schemes rarely meshed well the messy regulatory necessities of an ever-changing social reality. Mitrany presciently pointed out, for example, that even when extended to the supranational level, federalism might prove irrelevant or even counterproductive to the regulatory tasks of modern government: borders between and among distinct federal units were unlikely to correspond coherently to dynamic and rapidly changing networks of cross-border social and economic activity. Even at the supranational level, state borders might not overlap with relevant arenas for state regulation. As for Morgenthau, a main function of government was to allow for the peaceful adjustment to, as well as conscious organization of, social change; conventional constitutional and legal instruments often proved clumsy devices for doing so. In Mitrany's view, Roosevelt and the New Dealers had been right to deemphasize the necessity of formal constitutional changes to the US system,[34] but instead to advance creative new configurations of decision making, set up in response to concrete practical needs, which inexorably revolutionized the system's basic operations. As an attentive observer of one of the New Deal's greatest achievements, the Tennessee Valley Authority (TVA), Mitrany admired how the New Dealers tackled the practical necessities of economic development in the poor rural south by means of novel institutional devices (in this case, a massive federally owned corporation) that rapidly transformed the division of labor between the national and state governments. Yet they did so without openly pursuing express constitutional change. In Mitrany's view, this was not simply a matter of disingenuous politics, as right-wing critics of the New Deal clamored, but instead institutionally unavoidable in light of the stunning complexities of the concrete practical problems (for example, rural electrification) at hand, with which no "top-down" constitutional reform could effectively have dealt.

Mitrany believed that the institutional pragmatism of the New Deal could be successfully applied to international reform; Morgenthau thought he was right. He appreciatively cited Mitrany's insight that functionalism called for the quest to:

> overlay political divisions with a spreading web of international activities and agencies, in which and through which the interests and life of all nations would be gradually integrated. That is the fundamental change to which any international government must aspire and contribute: to make international government coextensive with [practical] international activities. . . . It must care as much as possible for common needs that are evident, while presuming as little as

possible upon a social unity which is still only latent and unrecognized. (*PAN*, 2nd edn., 493)

Stated in Morgenthau's conceptual language, when the national interest of an existing political entity leads to cooperation with other nation states in the satisfaction of some typically down-to-earth policy need, creative institutional mechanisms could be developed as a way of funneling and regularizing shared regulatory undertakings. However modest at first glance, such experiments could ultimately unleash a *"revolutionary* attempt at solving" age-old political problems (*PAN*, 2nd edn., 497, emphasis added). As Mitrany had argued, "by linking authority to a specific activity," international organization could decisively "break away from the traditional link between authority and a definite territory," the fundamental presupposition not only of the modern state system but also of many proposals for "either an association or federation of nations."[35] Institutionalized cross-border cooperation "would help the growth of such positive and constructive common work, of common habits and interests," ultimately making borders meaningless "by overlaying them with a natural growth of common activities and common administrative tasks."[36]

From this theoretical perspective, the key task facing reformers was not to transfer national sovereignty via constitutional *formulas*, but instead gradually to alter its basic workings "by entrusting an authority with a certain task, carrying with it command over the requisite powers and means." By means of a process of creative institutional trial-and-error, over time "a translation of the true seat of authority" might result, based on new forms of shared power exercised for common ends.[37] International organization would have to develop gradually and organically. Yet this by no means precluded active intervention in the social process, as the New Deal had demonstrated so clearly. Mitrany went so far as to speculate that the "most disruptive and intractable" of international dilemmas, namely the factual inequality of states, might someday "be tamed by specific functional arrangements which would not steal the crown of sovereignty while they would promise something for the purse of necessity." Even the great powers might be driven to pursue ambitious forms of interstate cooperation which could ultimately open "the path for a gradual progress towards a real equality of nations."[38]

Best of all, Morgenthau noted, this was no mere pie-in-the sky utopian dream, predicated on the improbable overnight transformation of contemporary political consciousness and existing structures of power. In the emerging specialized agencies of the UN (e.g. the International Labor Organization, International Monetary Fund [IMF], and World Health Organization), autonomous organizations devoted to the fulfillment of specific social functions and "owing their existence to particular agreements among a number of states whose identity differs from agency to agency" (*PAN*, 2nd edn., 492), the outlines of a working version of functionalism could already be discerned. Even more rich in possibilities, Morgenthau postulated, was NATO, which belonged "among the most ambitious of the new functional agencies that try to bring the new procedures of international government to bear on a specific technical field for a common purpose," and where one could begin to discern the outlines of a novel international organization resting on the fruitful "interplay between common supranational interests, separate national interests, and American power" (*PAN*, 2nd edn., 496). His greatest enthusiasm, however, was saved for the European Coal and Steel Community, the fundament of what later became the European Union, and about which Morgenthau mused appreciatively in ever more expansive detail in updated editions of *Politics Among Nations*. Describing it as "a revolutionary departure from the traditional methods by which inferior powers have tried to counter a superior one," he marveled at how the concrete task of creating a common market for steel and coal had dramatically minimized longstanding political tensions between Germany and its former enemies (*PAN*, 2nd edn., 498). Following Mitrany, he praised the Europeans for avoiding the "top-down" approach to international reform, allegedly tried unsuccessfully between the world wars, which meant ensuring European unity by means of an all-embracing legal and constitutional framework. They instead had opted wisely for the "bottom-up" creation of "a functional unity within a limited sphere of action, expecting that the operation of that unity within that limited sphere will lead, first of all, to a community of interest within that particular sphere, and that this example will then spread to other functional fields, such as agriculture, transport, electricity, military forces." Over time, Morgenthau speculated, sovereignty might be effectively transferred to an overarching European government, "without the individual nations really being aware of it" (*PAN*, 2nd edn., 498). To be sure, the emergence of a regionally based common European political and economic bloc contained its own implicit dangers, since it was conceivable that traditional nationalism, discredited in Europe as nowhere else by two horrible wars, might simply undergo replacement "by a more efficient vehicle for the crusading national- ism of our age" (*PAN*, 2nd edn., 313). New continental or regionalist political identities might potentially prove as destructive of univer- sal moral standards as earlier national ones. Nonetheless, it was in Western Europe where one could begin to witness the basic con- tours of a novel form of supranational society, and thereby the nec- essary building blocks for a feasible world state.

Of course, much of what Morgenthau had to say on such matters, even in the latest editions of *Politics Among Nations*, now seems somewhat out of date. Yet his general remarks remain remarkably prophetic. Organizations like the IMF and the World Trade Organi- zation (WTO)[39] have indeed taken on a substantial role in the regu- lation of the global economy. The fact that many scholars are now heatedly debating whether we should interpret them as traditional *inter*state or novel *supra*national organizations arguably confirms his expectation that they might someday come to fit poorly into the traditional rudiments of the Westphalian system and its commit- ment to national sovereignty. In contrast to contemporary Realists who even today downplay the institutional novelty of the European Union,[40] in the early 1950s Morgenthau was already explaining how the emerging European order might someday represent a dramatic challenge to the nation state. On this point as well, he was stun- ningly far-sighted. The European Union has in fact been built to a significant extent on a difficult and time-consuming process of insti- tutional experimentation along functionalist lines, with initially quite limited cross-border regulatory systems "spilling over" to encompass an ever broader range of policy arenas.[41] Only the most dogmatic observer can dispute the fact that something novel – a post-national polity perhaps – has emerged.

Of course, we can only speculate about what Morgenthau today might say about proposals to advance European unification, for example by means of an ambitious constitutional treaty. He said far too little about the proper relationship between "bottom-up" functionalist evolution and "top-down" constitutional reform. How functionalism could contribute to a strengthened European parlia- ment, for example, or a democratization of the UN, was left unstated. In a perceptive 1964 *New York Times Sunday Magazine* article, however, Morgenthau conceded that the functionalists at times "naively assume that the political unification of Europe will somehow take care of itself, and that this qualitative transformation will result from the quantitative increase of functional agencies."

Even those justifiably enamored of Mitrany and his ideas, he argued, should have no illusions that someday "European sovereignty must be made by an act of will," by means of a "political decision which coordinates the divergent interests of individual nations." To their credit, the functionalists were helping to construct "the indispensable material foundations for the political unification of Europe," which Morgenthau enthusiastically endorsed.[42] But at some point functionalist reform would have to be complemented by a clear institutionalized expression of a shared European political will.

Whether or not Europe at the outset of the twenty-first century has reached that stage and is now ready for an expression of common political will, to be codified via a new constitutional document, remains open to legitimate differences of opinion.[43] To his great credit, Morgenthau rightly recognized that humankind would need to discover new forms of political order beyond the nation state, and that Western Europe was the most obvious place to start.

5

Utopian Realism and the bomb

The specter of nuclear war haunted Morgenthau's reflections throughout the cold war. During the 1950s it encouraged him to articulate a rechristened Realist theory of international politics as part of his quest for a peaceful political settlement between the USA and USSR. The prospect of a devastating atomic conflagration also motored the crucial argument in *Politics Among Nations* that the gradual construction of a world state represented a moral imperative which humanity neglected at the risk of self-destruction. Until his death in 1980, Morgenthau continued to write on the arms race and nuclear strategy, commenting critically on the failures of US policy and especially its refusal to grapple sufficiently with the mortal dangers at hand. Morgenthau ultimately became one of the most astute critics of the widespread tendency among policy makers and scholars alike to obfuscate the radical novelty of nuclear warfare and the unprecedented existential challenges it poses for humanity. Although his wide-ranging writings on the topic reveal Morgenthau to be at least as deeply immersed as his professional colleagues in the complex technical details of nuclear strategy and disarmament, what always set them apart were the author's moral preoccupations, and particularly his deeply rooted anxiety that humankind had stumbled irresponsibly onto a suicidal political and military course.

Not surprisingly perhaps, Morgenthau's fears about the possibility of nuclear warfare motivated him to propose yet another reformulation of Realist theory. In a 1961 lecture given at the University of Maryland, with the deceptively bland title "The Intellectual and

Political Functions of a Theory of International Relations," he announced to his audience that the looming nightmare of nuclear warfare now demanded that international relations theory perform "a creative and vital task," consisting in nothing less than a merger of the "realistic and utopian approaches to politics in general and to international relations in particular."[1] International theory had yet to get to grips with the novelty of nuclear warfare and especially its obliteration of the "rational relationship between violence as a means and the ends of foreign policy." Because nuclear weapons would necessarily destroy the victor as well as the vanquished, they undermined any conceivable goals for which such a war could be fought. Many conventional assumptions about the operations of foreign policy, interstate relations, and even the nation state itself were now suspect. A new theory of international relations synthesizing realistic and utopian approaches was called for in light of the "drastic changes in the structure of politics and in the institutions which must meet a new need."[2] International relations scholars were still obliged to start from a sober assessment of existing power relations, but a superior theoretical synthesis would have to show how humanity might transcend existing political conditions "to anticipate in a rational way the intellectual, political, and institutional changes" potentially unleashed by "the unprecedented revolutionary force" of nuclear weaponry. International theorists should join the ranks of "great political utopians," Morgenthau added, who started with a "realistic analysis of the status quo" but then proceeded to suggest possibilities for moving dramatically beyond it.[3]

At precisely that historical juncture when many of his professional peers seemed bent on purging international relations theory of normative let alone utopian concerns, Morgenthau instead proposed a creative fusion of Realism with normative and indeed utopian political theory. He left no doubts in the minds of his listeners about its eventual goal: "a supranational community and a world government, a political organization and structure which transcends the nation-state," alone could solve the political problems posed by the nuclear revolution.[4] Only a theoretical alliance between Realism and utopianism might help to prepare the necessary intellectual groundwork for world government.

To be sure, Morgenthau's defense of a world state covered much terrain familiar from *Politics Among Nations*. Yet, beginning in the early 1960s, he briefly toyed with the idea that the specter of nuclear warfare, along with the moral necessity of world government, necessitated a restatement of Realism. Unfortunately, Morgenthau never accomplished the called-for theoretical revision. His readers will look in vain for a systematic follow-up to the rich insights of the Maryland lecture. Campbell Craig's harsh assessment that Morgenthau's honest intellectual confrontation with the nuclear revolution exploded the contours of his 1950s version of Realism contains more than a small kernel of truth.[5] To his enormous credit, however, Morgenthau seems to have grasped that some of his own previous theoretical positions required amendment. As he proceeded to demonstrate in his many writings on the atomic threat, strict dichotomies not only between Realism and Idealism, but also between the national and universal or humanitarian interests, no longer could be maintained. In the nuclear age, it turned out, fidelity to the national interest called for careful yet decisive reforms pointing towards the establishment of a new cosmopolitan political order. National self-preservation required nothing less than working towards the hitherto utopian quest for world government. The rational pursuit of the national interest necessitated the supersession of the existing state system.

Morgenthau's endorsement of the view that nuclear weaponry demanded a major reorganization of international politics by no means came naturally to an author who delighted in knocking down naïve visions of global reform. Perhaps by retracing the hesitant and by no means linear steps which led him to this position, we can highlight its intellectual plausibility. However incomplete, his reflections on nuclear weaponry provide a rich goldmine for those legitimately worried that too much international relations theory remains bogged down in a pre-nuclear mindset.

One step forwards, two steps backwards

Morgenthau's reflections on nuclear warfare during the late 1940s and 1950s suffered from an obvious conceptual tension. On the one hand, he recognized early on the striking novelties of the nuclear era, astutely observing that, when even localized conflicts threatened to become all-out atomic wars, "war is no longer, as it once was, a rational instrument of foreign policy, the continuation of diplomacy with other means."[6] The real possibility of thermonuclear destruction implied a qualitative and not simply quantitative shift in the nature of modern warfare. The risky quest for power and prestige among nation states might now erupt into a war that would decimate the human species. The means of warfare undermined the ends (e.g. the "national interest") since atomic warfare would destroy both the vanquished and victorious nation states. As Robert Jervis has similarly put it, "[b]ecause they render meaningful military victory impossible, nuclear weapons fundamentally alter the traditional relationship between force and foreign policy."[7]

For a Realist theory committed to advancing a clear-eyed *rational* pursuit of the national interest, the fundamental irrationality of military force clearly engendered novel enigmas. In the nuclear age, force not only potentially proved strategically counterproductive but might engender what Morgenthau described as "universal destruction."[8] What in fact did the national interest consist of when the nation state, Morgenthau declared in 1957, no longer could successfully provide for the "common defense of the life of the citizens and of the values of the civilization in which they live?" Echoing fellow Realist John Herz' landmark *International Politics in the Atomic Age*, Morgenthau asserted that the military revolution wrought by the taming of the atom "destroyed the protective function of the nation state."[9] Most nation states could no longer perform the minimal function of securing self-preservation. After Hiroshima and Nagasaki, the perennial laws of interstate rivalry potentially prepared the way for nuclear incineration. In part because he feared this prospect, *Politics Among Nations* advocated the gradualist construction of an international society and ultimately world government, hoping that Mitrany's evolutionary functionalist approach to institution-building might serve as its midwife.

On the other hand, Morgenthau's thinking on nuclear weapons remained mired in conventional categories which clashed with his own emphasis on their unprecedented and even revolutionary implications. As described in chapter 3, he looked askance in the late 1940s and early 1950s at many proposals for arms control and disarmament, accusing their advocates of closing their eyes to the uncomfortable fact that only a prior political settlement between the Soviets and Americans could guarantee success. Without a negotiated settlement, disarmament, even in the nuclear age, remained a mirage. When asked in 1950 whether the United States should develop the H-Bomb, he described the dilemmas at hand as "different only in magnitude, but not in kind, from the dilemmas with which all the modern instruments of mass destruction, from the machine gun onwards" confronted policy makers. Nuclear weapons, it seemed, were akin to mega-sized machine guns. Consequently, the United States could "no more afford to be without all the weapons which modern technology puts at its disposal."[10] Indeed, as Michael Cox has accurately observed, during the mid- and late 1950s "Morgenthau began to sound a series of decidedly alarmist notes," responding to signs of Soviet military strength with splenetic calls for Washington to replenish its purportedly dwindling military muscle.[11] In the immediate aftermath of Sputnik, he lamented alleged Soviet superiority in the development of intercontinental ballistic missiles (ICBMs), demanding that the United States overcome an emerging missile gap by "drastic measures necessary to restore the balance."[12] To be sure, this buildup should primarily entail the augmentation of *conventional* military forces in order to allow the USA to respond with greater flexibility to Soviet moves. "Morgenthau urged a conventional buildup more than a decade before Robert McNamara," Michael Smith has aptly noted, and his views from the late 1950s anticipated John F. Kennedy's criticisms of Eisenhower's foreign policy during the 1960 presidential campaign and the subsequent shift in US strategy towards so-called "flexible response."[13] Yet, as part of this strategic shift, Morgenthau still sought "a crash program which would bend the total resources of the nation toward achieving" ICBMs and other advanced nuclear devices, despite his own open admission that the arms race was both irrational and potentially suicidal.[14]

After the Geneva Conference in July 1955 momentarily reduced cold war tensions, Morgenthau accused the Eisenhower Administration of inadvertently heightening the probability of nuclear war by potentially communicating to the Soviets that the United States might not fight one: "Atomic power, monopolistically controlled by the United States and the Soviet Union and keeping each other's destructive capability in check, is a force for peace, however precarious."[15] To the extent that the Geneva meetings may have mistakenly implied that the USA would "under no circumstances . . . resort to all-out nuclear war," the USA had in fact destabilized the arms race and may even have condemned itself "to a policy of appeasement, inviting defeat after defeat." The paradox at hand, Morgenthau claimed, was that the only way to avoid full-scale nuclear war between the Americans and Soviets "resides in their willingness and ability to fight it."[16] Confusing signals to the contrary simply threatened to disrupt the complex dynamics of nuclear deterrence. In the *New Republic*, writing in the aftermath of the Suez crisis and Eisenhower's public renunciation of the use of force except in response to violent aggression, Morgenthau went so far as to denounce United States policy as portending nothing less than a

well-meaning but irresponsible "new pacifism" hearkening back to
the Briand–Kellogg Pact and its ill-fated illegalization of warfare.
The "pacifists" in the Republican White House, he asserted, invited
Soviet aggression by sending dangerous signals that the United
States might hesitate before employing the full array of available
power instruments. If US policy was now to employ force only
when attacked, the Soviets would likely "make its enemy ready for
the kill by means of economic strangulation, subversion or military
preparations."[17] Only able to respond militarily after the Russians
had fired the first shot, the Americans might soon find themselves
on the defensive, pinned down by a self-imposed strategy that
denied them the requisite flexibility. All-out nuclear war might
ensue as a desperation measure. Eisenhower's seemingly humanitarian declarations about the evils of aggressive force, Morgenthau
concluded, not only constituted further evidence of the politically
immature character of US foreign policy, but inadvertently increased
the probability of a devastating nuclear war.

Yet it still would be a mistake to describe Morgenthau, even in
the 1950s, as a consistent defender of a "militaristic cold war line."[18]
He vigorously criticized the US embrace of "instant retaliation,"
according to which Soviet aggression would meet with massive
rapid-fire atomic retaliation, underscoring its strategic inflexibility
as well as the ways in which it might invite nuclear attacks. Only
if there was no shadow of a doubt in the mind of a potential aggres-
sor that, even in the case of a local conflagration (e.g. Korea or
Berlin), its actions would generate a nuclear response, could the
policy succeed. But since some doubt in such cases was unavoidable
and even desirable, instant retaliation invited "that kind of miscalculation that has so often in the past led to the outbreak of a general
war."[19]

Even more provocatively, Morgenthau identified early on some
of the latent risks of nuclear deterrence. Deterrence posited that
"prospective opponents are kept constantly aware of the inevitability of their own destruction should they resort to all-out atomic
force, and this prevents them from resorting to it."[20] Although previous military strategies had integrated many psychological elements,
Morgenthau noted in 1957, deterrence rested on a psychological
function "pure and simple" since the threat of atomic force could
never really be put to use without risking universal destruction.[21]
In the pre-atomic era, threats and counterthreats were of course
occasionally put to the test, whereas in the nuclear era the very
rationale behind threat and counterthreats was to keep the actual

performance from *ever* occurring. Nuclear deterrence, to a greater extent than its strategic predecessors, depended on repeated recourse to an "element of bluff, either real or suspect," and thus a complex and risky psychological game. Its convoluted psychological dynamics rendered nuclear deterrence vulnerable to dangerous and potentially self-destructive miscalculations, however. No country could ultimately determine whether or not an opponent was bluffing other than by at some juncture calling the bluff; no responsible national representative could be expected rationally to succumb to a threat to vital interests that turned out to represent a mere bluff: "Miscalculation is bound to be fatal either to the interests of the nation concerned, if it yields to the bluff, or to its existence, if it stands up to an atomic threat that is not a bluff."[22] Yet the whole function of deterrence was to avoid any such test from ever taking place. In short, "[s]ooner or later someone will want to know whether the statesman approaching the brink is serious or bluffing, whether he will jump or pull back."[23] It was probably just a matter of time before one of the atomic powers tested its opponent's resolve.

To be sure, in the context of a bipolar nuclear monopoly, the possibility of miscalculations and psychological misunderstandings could at least be mitigated. Morgenthau implicitly qualified the harsh view of bipolarity found in *Politics Among Nations*, admitting that the nuclear stalemate between the Americans and Russians provided for some stability. The scary prospect of nuclear proliferation, however, would unavoidably add levels of complexity to a strategic game that very well might overwhelm the psychological and cognitive abilities of ordinary political actors and prepare the way for full-scale nuclear war. "Under the condition of dispersion of atomic capabilities among, say, six or ten different nations," a nuclear explosion could set off a perilous political and strategic chain reaction leading to all-out atomic war.[24]

To Morgenthau's credit, he firmly resisted the increasingly fashionable tendency in the late 1950s to advocate a winnable nuclear war and the limited employment of so-called "tactical" nuclear weapons. Although his nuanced reflections on limited nuclear war have generated some confusion in the secondary literature, Morgenthau consistently argued against the possibility of a "rational" and thus manageable employment of atomic weapons.[25] In "Has Atomic War Really Become Impossible?" penned in 1956 for the anti-nuclear *Bulletin of the Atomic Scientists*, he noted that the apparent renunciation of all-out nuclear war left the USA and USSR with two strategic options. They would have to rely on either conventional forces or tactical nuclear weapons. The Soviets already possessed superiority in the former, however. Unless the USA abandoned the mistaken policy of refusing to refurbish its conventional forces, it thus might be forced to "prepare for, and fight if necessary, a limited nuclear war." Yet not only did the looming embrace of limited atomic war rest on a failed policy of neglecting conventional armaments, it also inaccurately presupposed that political and military leaders would "bring to their tasks a blend of self-restraint and daring, which very few leaders in history have proven themselves capable of." Limited nuclear warfare was predicated on the fictional possession by all relevant actors of an infallible political and military judgment able to conduct "a war with just the right atomic dosage" employed at precisely the right moment, and capable of pulling back from the brink of nuclear holocaust at just the right time.[26] When push came to shove, however, could anyone be secure in the expectation that the losing power would refuse to start an all-out nuclear war? In the final analysis, the idea of a limited or graduated atomic war was a risky delusion opening the door to unintentional all-out nuclear war. The real problem, Morgenthau reiterated, was partial western disarmament in regard to conventional forces, which narrowly delimited strategic possibilities. "Yet the use of atomic force, however narrowly circumscribed by the initial intent," Morgenthau wrote in a companion piece from 1957, still "entails the enormous risk that it may develop, imperceptibly but ineluctably, into the use of all-out atomic force." If the USA and its western allies were instead to augment conventional armaments commensurate to the Soviet challenge, the panacea of limited nuclear war could be wisely taken off the nuclear strategists' table altogether. Defenders of limited atomic warfare promised peace, Morgenthau polemicized, but theirs was "the peace of Babylon and Carthage – the peace of total destruction."[27]

Dealing with novelty

Beginning in 1960, Morgenthau's views of nuclear armaments underwent a noticeable shift. Though he had had previously scolded politicians and strategists for failing to pay heed to the novelty of nuclear weaponry, only at this point did he systematically practice what he had always preached. Some of his new positions – e.g. his increasingly frequent attacks on nuclear "bean counters" – obscured the fact that Morgenthau himself had done some of his own bean counting during the 1950s. Nonetheless, a central theme in a flurry of lectures and publications from the early 1960s was that the unprecedented prospect of human annihilation required a major rethinking of virtually every aspect of international politics. Morgenthau now moved beyond the stock argument from the 1940s and 1950s that nuclear weapons had revolutionized *warfare* to the more far-reaching assertion that they generated the first significant revolution in *international politics* in human history. Only now could intense violent conflict result in humanity's extermination. As he commented in *Christianity and Crisis*, a journal edited by his Realist ally Reinhold Niebuhr, "no such radical qualitative transformation of the structure of international relations has ever occurred in history."[28] Throughout his long career, Morgenthau had taken to task scholars and statesmen who disparaged perennial and universal trends in history for naïvely ignoring the ways in which human nature circumscribed the scope of political action. *Politics Among Nations* went so far as to posit the existence of universal "principles of political realism," some of which approximated historically invariable laws. To a great extent, his mature 1950s version of Realism depended on providing frequent and occasionally dogmatic reminders of the continuities of human history, not the least of which were anthropological constants pointing to the unavoidability of intense strife. By the early 1960s at the latest, however, Morgenthau preferred to highlight the radical *discontinuities* in human experience engendered by the prospect of a suicidal nuclear war. A central preoccupation of his thinking henceforth was the potentially disastrous gap between our dominant modes of thought and political organization and the novelty of nuclear war. The nuclear threat in mind, he prophesized in 1961 that the "refusal to adapt thought and action to radically new conditions has spelled the doom of man and civilization before. It is likely to do so again."[29]

Morgenthau's theorizing had always struggled to integrate the deepest moral intuitions of the western tradition. Those moral impulses again took center stage in his reflections on nuclear warfare. He now wrote that the prospect of such warfare challenged not only the nation state and traditional modes of interstate conflict, but, if realized, would constitute an abominable moral evil. Of course, he noted in another contribution to *Christianity and Crisis*, countless evil acts had been committed in human history. Yet "the moral evil inherent in any act of violence" had sometimes been "mitigated by the end it serves." Evil acts remained immoral even when linked to noble political or social goals, yet their immorality was at least potentially minimized by the ends served. Tyrannicide remained murder, for example, yet nonetheless occupied a higher moral plain than murder committed during a bungled burglary. However, nuclear warfare necessarily "destroys the saving impact that good ends exert upon evil means."[30] Its occurrence would inevitably result in untold horrors and probably human annihilation. How could any of the great values of western civilization possibly justify such terrors? A nuclear war might be launched for the sake of Berlin under the banner of "freedom and equality," for example, but atomic war would necessarily extinguish any possibility of their realization.

At an October 1961 symposium on "Western Values and Total War" organized by *Commentary* magazine, Morgenthau responded derisively to a comment by the philosopher Sidney Hook that a nuclear war might be stupid yet somehow heroic: "I see no meaning in the reduction of tens of millions of people to atomic dust, of the monuments of a civilization to radioactive rubble. I see no meaning at all, I see no heroism in this." When classical writers like Aristotle preached the virtues of heroism, Morgenthau continued, they "had in mind individual acts of heroism – Leonidas being slain at Thermopylae and Socrates drinking the hemlock." Such deaths potentially carried a deep cultural and historical significance. They were freely willed, and their memory lived on, providing those making the highest sacrifice with some degree of cultural longevity. Yet "the extermination of eight million New Yorkers within a fraction of a second is an entirely different type of thing." We ignore the radical evil of nuclear warfare and thus misleadingly "talk about defending Western civilization against communism as the ancient Greeks used to talk about defending their civilization against the Persians."[31] The possibility of nuclear war dramatically alters the meaning of life and death:

> Nuclear destruction is mass destruction, both of persons and things. It signifies the simultaneous destruction of tens of millions of people, of whole families, generations, and societies, of all things that they have inherited and created. It signifies the total destruction of whole societies by killing their members, destroying their visible achievements, and therefore reducing their survivors to barbarism. Thus nuclear destruction destroys the meaning of death by depriving it of its individuality. It destroys the meaning of immorality by making both society and history impossible.[32]

The prospect of nuclear death reduces to absurd clichés martial appeals to noble traditional values like bravery, honor, or heroism.[33] They presuppose a degree of historical continuity or at least the survival of a culture that knows what such values mean, neither of which seems likely in the aftermath of a nuclear holocaust.[34] Indeed, the prospect of a nuclear death raises unsettling questions about everyday life from which most of us simply prefer to avert our vision: "Man gives his life and death meaning by his ability to make himself and his works remembered after his death."[35] Soldiers risk their lives in terrible wars with at least some hope that they will be remembered as patriots; parents bring children into the world aspiring to be remembered long after they have vanished; scholars and artists leave behind what they hope will be lasting contributions to the human spirit. In our relatively secular age, it is primarily the possibility that we might achieve some durable accomplishment by means of which, however fleetingly, we may be recalled by future generations that provides our pursuits with some meaning. Yet nuclear war would render even this impossible. Although we typically go on with our lives as though nothing new has happened, "as though the possibility of nuclear death portended only a quantitative extension of the mass destruction of the past and not a qualitative transformation of the meaning of our existence," its prospect potentially denies almost everything we do that has significance.[36] Why continue to live as we do, given the real possibility of a nuclear war destroying even the barest trace of our existence? "Perhaps in some faraway place some evidence would be preserved of the perished civilization and of the men who created it";[37] but this could hardly provide solace for the millions who perished, "not like men but like beasts, killed in the mass," merely "by somebody switching a key thousands of miles away."[38]

What brought on the increasingly philosophical – and, indeed, existentialist – tenor of Morgenthau's anti-nuclear reflections in the early 1960s? His preoccupation with the novelties of the nuclear era clearly built on key ideas found in previous writings. For that matter, his was by no means the only voice in the early 1960s expressing growing anxieties about the nuclear arms race. Previously moribund peace movements were again on the move in many parts of the world, and even popular culture gave reflection to burgeoning anti-nuclear sentiment with successful Hollywood productions like *Failsafe* (1964) and *Dr. Strangelove, or How I Learned to Stop Worrying and Love the Bomb* (1964). A direct inspiration for Morgenthau's own reflections was the heated public discussion in the USA in the early 1960s about a proposed atomic test ban treaty, which Morgenthau strongly endorsed. "Only a miracle will save mankind," he announced in a letter to the editor published simultaneously by the *New York Times* and the *Washington Post* on February 23, 1960, unless the arms race could be brought under control. A cessation of nuclear tests was "a first small step in the direction of the control of the arms race."[39]

Yet it remains difficult to escape the conclusion that Morgenthau's encounter with Karl Jaspers' influential *The Future of Mankind* helped to crystallize as well as funnel longstanding anxieties in a constructive theoretical direction. Jaspers' book had first appeared to popular acclaim in Germany in 1958, winning the coveted German Peace Prize at the Frankfurt Book Fair. Hannah Arendt, a former pupil of Jaspers, as well as Morgenthau's friend, helped to arrange for its translation and perhaps encouraged Morgenthau to write a review, which he was able to do for the popular *Saturday Review* on February 18, 1961.[40] As Morgenthau's brief but positive discussion attests, he was taken by Jaspers' main arguments, praising him for recognizing the singularity of the nuclear revolution and systematically drawing the logical "radical philosophic and political conclusions."[41] Morgenthau, in fact, quickly went on to make many of Jaspers' most telling points his own.

Even a cursory glance at Jaspers' volume intimates why it immediately appealed to Morgenthau. Jaspers had honed in on the unique character of nuclear weapons, vividly outlining manifold escape mechanisms by means of which the anxious inhabitants of the nuclear age disingenuously closed their eyes to the new perils at hand. Atomic weaponry may have simply represented the latest results of a long process of continuous technological development, yet it would be a mistake to underplay its novelty. In the past, even the greatest disasters could not wipe out humanity, but in the nuclear age, great powers were in fact accelerating the production of weapons to accomplish just that.[42] Given the dreary course of the arms race and the existence of explosive interstate tensions, Jaspers dryly noted, "on purely rational reflection it is probable that it will happen."[43] Obviously, this was a harsh fact with which to come to terms; most people understandably preferred to bury their heads in the sand, pursuing bustling lives void of any serious reflections about the historically unprecedented possibility of human extinction.

At the same time, Jaspers' alarmism was tempered by a skeptical assessment of grandiose plans for instant institutional change. A liberal democrat, Jaspers was a firm ally of the United States and of NATO, though hardly an uncritical admirer of either. He could hardly be accused of being "soft" on Soviet communism, which he described devastatingly as fundamentally totalitarian in character. Although the threat of total destruction ultimately required a new world community governed by law, "attempts at instant reformation would quickly produce total anarchy and despotism." In Jaspers' conceptual language, a "new politics" which took the possibility of suicide by atomic extermination seriously would first "have to move in the tracks of the old politics."[44] Reformers could simply not count on a sudden end to power politics or the pursuit of national interest, but instead would need to figure out how dramatic changes to the existing political universe could be engineered from within the confines of the political status quo.

Unsurprisingly in light of their shared debts to Max Weber, who had been Jaspers' mentor at Heidelberg, the book repeatedly echoed Morgenthau's own earlier attempts to refurbish Weber's ethic of responsibility. For Jaspers, as for Morgenthau, the necessity of circumventing the twin dangers of a cramped political realism as well as a naïve moralism was central. By itself, a narrow political realism or *Realpolitik* risked ignoring universal ethical and moral imperatives which alone could save it from moral nihilism. Notwithstanding "the extraordinary insights to be acquired by means of political realism," a conservative realism of "pure politics," "pointing to human nature, as it has always been and always will be," mistakenly discounted the "suprapolitical" or ethical element of human experience as well as the novelty of the present situation.[45] Unavoidably, it aggrandized the chances of nuclear destruction. No less perilous, however, was a crude moralism culminating in a naïve and counterproductive political and legal idealism: "In foolishly idealistic politics we act as if the condition we want had been attained already. In foolishly realistic politics we act as if it were unattainable. Both ways are irresponsible."[46] Only a third alternative which began with the harsh realities of present-day political life while keeping irrepressible moral laws in sight could motor the necessary institutional reforms which might allow humankind to survive the invention of nuclear weapons. However, even the most well-designed legal and political reforms by themselves might not do the job. Jaspers speculated that human nature itself would have to be directed in unprecedented ways if we were to survive: latent "forces in man" would need to "well up from such depths as to transform him in moral, rational, political aspects – a transformation so extensive that it would become the turning point of history."[47] The radical novelty of nuclear weapons would have to summon a no less dramatic revolution in the human condition. A first realistic step towards reform, fortunately, was offered by growing popular awareness of the nuclear dangers. The inchoate but ultimately rational fear engineered by the fear of atomic war, Jaspers hoped, provided a launching pad for creative reforms as well as broader shifts in human existence that might stem the approaching tide of the nuclear flood.

Shortly after reviewing Jaspers' *The Future of Mankind*, Morgenthau gave a series of lectures in late 1961 and early 1962, entitled "Reflections on the Nuclear Age," at major institutions of higher education including American University in Washington, D.C., and the University of Chicago.[48] Although never published in full, snippets did appear in journals and magazines, and a substantial portion was published pretty much unaltered a decade later, in Morgenthau's last major book, *Science: Servant or Master?* (1972).[49] The lectures reproduced many of Morgenthau's familiar arguments about nuclear weapons. They also discussed Jaspers' book at length, and in the process provide indelible evidence of Jaspers' deep impact, suggesting how the intellectual engagement with Jaspers' existentialist brew gave a new shape even to some of Morgenthau's stock positions.

The lectures and publications based on them vividly described the likely terrors of a nuclear war, building directly on Jaspers' reflections on the ways in which modern technological development culminates in the nuclear revolution, and even concluding with a cautious endorsement of Jaspers' suggestion that the nuclear revolution requires humankind to transform itself and its "very nature so as to come to terms with the nuclear age."[50] Most importantly, they adeptly employed Jaspers to assail prominent nuclear strategists whom Morgenthau now accused of irresponsibly underplaying the novelty of nuclear weapons. Morgenthau wrote that one could distinguish between two competing schools of thought on nuclear weapons: the "cataclysmic" school, under whose rubric he placed both Jaspers and himself, and the "complacency" school, which missed the novelty of the nuclear threat and whose patron saint was the controversial Herman Kahn, whom he acerbically admonished for failing to discriminate nuclear from conventional warfare. Morgenthau accused Kahn not only of defending an unrealistic vision of how a limited nuclear war might be won, but also of succumbing to a hyper-rationalistic model which downplayed the unpredictable and unavoidably contingent character of crisis-level decision making. Kahn's picture of human society was akin to that of a primitive ant colony, whose recuperative capabilities even in the aftermath of unprecedented destruction were simply taken for granted. His expectation that humanity could somehow survive a massive nuclear war neglected the fact that "societies have a breaking point as do individuals, and there may be a point beyond which human endurance does not carry . . . in the face of such unprecedented devastation."[51] The same critical line, by the way, was taken in response to Edward Teller in a 1962 review published in *Bulletin of the Atomic Scientists*, where Morgenthau pilloried Teller's defense of limited nuclear war, arguing that his Panglossian faith in the nuclear arms race missed a decisive historical shift: "once a nation has acquired a nuclear arsenal which is both indestructible and capable of destroying the enemy," the continuation of the nuclear arms race no longer served rational purposes.[52] The nuclear bean counters delighted in tallying up comparative missiles for both sides, pretending that nuclear weapons are ultimately no different from troop totals or counts of armored vehicles. They, like Kahn and Teller, remained prisoners of the outdated and deeply irresponsible view that nuclear weaponry represented a mere quantitative extension of its conventional cousin.

The same failure to tackle the novelty of our historical situation head-on was the source of what "Reflections on the Nuclear Age" attacked point blank as the "Alice in Wonderland" quality of US and Soviet foreign policy. In the recent conflict over Berlin, Morgenthau reminded his listeners at American University in November, 1961, the USA was forced to suggest to the Soviets that it would wage nuclear war if necessary in order to maintain the autonomy of West Berlin, while the Soviets similarly tried to bluff the West into believing that it would fight in order to close off access to Berlin. But both sides simultaneously assumed that the other side would not risk blowing up the world in order to advance policy aims: "So we are dealing here with a strange paradox . . . Both sides maintain their determination to engage in one [i.e., nuclear war] on certain conditions and both sides maintain that the other side will never do something like that."[53] The fundamental problem, Morgenthau asserted, derived from a gap or discrepancy between conventional modes of diplomatic procedure "which have been transmitted to us from the pre-nuclear age" and their employment in the novel nuclear context.[54] The result, he concluded, was an extremely perilous game of psychological bluffs and counterbluffs, which risked getting ratcheted up to a point of no return. The lectures repeated his earlier assessment that, in a bipolar environment, the nuclear game might potentially take a relatively predictable form. But what if ten powers possessed nuclear weapons, for example, and three of them were hostile to the United States? How much rationality could then reasonably be expected of policy makers faced with a sudden nuclear attack on a US or Western European city? What was needed, in short, was nothing less than a "radical rethinking of the relations which ought to exist between violence as a means and the ends of foreign policy."[55] At the very least, this radical revision would need to close the gap between the objective conditions of contemporary life and the predominant modes of thought and political practices.

Precisely this misfit between the objective conditions of the nuclear age and contemporary thought and practice lay at the base of what Morgenthau dubbed the "four paradoxes of nuclear strategy" described in a major 1964 *American Political Science Review* article. Although restating some familiar positions, the article refined them, situating them more clearly in the context of Morgenthau's diagnosis that nuclear strategy remained mired in a pre-nuclear mindset. The first paradox referred again to the continued employment of the pre-nuclear diplomatic ploy of bluffing by nuclear powers which simultaneously claimed that neither side would rationally unleash a suicidal atomic war. Morgenthau now deepened the original argument by noting that the dynamic of nuclear bluffing and counterbluffing was likely to erode over time:

> With every demonstration of its emptiness, the nuclear threat will lose a measure of its plausibility . . . Inherent in that dynamic is . . . a dual escalation, one feeding upon the other: the ever-diminishing plausibility of the nuclear threat and ever bolder challenges to make good on it. The effects of deterrence are likely to decrease with the frequency of its use, to the point where, as it were, the psychological capital of deterrence has been nearly expended and the policy of deterrence will be close to bankruptcy.[56]

Hitherto, the psychological dynamics of deterrence had helped tame the two nuclear superpowers. However, deterrence necessarily remained a limited answer to the massive challenges posed by nuclear weaponry – in the final analysis, it was nothing but a strategic device by which political actors circumvented the necessity of far-reaching policy and institutional changes. Although possessing some rational basis given the structure of the existing state system, deterrence in the long run was likely to prove self-destructive.[57]

The second paradox reiterated Morgenthau's earlier criticisms of limited nuclear war, reminding his readers of the hazards of treating atomic weapons as mere technological extensions of conventional weaponry. No nuclear war was likely to remain limited; escalation was "built into the very dynamics of nuclear war, as the maximization of violence is built into the dynamics of any war."[58] The third paradox consisted of the fact that policy makers myopically insisted on stockpiling ever more deadly nuclear weapons, as though bigger and better weapons of mass destruction inevitably implied, as with conventional weaponry, greater prowess. In a detailed critique of Kennedy-era US nuclear policy, Morgenthau scattered the main US justifications for the arms race, expressing deep skepticisms that even the prospect of path-breaking technological innovations countered the new but decisive fact that, once each side was capable of destroying the other, there were rational limits to how many additional nuclear weapons were necessary. Kennedy's widely touted "counter-force" policies conflated nuclear and conventional weapons and thereby remained imprisoned in the complacency school of nuclear thought.[59]

Finally, he noted that the nuclear revolution dismantled traditional ideas about military alliances. Although contemporary diplomatic practice tended to ignore this novel fact, conventional military alliances were undermined once good reasons could be identified for questioning whether any nation state in the nuclear age would sacrifice its own existence in order to aid an ally. To Charles de Gaulle's credit, Morgenthau admitted, he had grasped the fragility of a military alliance dependent on the dubious assumption that a dominant power might risk nuclear suicide for the save of upholding an alliance. Unfortunately, de Gaulle's medicine was worse than the disease: if other countries followed France's model and anachronistically decided that nuclear weapons could be used as more or less conventional instruments of national policy, the precarious bipolar model of nuclear deterrence would be quickly undermined. Global nuclear proliferation would make any attempt to mitigate the dangers of nuclear weapons impossible, destabilizing the fragile nuclear balance and opening the door to a disastrous war. The basic dilemma here remained the failure to undertake, as Jaspers had similarly advocated, a "psychologically painful and politically risky" but urgent "radical transformation" of conventional modes of strategic thought and political practice. As Morgenthau concluded, "short of such a transformation, there will be no escape from the paradoxes of nuclear strategy and the dangers attending them."[60]

Towards limited world government?

So what radical changes were to be pursued? Morgenthau's American University lectures directly named his proposed antidote to the creeping possibility of nuclear war. As in many writings from the late 1950s onwards, he eulogized the Baruch-Lilienthal Plan of 1946, which had called for an international agency, or Atomic Development Authority, with a monopoly on all atomic energy activities, now openly admitting that he initially had been too slow to recognize the greatness of the failed US proposals. Indeed, his first published appraisal of the US proposals for supranational control of nuclear weapons had been at best ambivalent (*PAN*, 1st edn., 297–300).[61] Here again, he preferred to downplay a subtle but decisive shift in his own thinking. But by 1960, however, Morgenthau was calling unabashedly for a revival of the supranational control of nuclear power: *Purpose of American Politics* included a detailed defense of the "sound and bold assumptions" behind the original Baruch-Lilienthal proposals, now described with enthusiasm as an "unprecedentedly radical step towards a limited world government" (*PAP*, 173). Such a government could obviously not be established overnight. Yet Morgenthau declared that in the final instance it alone was commensurate with "the existential threat atomic power poses to all nations" (*PAP*, 169). The USA had been right in 1946 to acknowledge that the "competitive development of atomic energy was fraught with incalculable danger for all mankind and therefore ought not to be at the discretion of national governments." As Morgenthau appreciatively recalled, this insight had led postwar policy makers to advocate supernational supervision of nuclear development, research, and mining, as well as "the cessation of the manufacture of atomic bombs and destruction of existing ones" (*PAP*, 173). Given the centrality of nuclear weaponry to military power, he noted, for all effective purposes such a body would ultimately function as a world government. Yet in contradistinction to competing plans for global government, Baruch-Lilienthal made no unrealistic call for a mammoth global police force or military, neither of which Morgenthau deemed imminently achievable or perhaps even desirable. Even though the ADA would be outfitted with extensive inspection authority, in the event of a violation states could simply withdraw from it and advance unilateral measures.

Although outmoded conceptions of national sovereignty and especially Stalin's refusal to accept intrusive international inspections had prevented their approval, Morgenthau argued, the Baruch-Lilienthal Plan still pointed would-be international reformers in the right direction. Yet what if the Soviets again refused to endorse a strict supranational system of nuclear regulation? *Purpose of American Politics* also briefly considered the possibility of an alternative supranational "free-world association" of liberal democratic states, under US leadership, whose main achievement would be to take the first decisive step towards breaking the explosive chain between national statehood and the monopoly on violence by placing the control of nuclear weapons in its shared hands. Resting on a modicum of philosophical and institutional homogeneity, this free-world association would be "more intimate" than traditional alliances or ad hoc alignments (*PAP*, 308–9). While a universal system of supranational atomic regulation might presently prove unrealistic, a more limited yet potentially trendsetting association of liberal democratic states could serve as a stepping stone to more ambitious varieties of supranational atomic regulation.

Morgenthau was again inspired by Mitrany's functionalist theory, even though he failed to mention his name. The 1946 US proposals, Morgenthau reiterated, pointed to the necessity of creative institutional experiments in the global oversight of nuclear power, at the very least a "beginning, a pattern to be duplicated in other fields" (*PAP*, 173). In fact, the proposed ADA was modeled in part on the New Deal Tennessee Valley Authority (TVA), a direct inspiration as well to Mitrany. David Lilienthal, or "Mr. TVA" as he was widely known to Americans at the time, chair of the panel which proposed the ADA, had been Director of TVA and was closely identified with its accomplishments. For Morgenthau, here again was an arena of social activity crying out for sensible institutional experiments which might tap into shared regulatory needs, while moving beyond outmoded configurations of territorially based decision making. Despite their many differences, the United States and the Soviets possessed a common interest in keeping nuclear weapons out of the hands of other countries. Their respective national interests, rightly understood, meshed considerably with an international system sharply limiting the spread of atomic weapons. Speaking to a US

Senate Committee about the dangers of proliferation, Morgenthau reported that this was "one area of disarmament where the vital interests of the United States and the Soviet Union coincide."[62] In the same vein, a proposed atomic test ban treaty could hardly achieve much on its own, he told his listeners at American University. Yet it might come to represent a symbolically consequential stepping stone beyond the principle of unabashed territorial sovereignty in security policy: "An example would have been established to the effect that it is possible to create and make work supranational agencies and supervising at least one small technically-limited segment of this enormous new force of nuclear power."[63] Its success might at least have left the door open for more far-reaching experiments with the supranational regulation of atomic weapons. Since control over nuclear weapons constituted a decisive attribute of effective state sovereignty, supranational oversight of it would entail a more dramatic move towards a cosmopolitan world state than global oversight of international postal services, for example, or even international trade. Nonetheless, the supranational regulation of atomic power might still emerge organically out of a series of ever more far-reaching institutional experiments, designed for concrete cross-border regulatory tasks, undertaken on the basis of overlapping national interests.

Morgenthau frequently listed the many familiar obstacles to the effective supranational control of nuclear weapons. By the early 1960s, however, he also tended to underline the existence of shared or common interests between the United States and the Soviets which provided at least some glimmer of hope for would-be reformers: "That common interest is the common fear of atomic destruction, the danger of which is inherent in the atomic armaments race and is enormously increased by the impending dispersal of atomic weapons into the hands of any number of governments. On rational grounds, that common fear ought to outweigh even the fear of each other."[64] To be sure, there was no guarantee that the existing nuclear powers would recognize either the dangers of the arms race or the overall irrationality of deterrence. Yet a historical situation in which "so powerful a nation as the United States is no longer able to . . . protect its interests vis-a-vis nations which by any standard of comparison are infinitely weaker" might lead even the great powers to experiment with potentially far-reaching shifts to the international system.[65] In this view, "the desire, innate in all men, for self-preservation" could be funneled in creative institutional directions by political leaders who were beginning to understand that only the abandonment of nuclear weapons as an instrument of national policy could provide real national security.[66]

For untold eons, cosmopolitan visions of world government had indeed been utopian. But now that only an effective global monopoly over nuclear weapons could successfully mitigate the specter of nuclear holocaust, world government had become an existential necessity. To the extent that the most basic element of the national interest was self-preservation, in the nuclear age pursuit of the national interest called for gradual movement towards a worldwide system of nuclear controls capable of preventing a devastating war. As Morgenthau observed in a relatively hopeful comment published in a Catholic student journal in 1963, "the governments of the Great Powers are aware of the irrationality of nuclear war which would destroy at the very least all belligerents." Even though success was by no means assured, "they are groping towards translating this rational awareness into political action."[67] What action should they then pursue? Morgenthau again declared that only the establishment of supernational control of the production and employment of nuclear energy could do the job.

Morgenthau never abandoned the fundaments of this position. In a 1974 interview for the left-leaning *War/Peace Report*, devoted to an ongoing exchange between Andrei Sakharov and Aleksandr Solzhenitsyn, Morgenthau sided with Sakharov's embrace of world government, noting again that the gulf between existing political practice and the "objective technological conditions under which we live" could only be bridged by it. Of course, he quickly added, the question of whether it "is likely to be achieved is something else again."[68] In 1975, writing for the *New Republic*, Morgenthau claimed that the US national interest, sensibly defined, required "support of supranational institutions and procedures capable of performing the functions that in view of modern technological developments the individual nation-states are no longer able to perform."[69] In the nuclear era, small and medium-sized nation states lacking a sufficient nuclear arsenal could no longer defend themselves effectively. As for those possessing nuclear weapons, it was high time for them to grasp the crucial point that proliferation and the arms race risked suicide. Morgenthau also continued to speak out loudly and oftentimes unfashionably on the perils of nuclear war, telling an audience at Lehigh University in 1976, for example, that, unless humanity drastically changed course, it remained "virtually inevitable that sooner or later there will be a general nuclear war and such a war would certainly mean the end of civilization and of mankind."[70]

As he had spent much of his career documenting the *irrationality* of foreign policy making, Morgenthau's rare hopeful comments unavoidably tended to take a back seat to his growing anxieties and even despair about the improbability of supernational nuclear oversight. As he understood far too well, the rational necessity of a fundamental reordering of the international order hardly ensured its practical realization. Even when referring to the relatively successful Nuclear Non-Proliferation Treaty (NPT) in a 1976 interview, he identified its Achilles' heel, predicting that the refusal by the great powers to cut their own nuclear arsenals would soon lead aspiring nuclear powers to circumvent it:

> For the nonproliferation treaty has only been a temporary success while the prospective new nuclear powers waited for the old, established nuclear powers to take care of nuclear arms control and disarmament. When this appears to be out of the question, they will ask, as India has asked, Why should we not have nuclear weapons . . . ? And if the Pakistanis will ask tomorrow, Why shouldn't we have them? When the Pakistanis have them, the Afghans will ask, Why shouldn't we have them? [*sic*][71]

Perhaps this is also why Morgenthau's many comments on issues like the proposed atomic test ban treaty were so heated: unless room was made for minimal attempts at the global regulation of nuclear weapons, there would simply be no real chance for humanity to pursue the more extensive experiments which alone could secure peace, "and the only issue remaining to be settled will be how and when we shall be doomed."[72]

Morgenthau's reflections on what he dubbed *limited* world government also inadvertently generated an internal theoretical incongruity. Because indivisibility and supremacy made up constitutive features of sovereignty, Morgenthau categorically stated in *Politics Among Nations*, proposals for supranational government that fell short of a powerful world state with a legitimate monopoly on force were intrinsically incoherent:

> We have heard it said time and again that we must "surrender part of our sovereignty" to an international organization for the sake of world peace, that we must "share" our sovereignty with such an organization, that the latter would have a certain "limited sovereignty" while we would keep the substance of it . . . We shall endeavor to show that the conception of a divisible sovereignty is contrary to logic and politically unfeasible. (*PAN*, 2nd edn., 303)

Not only is divisible – or in more recent parlance, differentiated – sovereignty inconsonant with effective state action, but supranational political and legal institutions committed to realizing confused ideas about sovereignty were destined to founder in the face of war or dire crisis. For Morgenthau, the League of Nations' failure to act in the face of Japanese and German aggression represented paradigmatic examples of such failures. The necessary indivisibility and supremacy of sovereignty manifested themselves most clearly in the emergency or crisis situation, when "a man or a group of men" – Morgenthau's favorite examples for his primarily US audience were Lincoln, Wilson, and the two Roosevelts – inevitably exercised unlimited power. Democratic systems "purposefully obscured the problem of sovereignty and glossed over the need for a definite location of the sovereign power" with legalistic and constitutional niceties masking the real nature of power (*PAN*, 2nd edn., 305). At times echoing Schmitt's view of sovereignty as the capacity to act effectively during a crisis, Morgenthau doubted that it could "be vested in the people as a whole, who, of course, as such cannot act" coherently, especially during an emergency (*PAN*, 2nd edn., 306).[73] If states are to counter dire existential threats, supreme power must be placed in the hands of some individual or small group.

This conception of sovereignty, like its Schmittian cousin, suffered from a misleadingly one-dimensional preoccupation with the emergency situation. Its personalistic emphasis on the necessity of decision making by "a man or a group of men," along with its anti-democratic overtones, provides additional evidence for Morgenthau's misplaced historical nostalgia: his ideas about sovereignty were modeled sometimes on notions of statehood derived from the historical experience of European Absolutism.[74] Consistent with this view, Morgenthau was skeptical of proposals for pacific *federations* or *confederations* of states (*PAN*, 2nd edn., 482–3). This is, of course, unfortunate, because many, if not most, modern cosmopolitan theorists – beginning with Kant – have advocated something along these lines, rather than a world state, as the best way to preserve peace.[75] In short, this conceptual move precluded him from offering a sufficiently subtle analysis of institutional proposals, *short of a more or less centralized world state*, for securing peace. As Daniel H. Deudney has analogously noted, Morgenthau's problematic ideas about the nature of the state led him prematurely to exclude the possibility of a federal and republican model of world government which might flourish without the attributes of a centralized world state which have understandably worried some.[76] A suspect definition of sovereignty outfitted Morgenthau with a counterproductive intellectual straitjacket.

Making matters even more enigmatic, Mitrany's functionalist model of sovereignty got a free pass in Morgenthau's analysis even though it surely broke no less decisively with traditional conceptions of state sovereignty. Morgenthau's own functionalist-inspired vision of reform, after all, was predicated on the possibility that national sovereignty might be gradually transformed in synch with concrete cross-border regulatory needs that slowly but inexorably undermined it. In this view, some elements of sovereignty *could* in fact be carefully "surrendered," *if* this was undertaken in accordance with functional needs, national interests overlapped, and reformers shied away from grandiose models of top-down constitutional reform. Tellingly, Morgenthau sometimes described his own institutional goal as a *limited* world state, in part as a way of expressing the hope that the supranational coordination of nuclear power might leave other fundamental government tasks in the hands of existing nation states. Nor did it perhaps require, as the Baruch-Lilienthal Plan had tentatively intimated, a massive accumulation of force at the global level. The functionalist vision articulated by Mitrany and espoused by Morgenthau, in reality, implied both the desirability and feasibility of complex modes of functionally differentiated sovereignty.

When pondering the possibility of the supernational control of nuclear weapons, Morgenthau was right to ignore his own dogmatic strictures about state sovereignty. Yet they still worked to narrow the horizons of his institutional imagination. In the final analysis, Morgenthau was only able "to glimpse – not to design, to glimpse – a *new*, that is, unforeseen political process whereby a condition of anarchy evolves in a new Leviathan; a world state that comes into being merely because of the *prospect* of a nuclear war of all against all."[77]

Buying time

Morgenthau's final writings on the nuclear threat tended to focus on the continuing perils of the atavistic mindset – commonplace on both sides of the Iron Curtain – that nuclear war remained winnable. This reckless illusion, he repeated in numerous publications for both academic and popular journals in the late 1960s and 1970s, destabilized superpower relations and brought humanity closer to the nuclear brink. The complacency school of nuclear thinking incited politicians to seek ever more destructive weapons, a superior first-strike capacity, and fanciful visions of nuclear defense.[78] The result was a wasteful arms race that plundered scarce resources and threatened to deliver humanity "helplessly to the prospect of nuclear destruction," as he noted nervously in a 1979 *New Republic* article on the SALT II negotiations.[79] Many politicians, strategists, and military officials still missed the novelty of nuclear weaponry:

> The military balance as bean-counting exercise is just one concept among many, hallowed by tradition, that have been rendered obsolete by the nuclear revolution. Defense, limited war, victory, alliances, and the distinction between combatants and non-combatants also have lost most practical meaning. Yet our strategic experts disquietingly continue to think in obsolete terms, and thus construct obsolescent policies concerning the nuclear weapons that have transformed the condition of our existence.[80]

Sadly, over the course of the cold war, an insidious but influential system of social and political interests had emerged to provide ready support for obsolescent policies.

Beyond an atomic test ban and nuclear non-proliferation, what nuclear policies should sensible politicians and diplomats advance? Even under ideal circumstances, the creation of an effective supernational system of nuclear controls would take time. As the chances for its emergence remained dim, the elderly Morgenthau forced himself to offer additional policy suggestions. Only some form of world government, based on the supernational oversight of nuclear weapons, could secure lasting peace. In the meantime, political officials would need to pursue other policy options.

First, Morgenthau proposed a modification of existing forms of nuclear deterrence. Even if deterrence in the long run was "a self-defeating and ultimately, I am convinced, a suicidal policy," it had in the short run countered Soviet aggression and performed stabilizing functions.[81] Absent fundamental changes to the state system, it remained a necessary albeit unfortunate component of sound foreign policy. As Richard Ned Lebow and Janice Gross Stein have argued more recently, "deterrence should be viewed as a powerful but very dangerous medicine."[82] The immediate task at hand, then, was to minimize its deadliest features. Both the USA and the USSR, Morgenthau stated succinctly in 1971, have "pursued the rational goal of nuclear deterrence with the irrational means of an unlimited nuclear arms race." They falsely presupposed that the rational functions of nuclear deterrence necessitated an (irrational) arms race which had long since spiraled out of control. They missed the existence of "an optimum of nuclear preparedness sufficient for deterrence," determined by whatever weapons would be necessary effectively to cripple the other side.[83] In his more radical moments, Morgenthau appeared to be moving towards an endorsement of "finite deterrence," according to which a relatively limited number of nuclear missiles would suffice to deter great-power rivals.[84] In the same vein, the dangerous political gamble of nuclear bluffs and counterbluffs had to be closed down. Morgenthau feared that it was simply a matter of time before a bluff was called, and an unintended nuclear war ensued. Writing in the *Bulletin of the Atomic Scientists*, he proposed that nuclear bluffing "ought to be eliminated from diplomatic practice" since it was now "inherently lacking in credibility." More fundamentally, strategists ought to remove nuclear weapons not only from normal diplomatic practice, but also from standard military planning. In contrast to conventional weapons, their indiscriminate destructive character meant that they could never serve as normal instruments of national policy. Policy makers should assign to a limited number of nuclear weapons, adequate to threaten rivals with the possibility of destruction, "exclusively the function of a deterrent, to be used only in suicidal desperation."[85]

Second, Morgenthau jettisoned any remaining doubts about the necessity of multilateral nuclear disarmament. The political tasks of nuclear disarmament and arms control were now described as dwarfing all others.[86] Whereas in the 1950s he had posited that only a political settlement would permit lasting success in limiting nuclear arsenals, he now insisted that this position only obtained for *conventional* weapons. To be sure, in "Four Paradoxes of Nuclear Strategy" and elsewhere, he had already begun to provide a firm grounding for disarmament. The early 1970s, however, found Morgenthau hammering away stubbornly at the irrationality of the atomic arms race: even if basic political conflicts between the superpowers remained unresolved, they possessed a rational common interest in reducing existing arsenals as well as preventing the creation of new weapons of mass destruction. Unless halted, nuclear proliferation would place dangerous weapons in the hands of irresponsible governments which might use them disastrously as weapons of national policy.[87] Proliferation could inadvertently "involve the major nuclear powers in a nuclear war against their will," and they consequently shared a clear interest in preventing any such nuclear "catastrophe not of our own making."[88] As long as one superpower was capable of destroying its rivals, Morgenthau reported on the latest Pugwash Conference for the *New York Review of Books* in 1970, it gained no advantage militarily by augmenting the quality and quantity of its nuclear weaponry.

To be sure, every arms control or disarmament agreement contained risks. Yet those who assumed that the Soviets would necessarily pursue the most diabolical course not only failed to provide sufficient evidence that the Russians either could get away with cheating or even possessed an adequate incentive to do so, but disregarded the even more horrendous risks of an unlimited arms race increasing the probability of war.[89] A large part of the blame should be laid at the door of elites in both the USA and USSR who had succumbed to an irresponsible passivity in the face of scientific and technological development: "what seems to be technologically possible is put into practice for no better reason but because it can be done," despite its political and sometimes even military irrationality.[90] Hearkening back to *Scientific Man*, Morgenthau saw in this ominous trend the latest and perhaps most hazardous consequence of a myopic and deeply anti-political faith in science and technology as a panacea for social and political ills. Yet policy makers who falsely assumed that if a prospective innovation in weapons technology was *conceivable*, then it *necessarily* must be pursued regardless of costs, were simply forging nails for their own coffins.

How Realism (after Morgenthau) learned to love the bomb

Living in the shadows of the cold war and a terrifying nuclear arms race, Morgenthau worried deeply about "the bomb." After the revolutions of 1989 and the dramatic disarmament measures initiated chiefly by Mikhail Gorbachev, we have become more complacent. Like Dr. Strangelove, many of us apparently have learned to stop worrying about the bomb, or at least accept the existence of substantial nuclear arsenals as a necessary feature of political life. More recent Realist theorists have even tried to make a virtue out of a vice, arguing that the apparent successes of cold war nuclear deterrence can be readily extended to the post-1989 setting. In this view, nuclear proliferation is no peril to humankind, but instead a potentially positive development. In the unforgettable words of Kenneth Waltz, "more may be better" in nuclear weaponry, since new nuclear states, like the old ones, will quickly grasp that "possible losses in war overwhelm possible gains."[91] For Waltz and other prominent present-day Realists, the acquisition of second-strike nuclear arsenals renders attacks on countries possessing them irrational. Ownership of a sufficient nuclear arsenal obliterates the possibility of the country in question being conquered and thereby helps to stabilize interstate relations between and among new nuclear powers, just as it provided a modicum of order in relations between atomic powers during the cold war. If properly managed by the great powers, nuclear proliferation might aid rather than undermine international order.

This position, widely associated with contemporary Realism, has already helped to shape foreign policy. It has influenced recent shifts in US policy towards India, for example, which have increased the likelihood of a far-reaching expansion of India's nuclear arsenal.[92]

From the perspective of recent Realism, Morgenthau's reflections on nuclear warfare appear quaint, unscientific, and unduly moralistic. This is not the place to examine the complex twists and turns in the development of recent Realist theory which resulted in its stunning intellectual change of course. Nonetheless, there are sound reasons for questioning the widely held assumption that present-day Realists are more sophisticated than their founding father.

Morgenthau's anxieties about nuclear deterrence have been substantially corroborated by recent research. Not only was the nuclear arms buildup astonishingly costly in social and economic and thereby human terms for both the Soviets and Americans, but deterrence strategy at key junctures aggrandized tensions and "likely prolonged the Cold War."[93] Morgenthau also worried about its costs to *democratic* politics; on this matter as well, his analysis was far-sighted. Contemporary Realism offers at best a one-dimensional, and at worst a romanticized, view of Soviet–US relations during the cold war. We now know that both sides too often came perilously close to stumbling accidentally into nuclear warfare.[94] The blame for at least some of those near-misses can be placed at the feet of deterrence strategy. If Scott Sagan is correct, one decisive source of the relative "success" of postwar nuclear deterrence was that effective mechanisms of civilian control, however flawed, functioned to rein in military elites typically more likely to start either accidental or deliberate nuclear wars. Mechanisms of civilian control seem more fragile in many new and prospective nuclear states.[95] Despite Morgenthau's own occasionally crude criticisms of proliferation, he accurately glimpsed that a pivotal threat posed was not that new nuclear powers might attack a great power like the United States, but instead that proliferation would potentially engender new sources of unexpected and unpredictable instability. As Joseph Cirincione, a leading arms control expert, has observed in the context of Iran's quest for nuclear weapons:

> what a state like Iran might see as a defensive move [for example, as an answer to the possibility of US attack] would provoke dangerous reactions from other states in the region. A nuclear reaction chain could ripple through a region and across the globe, triggering weapons decisions in several, perhaps many, other states . . . The spread of nuclear weapons to multiple states throughout an already tense region could bring increased rivalry, greater friction, and quite possibly nuclear catastrophe . . . It is possible that the Middle East could go from a region with one nuclear weapon state (Israel), to one with two, three, or five such states within a decade – with all the tensions of the existing political and territorial disputes still unresolved.[96]

Faced with this scenario, even a great power like the United States would have a hard time managing it, in part because the resulting distribution of nuclear weaponry would fail to reproduce the dynamics of the *bi*polar cold war system. Given the many vital interests at stake in the Middle East, a "localized" atomic war might easily uncork a worldwide nuclear conflagration. If Iran were to launch nuclear missiles against close US allies like Israel or Egypt, would the United States remain on the sidelines? If a war erupted between North and South Korea, would China and the USA remain uninvolved? Morgenthau wrote in 1975 that "the fact that we have lived with the nuclear arms for more than twenty years now is no reason to assume that we can live forever in this kind of semi-orderly and peaceful world."[97] By the same logic, there is no reason to presuppose that an idealized interpretation of postwar bipolar nuclear deterrence can be easily transferred to the novel conditions of the twenty-first century.

Morgenthau also anticipated the legitimate anxiety that deterrence overstates the likelihood that nuclear states will act rationally and avoid policies risking their own destruction. His worries about the convoluted psychological dynamics of deterrence are echoed by those who have pointed to dangerous brinkmanship contests which tie the hands of political leaders, committing them to reckless courses of action from which they see no viable escape. Nor would Morgenthau have been surprised by those who have noted that nuclear deterrence is unlikely to operate usefully against radical and millenarian regimes whose leaders may opt for self-destruction over military defeat and occupation.[98]

The tendency among contemporary Realists to serve as intellectual apologists for nuclear proliferation would surely have reminded Morgenthau of the complacency school of nuclear thinking which he criticized. It suggests that he was probably right about the need to revise conventional Realist theory: one obvious source of recent Realist complacency about nuclear weaponry is a stubborn refusal to tackle the fundamental *normative* and even *utopian* institutional questions posed by the possibility of human extermination.[99] For many of Morgenthau's academic offspring, such questions simply do not rightfully belong to a scientific model of international relations preoccupied with identifying universal nomological laws. Without facing them, however, it is hard to see how *any* theory of international relations, Realist or otherwise, can make sense of the dangers posed by the nuclear revolution, most of which concern the prospective implications of a barely fathomable horrific event which *has never* – and hopefully *will never* – occur. Pinned down by a dogmatic adherence to studying *existing* empirical regularities, Morgenthau's children not only ignore his own methodological strictures about the limitations of a social science modeled on the natural sciences, but inevitably restrict themselves to a cautious but ultimately misleading restatement of the "facts" of postwar deterrence. The possibility that we may only have survived the cold war because of contingencies – in short, because of *luck* – necessarily gets left at the wayside by a theory preoccupied with determining universal regularities and patterns. The prospect that the only means by which we might effectively circumvent nuclear disaster is via historically unprecedented modes of supranational political organization, from the perspective of contemporary "scientific" Realism, does not even warrant systematic examination.

Morgenthau would have directed tough questions at the latest exponents of the complacency school of nuclear thought. So should we.

6

Vietnam and the crisis of American democracy

Morgenthau's opposition to the Vietnam War, one of the worst debacles of modern US foreign policy, overshadowed his reflections on the nuclear arms race. Throughout the 1950s, Morgenthau vehemently criticized US policy in Southeast Asia, pillorying US policy makers for ignoring the political complexities of the region in favor of embracing another misconceived Manichean crusade. As US military involvement intensified under the Kennedy and especially the Johnson Administrations, Morgenthau became one of the most outspoken public intellectuals critical of US intervention in Vietnam: a 1972 survey ranked him, among intellectuals, just behind Noam Chomsky as its most prominent opponent.[1] A flurry of critical articles in major newspapers (including the *New York Times* and *Washington Post*) and liberal news-weeklies and journals, a vocal role in the peace movement along with many public appearances on its behalf, and participation in a nationally televised 1965 debate with McGeorge Bundy (one of the Johnson Administration's most aggressive hawks) catapulted Morgenthau into the national spotlight. In contrast to many left-liberal US intellectuals who preferred looking away as two Democratic presidents deepened US military commitments in Vietnam, Morgenthau opposed the war early on and was consistently one of its most far-sighted critics.

In the 1950s, Morgenthau had aspired to shape decision making in Washington's inner sanctum, eagerly cultivating influence with Dean Acheson, George Kennan, and other members of the Democratic Party foreign affairs establishment whom, he believed, had been unfairly booted from office by Eisenhower and the Republicans. He may even have hoped to gain a position of influence when the Democrats regained the White House in 1960.[2] Ironically, it was only in the mid-1960s, in a new and unexpected role as intellectual and political apostate suddenly at odds with former allies, that Morgenthau gained national attention.[3] Even more ironically perhaps, his fame came at a high price: he became the regular recipient of vicious hate mail, and was soon the subject of a nasty campaign by the White House to discredit him.[4]

A number of scholars have already provided helpful surveys of Morgenthau's role in the movement against the Vietnam War.[5] Rather than repeat what has been said elsewhere, this chapter focuses on the ways in which Morgenthau's dissident position on Vietnam built on his analysis of democratic politics, in general, and US democracy, in particular. At first glance, this might seem like a strange place to conclude our analysis of Morgenthau's international theory. After all, Realist theory – or so it is widely asserted – downplays the importance of what Kenneth Waltz has famously described as the "second image," or internal structure of states, instead emphasizing the unchanging laws of interstate competition in the context of anarchy.[6] In many influential versions of Realist theory, domestic politics indeed takes an explanatory back seat to the universal laws of the international system. As noted in chapter 3, Morgenthau's own defense of the primacy of the national interest at times could easily be adduced as support for the view that the laws of interstate rivalry constitute the primary driving forces behind foreign affairs. Morgenthau frequently noted, for example, that Soviet foreign policy in Eastern Europe cohered with a long tradition of Russian great-power politics: communism had limited bearings on Russian foreign policy. Yet to the extent that he conceded that the pursuit of the US national interest required preservation of the integrity of the American experiment in self-government and thus basic US political ideals, Morgenthau's *own* definition of the national interest implicitly recognized the centrality of distinctive moral, political, and cultural traits. Defense of America's special normative attributes constituted a core component of the US national interest and, by implication, was pivotal to a proper understanding of its foreign policy.

Not surprisingly, one of Morgenthau's most impassioned but also least appreciated books, *Purpose of American Politics* (1960), focused on the fundamental normative aims of US liberal democracy. This "national purpose" – most importantly, what he dubbed "equality in freedom" – was directly related to the successful pursuit of the national interest. As the body count from Vietnam mounted, and then as the Watergate scandal broke, Morgenthau developed a probing analysis of the pathologies of American democracy. By the end of the Vietnam disaster, he had reached the conclusion that far-reaching reform was imperative if the USA were to alter its foreign policy, whose stunning irrationalities in the bloody jungles of Vietnam had become manifest even to mainstream public opinion. Although Morgenthau would continue to write widely on foreign policy, by the end of his career he was also one of America's most astute political and social critics, and a consistent defender of what he dubbed "radical reform."[7] For the mature Morgenthau, these two roles were inevitably interlinked.

Contemporary international relations theorists typically ignore Morgenthau's wide-ranging writings on US democracy, in part because of their unsystematic and journalistic character. By doing so, however, they ignore his provocative attempt to link sensible foreign policy to domestic political and social reform. In the twilight of his long career, Morgenthau endorsed the position that a rational foreign policy required a no less rational, or at least decent, society. Unlike many liberal and left-leaning intellectuals driven by the radical movements of the 1960s and early 1970s to the political right, Morgenthau insisted that the achievement of such a society demanded far-reaching social and political reform. At least in this version of Realism, the "second image" of politics remained congenitally tied to the proper analysis of international relations.

Vietnam and the national interest

In a 1978 interview, Morgenthau modestly claimed that his writings on Southeast Asia and Vietnam were lacking in originality: "I simply applied certain basic principles of foreign policy which I had formulated almost twenty years earlier to the situation in Vietnam."[8] From the perspective of his overall theory, this self-assessment is probably accurate. Unfortunately, what seemed relatively plain from the perspective of Morgenthau's Realism was hardly self-evident to US policy makers or the public.

In a prescient early discussion of the foibles of US Asian policy in *In Defense of the National Interest*, Morgenthau laid out much of the intellectual terrain he would cultivate in his subsequent writings on Vietnam. In contrast to Eastern Europe, where talk of revolution was fundamentally an ideological cover for Soviet domination, the revolutions breaking out in Asia were genuine popular upheavals oriented towards venerable western ideals of national self-determination and social justice. Although revolts against the West, they were undertaken under the auspices of familiar ideals. Such revolutionary movements were hardly puppets of Moscow or even, as he argued later, Beijing: even before Tito and Mao proffered concrete evidence of deep fissures in the communist world, Morgenthau accurately predicted what many scholars soon described as *polycentrism*. He also questioned whether military means could successfully ward off the revolutionary tide. The United States and its allies would instead have to employ a full range of supple ideological and political devices so as to minimize the domination of revolutionary and anti-colonial movements by hostile foreign powers: their dependence on the Russians or Chinese might *result* from inept US foreign policy, but did not, as many in the United States dogmatically propounded, already represent a fait accompli that could only be effectively opposed by military means (*IDNI*, 201–12). A proper response called for more than Madison Avenue public relations coupled with a show of military muscle: the USA would have to make its case via policies that evinced sympathy and, in some cases, even direct support for peoples throwing off the shackles of western domination. Key to US success in Asia, he wrote in 1953, was "our willingness and ability to support effectively the national and social aspirations of the peoples of Asia," not chiefly due to humanitarian reasons, but because such policies best advanced the US national interest.[9] This meant conceding that some of the formal mechanisms of western-style liberal democracy might "be used for undemocratic and even anti-democratic ends" (*IDNI*, 215). Desirable political and social reform should not be conflated with the pursuit of counterproductive institutional implants from western political and social life.

US policy makers were failing to recognize the novelties at hand. A strategy of military containment made sense in the European context. However, the attempt to universalize it into a cure-all for political conflicts elsewhere was misconceived. The most obvious problem was that US policies in Asia and in other parts of the developing world had been rendered as "hardly distinguishable from a counterrevolutionary position per se," which conveniently played into the hands of communists.[10] US policy makers predictably envisioned foreign policy there as "a struggle between good and evil, truth and falsehood" (*IDNI*, 215) – in short, as just another (primarily military) front in the worldwide crusade against communism.

Their vision of democracy and social justice, however, was colored inordinately by the peculiarities of US experience. Not surprisingly, US political and economic appeals tended to fall on deaf ears in Asia. In contrast, the communists were speaking effectively to legitimate demands for social justice. Not only did the familiar relapse into a simplistic moralism preclude the possibility of creative political and ideological responses to revolutionary movements, but it had already led the United States ill-advisedly to take on the flawed mantle of European colonialism. In contrast to the situation in India, where the British exchanged "a tenuous military and political advantage for a great moral and political triumph," the USA "did not understand these alternatives when it intervened in the Chinese and Indo-Chinese civil wars, and thus gained nothing and lost almost everything" (*IDNI*, 209).

In 1955 Morgenthau visited Vietnam. Unlike those who toed the cold war line, he was unimpressed by President Diem. An article in the *Washington Post* from February 2, 1956, prophetically entitled "Background to Civil War," underscored the repressive nature of Diem's regime, identifying what Morgenthau bluntly described as its "totalitarian" elements (*VUS*, 21–4). A central theme in many of Morgenthau's pieces, in fact, was the fragility of the US-backed government in South Vietnam. It was Ho Chi Minh and the Vietcong who were successfully addressing the masses' political and social aspirations; single-minded US support for the repressive and reactionary Diem played into their hands. Later on, as the USA became entangled in Vietnam, he toyed with the prospect of a Titoist outcome: a communist state under Ho Chi Minh was probably inevitable, but, as in Yugoslavia, the regime might achieve a modicum of independence vis-à-vis China and Russia. Unfortunately, simplistic US anti-communism worked to foreclose the possibility of a Titoist path, counterproductively driving the Vietcong to seek aid from established communist powers and thereby helping to realize the worst fears of US policy makers (*VUS*, 68). If the United States were to continue blindly shoring up another repressive anti-communist government, Morgenthau observed in "Vietnam: Another Korea?" (1962), we would "commit ourselves militarily beyond what our national interest would require" (*VUS*, 25). Writing before the Johnson Administration dramatically ratcheted up military involvement, he still hoped that the USA might break with Diem or at least push for a political alternative more open to legitimate social and national demands. Repeating earlier arguments from *In Defense of the National Interest*, he asserted that it was mistaken to apply mechanically the lessons of containment to Asia and Chinese communism, or to believe that US *military* muscle in Vietnam, in contrast to an effective employment of *political* advantages, could restrain the Chinese. A policy of military containment which depended on maintaining a foothold in Vietnam risked a full-scale military conflagration with China (*VUS*, 43–9). In Morgenthau's assessment, the price was simply too high given Vietnam's limited strategic value to the USA. Even if desirable, the prevention of a communist takeover in Vietnam was simply not worth the sizable political and military perils. The *real* danger faced by the USA in Asia was an "American Algeria," in which crude anti-communism coupled with military hubris might unleash political havoc and perhaps even disorder at home.[11]

As the war escalated, Morgenthau added a number of arguments to his litany of complaints. To those who worried about a possible loss of prestige if the USA pulled out of Vietnam, Morgenthau countered in 1965 that any such loss was more likely to ensue "from the continuation and escalation of a losing enterprise" (*VUS*, 12). *Pace* the Administration's interpretation of the war as stemming from foreign aggression, he correctly insisted that the conflict was a *civil* and indeed *guerrilla* war abetted by North Vietnam. As the disastrous French experience in Algeria had demonstrated, a guerrilla war could only be effectively countered "by the indiscriminate killing of everybody in sight" and ultimately "by genocide." In guerrilla warfare, the distinction between combatants and non-combatants was necessarily blurred. US troops in Vietnam would likely "go on torturing, killing, and burning, and the more deeply we become involved in Vietnam, the more there will be of it" (*VUS*, 20). Although prior US presidents too often had subscribed to a crusading moralism, and even though Johnson was not the first occupant of the White House to imply that containment was a worldwide doctrine, only he disastrously pursued what his predecessors had preached but in fact inconsistently practiced: "What in the past we said we were doing or would do but never did, we are now in the process of putting into practice: to stop the expansion of Communism on a global scale by force of arms" (*VUS*, 84). Johnson's misadventures seemed to build directly on the Truman Doctrine, but in actuality represented its senseless radicalization.

Morgenthau did more than underline the strategic and political irrationality of the Vietnam War, however. By the mid- and late 1960s, his criticisms overflowed with expressions of moral outrage: the familiar hostility to moralism, once again, did not preclude him from advancing an ethical or moral critique of US policy. As the USA "took off the gloves" and embraced counterinsurgency strategies, he argued, the pigeons were coming home to roost. US liberal democracy was suffering badly: the Vietnam War had already altered the American polity, and the resulting changes were unmistakably for the worse. In order to conceal their mistakes from public scrutiny, Johnson and then Nixon reverted to lying and deception as a matter of course. Uncomfortable empirical facts had to be obliterated from the public record, and those who dared to recall them were accused of treason. In order to prevent the world of facts from piercing the simplistic fictions which politicians peddled to a bewildered public, political leaders reverted to devices which hearkened back to the ugliest practices of tyrants and political thugs.[12] As Morgenthau recorded with growing alarm, the war coarsened political discourse as leaders tested out new forms of McCarthyism, demanded anti-democratic forms of executive prerogative, and perilously debilitated Congress and other popular institutions. US brutality in Vietnam was undermining respect for its power abroad, inspiring hope among movements elsewhere wanting to weaken the USA, and raising legitimate concerns among both rivals and allies about the soundness of US political judgment.

The ethical tenor of Morgenthau's critique in part stemmed from a straightforward political calculation. As the US military stumbled in the jungles of Vietnam, Americans heard ever louder calls to deploy more troops, drop more bombs, and perhaps even use weapons of mass destruction; the war could be "won" if the USA were simply allowed to unleash every instrument in its military tool kit. Morgenthau recognized early on that Nixon's domestically popular decision to minimize US casualties, for example, might logically lead him to embrace this path. In a 1971 article for the *New Republic*, he speculated that Nixon and Kissinger might go so far as to employ tactical nuclear weapons in order to ensure some measure of US "success."[13] In this context, it made perfect sense for Morgenthau to argue that, even if the USA militarily eliminated communism from Vietnam, it still entailed "unreasonable moral liabilities and risks" (*NFP*, 129). The most obvious risk was a potentially catastrophic and probably unwinnable war with communist powers like China. But the moral costs were no less noteworthy. To be sure, the United States might employ its technological prowess to bomb Vietnam back into the Stone Age. Yet, for a nation "founded as a novel experiment in government, morally superior to those that went before it, and which has throughout its history thought of itself, and was regarded by the other nations of the world, as performing a uniquely beneficial mission" (*NFP*, 138), the results would prove cataclysmic. Any lingering ideas about the United States as "the last best hope of the downtrodden and enslaved, to which men of good will throughout the world have looked as a shining example," would be decisively put to rest if the USA continued "trying to force a primitive nation of peasants into submission by the massive use of all the modern means of mass destruction" (*NFP*, 138–9). As a physical and geographical entity, the United States might persevere. But it could no longer exercise a moral appeal to "men of good will" elsewhere. Policies which undermined the moral fiber of the United States weakened it abroad as well. Having betrayed what was normatively attractive about its political identity, US prestige abroad would inevitably suffer.

Politics Among Nations had vehemently criticized one-sided accounts of national power exaggerating the role of military brawn: national character, morale, and even the quality of government remained constitutive components of national power.[14] In a similar spirit, Morgenthau now declared that a central source of abiding American strength had always been the moral example it had regularly "presented to the rest of the world." Since Tom Paine, American thinkers had portrayed their republic as a special experiment based on principles "on which no other political commonwealth had ever been founded." Of course, this self-understanding contained a measure of hubristic self-congratulation; too often it had paved the way for foreign policy mishaps and even military adventurism. Nonetheless, Morgenthau stubbornly insisted, the mixed record of US foreign policy should not blind observers to the fact that the fate of the American experiment "was not just of relevance to the parochial interests of the United States."[15] Unavoidably, other countries judged America according to the high moral standards it proclaimed for itself. US influence depended to a unique extent on whether it proved deserving of the sympathy of people of good will. As Morgenthau similarly noted in 1974, "it is a peculiarity of the United States that its effectiveness in the world is profoundly and organically connected with the domestic picture and decencies it presents to its own people and to the world."[16] In this account,

> [t]he United States is not judged in view of its domestic situation as other countries are. We are not judged as the British are judged with regard to, say, the race problem, or as the French were with regard to Algeria. We are judged in a rather peculiar sense, which is a reflec-

tion of the particular moral virtue which we have represented to the rest of the world and which [in Vietnam] we have not only neglected but have badly shoved aside.[17]

When outsiders seemed to hold the USA to high moral standards, their views derived from the unusual and perhaps unique manner in which the United States had always depicted itself as a beacon of light in a dark world. The betrayal in Vietnam of the faith others had placed in America entailed not only the abandonment of its special moral status, but also a loss of power advantages it had gained from their trust.

Not surprisingly, Morgenthau's outrage over Vietnam led him to raise tough questions about US democracy. The second or domestic image of politics, as Waltz has called it, counted decisively for the analysis of foreign policy. The crisis of American democracy enervated US foreign policy. As Morgenthau commented in 1969:

> [w]hen a government composed of intelligent and responsible men embarks upon a course of action that is utterly at variance with what the national interest requires and is bound to end in failure, it is impossible to attribute such persistence in error to an accident of personality and circumstance. Nor is it possible to make such an attribution when the preponderance of public opinion – political, expert, and lay – for years supports such a mistaken course of action. When a nation allows itself to be misgoverned in such a flagrant fashion, there must be something essentially wrong in its intellectual, moral, and political constitution. (*NFP*, 139–40)

The débâcle in Vietnam could not be attributed solely to any single individual or even a particular political or social group; complicity in it was deep and widespread in American society. Something had gone badly wrong: Vietnam was a result of an intense social and political crisis even as it simultaneously aggrandized that crisis. Foreign policy mistakes were intertwined with the pathologies of American liberal democracy.

By the late 1960s and early 1970s, Morgenthau had determined that the United States was in a profound crisis, of which the disaster in Vietnam was the most striking manifestation. Always an astute critical observer of his adopted homeland, his writings from the late 1960s and 1970s nonetheless now encompassed radical hues generally missing elsewhere. In an enthusiastic foreword for Arnold Kaufman's *The Radical Liberal* (1968), a volume widely read among student advocates of radical participatory democracy, Morgenthau called for the abandonment of obsolescent political thinking on both the left and right and endorsed Kaufman's attempt to reformulate liberalism in a radical direction.[18] Most unmistakably in *Truth and Politics* (1970), a collection of essays written in response to the upheavals of the 1960s, Morgenthau lamented the failures of successive US governments to deal effectively with racial injustice, urban decay, and poverty, as well as the disintegration of the political system. Apathy and political alienation were ascendant, as political power shifted from the hands of the people to their government. Meanwhile, the executive branch demanded blind obedience, trivialized meaningful political discourse, manipulated real dangers for partisan purposes rather than counteracting them, and struggled to keep elected representatives out of the decision-making loop. Morgenthau went so far as to accuse Johnson and Nixon of harboring totalitarian and even fascistic tendencies.[19] Police-style tactics – the brutality of the Chicago police at the 1968 Democratic Convention was one example – were becoming increasingly widespread in political life. Militarism was rampant.[20]

The Keynesian model which had inspired the welfare state was exhausted as well: despite the fact that "we will have to transform radically our economic system and social organization" in light of novel technological and social changes, politicians plodded on with mantra-like recitations of anachronistic slogans.[21] The predominant conceptions of the proper relationship between state and economy were inadequate in the face of new problems, foremost among them being the "conjunction of ever-increasing productivity with large-scale obsolescence of human labor."[22] The USA had succumbed to a "hedonism of production and consumption" which contributed to "the ruination of the national environment."[23] Notwithstanding attempts at social and economic reform, vast concentrations of economic power continued to exercise disproportionate influence over the political machinery: reforms would have to tackle a "new feudalism" in which public and private authority were fused together in complex but deeply perilous ways. US political leaders continued to rack up points in popularity polls by advancing an irresponsible "demonological conception of the world, which assigns to the United States the mission to defend the 'Free World.'"[24] Conformism among intellectuals prevented a serious discussion of the challenges at hand even in the protected halls of the academy.

In the prologue to *Truth and Politics*, Morgenthau retrospectively conceded that many of the essays in the volume had initially been penned in a naïve spirit, as though "one only needs to call the

President's attention to the probable consequences of certain policies . . . and he will choose a policy most likely to serve the national interest."[25] This spirit still suffused his preface to the *Crossroads Papers* (1965), a volume edited by Morgenthau under the auspices of the liberal anti-communist Americans for Democratic Action, which included a contribution by Senator Hubert Humphrey of Minnesota, the standard bearer for the liberal wing of the Democratic Party.[26] Just a few years later, revealingly, Morgenthau authored a devastating critique of Humphrey, the Democrats' unsuccessful candidate for the presidency in 1968.[27] By 1970, Morgenthau would openly declare that he no longer shared the implicit assumption that the most important function of the public intellectual was to provide sound advice to political leaders who, though oftentimes mistaken, could be swayed by rational discourse. To be sure, the intellectual must still speak truth to power, but "it has become obvious that the great issues of our day . . . are not susceptible to rational solutions within the existing system of power relations." Although the crisis of US democracy took many forms, "the overriding single issue, of which all the others are but specific manifestations, is the distribution of power in American society," which not only remained deeply unjust, but which would have to be fundamentally changed if the USA were to grapple successfully with social and political ills whose resolution called for a new "system of power relations."[28]

Despite skepticism that attacks on the university would generate desirable changes, *Truth and Politics* expressed sympathy for the burgeoning student movement, noting in an epilogue that Americans faced a stark choice: radical reform or continued decay? A gap between democratic pretense and performance had understandably led many young people to embrace a radical critique of society. Living "in something approaching a Kafkaesque world, insignificant, and at the mercy of unchallengeable and invisible forces," they might be mistaken in many of their specific views; Morgenthau did not share their increasingly Marxist theoretical proclivities. He also occasionally described their efforts as apolitical, immature attempts to flee from the difficulties of social and political reform. Yet they were ultimately justified in putting the pressing question of social and political reform on the agenda.[29] They had at least identified the options confronting America: "a new society, with a new purpose, will be built upon the ruins of the old; or perhaps nothing will be left but ruins for later generations to behold."[30] Unfortunately, "the virtual assurance of atomic destruction under present conditions" implied that the latter was more likely than the former.[31]

Democracy against the national interest?

Reflecting on his political thinking from the 1960s and early 1970s, Ellen Glaser Rafshoon has argued that "Vietnam led Morgenthau to expand his notion of the national interest," with his late writings formulating a revised definition of the national interest that accentuated the need for the United States to "uphold its exceptional moral stature as a model of integrity."[32] On this interpretation, Morgenthau was forced by the Vietnam debacle to reformulate the idea of the national interest to include "moralistic" elements previously lacking from it. This expanded notion of the national interest alone allowed him to tie his critique of the Vietnam War to a broader agenda for radical social and political reform.

Morgenthau's earliest postwar discussions of the nexus between democratic politics and sound foreign policy indeed seem to buttress the claim that his basic theoretical framework underwent a fundamental transformation in the 1960s. To be sure, *In Defense of the National Interest* had placed matters of political and cultural identity, and hence "the integrity of the American experiment," directly under the rubric of the national interest. Yet as noted in chapter 3, Morgenthau's suggestion that the national interest encompassed normative elements tended to get subsumed under a competing tendency to associate it with core strategic and even geopolitical interests. The dominant reading of Morgenthau's view was soon an interpretation deemphasizing moral and ethical matters. Consistent with this second strand in his thinking, his writings from the late 1940s and early 1950s repeatedly pointed to deep *tensions* between sound foreign policy and democratic politics. In a line of argumentation which decisively influenced subsequent Realist theorists, democratic politics constituted a fundamental *threat* to rational foreign policy and the quest for the national interest.

Politics Among Nations thus highlighted democracy's culpability in the decay of international morality, which in Morgenthau's eyes had once functioned to civilize interstate affairs but in the twentieth century found itself under siege. Dependent on an "Aristocratic International," a cross-border but deeply interconnected class of European aristocrats "joined together by family ties, a common language (French), common cultural values, a common style of life, and common moral convictions," a shared system of mores and norms had restrained state actors during the heydays of the Westphalian system (*PAN*, 2nd edn., 221). This homogeneous social class staffed European governments and dominated diplomatic inter-course until the twentieth century, when the ascent of democracy drove its representatives from office and revolutionized interstate affairs. *Politics Among Nations* focused on three aspects of this transi-tion. First, the recruitment of government and especially foreign policy officials from the entire population meant that foreign affairs was subsequently pursued by practitioners whose values were as heterogeneous as those of society at large. Moral and political plura-lism demolished the relatively uniform normative outlook on which much of international society had depended. Second, democracy destroyed the stability and constancy that had characterized foreign policy making in the golden age of the Westphalian system, with state officialdom rendered subject to sudden turnovers and fluctua-tions in both personnel and policies. A democratically induced revolving door in the foreign ministry was incongruent with intel-ligent foreign policy. Inexperienced nationally rooted amateurs, rather than professionals steeped in the mores and mindset of an aristocratic elite having cosmopolitan interests and ties, came to dominate foreign affairs. Finally, democracy was closely connected to modern *nationalism*, which contributed decisively to the deep political and moral fragmentation of what previously had been a widely shared and – at least for the European context – universal-istic system of norms concerning warfare, the treatment of non-combatants, and other issues of life or death. Modern mass-based nationalism tended to engender new political religions, in which parochial values claimed universal validity: "Thus, carrying their idols before them, the nationalistic masses of our time meet in the international arena, each group convinced that it executes the mandate of history . . . and that it fulfills a sacred mission ordained by Providence" (*PAN*, 2nd edn., 234). In an era of popularly based political religions, which for Morgenthau included US democracy no less than it did Soviet communism and Nazism, both inter-national ethics and ultimately international law suffered severe injuries.

In Defense of the National Interest then built on this anti-democratic critique. Relying on Tocqueville's famous analysis, Morgenthau endorsed the view that foreign policy demanded an appreciation for long-term trends, while democracy called out for immediate or short-term results. Thoughtful foreign policy necessitated states-men who could think in terms of the national interest, whereas the masses preferred simple moralistic and legalistic crusades. Mass opinion was subject to emotional swings and rapid mood shifts, yet sensible foreign policy demanded constancy and the ability to "stay the course" despite popular pressures. Removed from foreign affairs, the populace tended inevitably to project provincial national ideals onto the international scene. In short, the "kind of thinking required for the successful conduct of foreign policy must at times be diametrically opposed to the kind of considerations by which the masses and their representatives are likely to be moved" (*IDNI*, 223). Elected representatives were no less susceptible to the ills of popular thinking: they had to compensate for the mundane and morally deadening daily routines of government affairs, typically lacking in intellectual substance or moral appeal. Projecting their suppressed intellectual and moral desires onto international affairs, they too often made "foreign policy . . . into a sort of fairyland where virtue triumphs and vice is punished" (*IDNI*, 222).

Although *Politics Among Nations* described democracy as one source of national power, and even though its author regularly excoriated authoritarian alternatives, readers might look in vain for a systematic defense of democratic politics in Morgenthau's writings during the 1940s and early 1950s.[33] On the contrary, democracy typically appeared as little more than a nuisance, as what Churchill famously described as the worst form of government except for all the others, a political system that could only work well when guided by responsible leaders who somehow avoided kowtowing to mass opinion. In contrast to democratic demagogues, the rare responsible democratic leader educated public opinion in support of unpopular foreign policies, refusing to follow the ever-changing barometer of public opinion. Only if elected government grasped "that it is the leader and not the slave of public opinion" could it counteract the kneejerk preference among modern democratic foreign-policy makers for publicity and majority rule, neither of which was conducive to the national interest (*PAN*, 2nd edn., 134).

Morgenthau's initial forays into democratic theory brought attention to serious enigmas. Modern democracies, in fact, have oftentimes pursued counterproductive foreign policies: even if Morgenthau overstated the point and misleadingly romanticized pre-democratic foreign policy, committed democrats need to proffer a convincing retort. Fortunately, the assumed correlation between irrational foreign policy and popular control turns out to be empirically unfounded.[34] His anxieties about democratic politics also engendered an internal theoretical and political problem. The fundamental political inspiration for virtually *everything* he wrote during the cold war was fear that the United States and its allies might succumb to blunders akin to those committed during the 1930s, when incompetent democratic foreign-policy makers helped to prepare the path for German aggression and the rise of fascism. But how could Morgenthau's preoccupation with preserving liberal democracy – and especially the American experiment in self-government – be justified, given his overwhelmingly critical discussion of democratic politics during this period? No wonder that so many readers of *In Defense of the National Interest* overlooked the normative attributes of the national interest: Morgenthau himself regularly devalued democratic politics and accentuated its animosity to rational foreign policy. But without a firm defense of modern democratic politics, why protect the United States and its allies from dictatorial rivals in the first place? Since Morgenthau sometimes unfavorably contrasted the irrationality of US policy to the relative "realism" of Soviet policy, his own reflections cried out for a stronger defense of modern democracy.

Despite such unanswered questions, it was this anti-democratic strand in Morgenthau's thinking which substantially influenced mainstream Realism in the postwar USA, which built enthusiastically on Morgenthau's anti-democratic nostalgia for nineteenth-century European diplomacy.[35] Such ideas probably helped to justify "the concentration of very substantial foreign policy power in the hands of the executive branch of the government, the presidency in particular, as well as a measure of domestically directed deception" – in other words, precisely those trends that so alarmed Morgenthau in the 1960s and 1970s.[36] Perhaps cognizant of the limitations of his initial discussions of democracy and foreign affairs, Morgenthau substantially modified his views in the late 1950s and early 1960s.

The national purpose: equality in freedom

International relations scholars tend, as with his writings on Vietnam, to neglect *Purpose of American Politics* and his related writings on democracy, seeing in them little more than a foray into partisan political debates unrelated to the core of Morgenthau's Realism. This view occludes not only the degree to which Morgenthau's democratic theory grew immanently out of his writings on international politics, but also the ways in which they posited a close link between democratic and international political theory. Here as well, Morgenthau found himself drawing an integral connection between the "second image" or domestic facets of politics and international affairs. A careful examination of Morgenthau's democratic theory also permits us to see why, at least from his viewpoint, subsequent criticisms of the US misadventure in Vietnam by no means represented, contra Rafshoon, a major break in his thinking. At the very least, his radical critique of US democracy was foreshadowed by his writings from the late 1950s and especially *Purpose of American Politics*.

As we have periodically noted, Morgenthau's initial conceptualization of the national interest encompassed crucial normative and moral elements but left their precise analytic status up in the air. The main conceptual innovation of *Purpose of American Politics*, the idea of a "national purpose," offered a creative attempt to move beyond this ambiguity. The volume's opening pages recalled Morgenthau's conventional identification of the national interest with the ability to "maintain or increase the power of a nation, acquire territory, conclude alliances, wage victorious war, and conclude advantageous peace" (*PAP*, 8). Congruent with the core argument of *In Defense of the National Interest*, every political community was conceived as possessing some rational and objective national interest which should guide policy. In a Hobbesian spirit, the national interest was married directly to the quest for basic survival. Yet Morgenthau now made an important addendum to this familiar view:

> In order to be worthy of our lasting sympathy, a nation must pursue its interests for the sake of a transcendent purpose that gives meaning to the day-by-day operations of its foreign policy. The empires of the Huns and Mongols, eminently successful in political and military terms, mean nothing to us; but ancient Greece, Rome, and Israel do. We remember Greece, Rome, and Israel . . . because they were not just political organizations whose purpose was limited to their survival and physical growth but civilizations, unique realizations of human potentialities that we have in common with them. (*PAP*, 8)

Referring to the unique aspirations embodied by concrete political entities, the "collective work of generations" by means of which a unique purpose manifests itself over the course of generations, national *purpose* transcends national *interest*. Only reference to some historically based normative purpose can help us answer the perennial question, why should I pursue *this* national interest (e.g. that of the Americans or British) and not *another* (e.g. that of the Germans under Hitler)? Not every national interest, Morgenthau now unmistakably noted, is of equal value: only some are tied to a worthy normative purpose, or some concrete way by which a people or nation achieves otherwise unexplored possibilities for human self-realization. The national purpose, Morgenthau argued, stems from "a continuum of actions that reveal a common and unique pattern" in which the special contributions to the human experience by a particular nation are manifested. Consequently, the national purpose is best discerned by studying political *action*; in most cases, "awareness of the national purpose in conscious thought . . . followed upon its achievement in action." Previous patterns of political action can also help us to predict the future trajectory of any given political community: we can "read in their past deeds a purpose to which we expect future deeds to conform" (*PAP*, 10).

Many had become justifiably skeptical of any discourse about national purpose, Morgenthau conceded, because of its frequent misuse in conjunction with simplistic theology, bad metaphysics, and crude nationalistic mythmaking. According to critics, "the idea of the national purpose is a political ideology to which nothing corresponds in verifiable experience." Yet such skepticism threw the baby out with the bathwater, obscuring the valuable intuition that political communities sometimes made a special contribution to humanity and thereby transcended the mere dictates of survival and pursuit of the national interest narrowly conceived. Even thousands of years after their demise, Morgenthau declared, we still identify Rome as the birthplace of the rule of law, and ancient Israel with religious monotheism. Those too quick to discard ideas of national purpose also ignored the harsh fact that some political communities succeed in providing an exceptional expression to human potentialities, while others – like the Huns and Mongols, he ethnocentrically noted – were destined to founder (*PAP*, 7–8).

Even though Morgenthau's reflections in the crucial opening of *Purpose of American Politics* cried out for elaboration, beyond a quick reference to Hegel he failed to offer his reader much with which to work.[37] Why speak of *national* purpose and not instead a more generic idea of political identity? After all, Morgenthau conceded that the nation state was already declining. And how exactly could nations successfully instantiate both particularistic *and* universal human traits? Also curious was Morgenthau's self-assured assertion that some nations were destined to fail in realizing a national purpose. Even ignoring its Eurocentrism, his position at times seemed overly Burkean and rather conservative: national identity seemed to represent a constant, composed over the course of many generations. How then to make sense of rapid shifts in political identity, for example between Nazi and postwar democratic Germany?

For better or worse, Morgenthau's preoccupations were political and practical rather than philosophical. What the idea of the national purpose seemed to offer, at least from his perspective, was probably twofold. First, it supplied a better tool for discussing the normative identity of political communities than the slippery and potentially misleading idea of the national interest. At least implicitly, he seemed to concede that his earlier writings had not done justice to the special problems posed by the constitutive role of norms and ideas in political life. *Purpose of American Politics* should be read as an attempt to overcome such weaknesses: it foregrounded the normative core of political identity along with its intimate links to foreign policy. To be sure, he continued to see the two concepts as interlinked, frequently placing them alongside one another and even mentioning them in the same breath. His own writings were hardly as consistent in their employment of the two terms as readers might legitimately hope: when criticizing US intervention in Vietnam, for example, any distinction between them became so blurred as to invite critical interpretations, like Rafshoon's, according to which Morgenthau had simply abandoned previous theoretical ideas. In fact, he had *always* conceived of the defense of distinctive moral and cultural ideas as part and parcel of intelligent foreign policy, despite his own sometimes misleading polemics against moralism and idealism. Second, and most importantly for Morgenthau, the idea of a national purpose permitted him to raise the chief question to which *Purpose of American Politics* was chiefly devoted: what then was the special national purpose of the United States of America, and how could an understanding of it contribute fruitfully to a reformulation of policy goals?

In responding to this question, Morgenthau was led onto the terrain of democratic theory, in general, and an analysis of US liberal democracy, in particular. America's contribution to the possibilities of human flourishing, in this view, has been an ambitious experiment in what he called "equality in freedom," embodying a particular rendition of liberal democracy suited to North American conditions.

A brief 1957 *American Political Science Review* article, and then the more ambitious *Purpose of American Politics*, offered Morgenthau's first systematic normative defense of liberal democracy. Morgenthau's interlocutor from the 1930s, the great legal theoretician Hans Kelsen, haunts these writings.[38] In his own reflections on democratic theory, Kelsen had argued that modern democracy was well suited to a relativistic worldview that could no longer depend on a belief in absolute values. Liberal democracy and what Weber famously diagnosed as the modern condition of disenchantment were closely allied. A commitment to moral absolutes leads to political authoritarianism, Kelsen claimed, whereas an open recognition of the prospect of intellectual fallibility implies the necessity of political tolerance, free speech, and political equality: anyone's views, after all, could turn out to be correct. Morgenthau shared Kelsen's core insight: democracy and a pluralistic conception of truth, according to which we reject the possibility that anyone could possess a monopoly on political truth, go hand in hand. Once we abandon the position that a particular individual or group could ever monopolize political or moral wisdom, and accept that "all members of society as rational beings have access to a measure of political truth," we can ground egalitarian norms on which modern democracy rests.[39]

Most importantly, Morgenthau implied, this view of democracy required a corresponding interpretation of majority rule. The most common means by which competing political groups are invited to test the soundness of their views is by a majority vote which temporarily decides the controversy at hand. Since we cannot assume that even large political majorities a priori possess more wisdom than outvoted minorities, however, majority rule only makes sense if reversible: today's minority must have a real chance of becoming tomorrow's majority. Fair and equal political competition, preventing majorities from making their temporarily privileged position permanent, as well as robust protections for political minorities, are indispensable if democracy is to operate as a dynamic, self-correcting system.

For Morgenthau, Kelsen's vision offered an attractive theoretical starting point for conceiving democracy in sober but still sufficiently demanding terms. By describing democracy primarily in *epistemological* terms, this view was able to move away from exaggerated and potentially misleading ideals of popular sovereignty, instead envisioning democracy as a representative republican government resting on the consent of the governed. Sovereignty cannot in fact "be vested in the people as a whole" (*PAN*, 2nd edn., 306). In contrast, in this model "[t]he power to govern is vested by the people in certain persons . . . The rulers, in order to continue to rule, must retain the confidence of the majority, if not in their policies, at least in their persons" (*PAP*, 245). Morgenthau favorably contrasted the Anglo-American and Lockean ideals of representative democracy with what he harshly (and one-sidedly) decried as a competing "degenerate" majoritarian Jacobin view, whose implicit authoritarianism purportedly had poisoned much of modern democratic practice. The latter, he insisted, conflated majority preferences with the *vox dei*, while the former admirably refused to do so. Morgenthau struggled to circumvent the self-congratulatory implications others typically drew from the rather conventional juxtaposition of ("healthy") Anglo-American with its ("degenerate") French or continental rivals. Democracy was more than mere elite competition in which irrational appeals to the congenitally ignorant masses determined political outcomes.[40] On the contrary, it suggested the possibility of sound and potentially rational policies. In light of their mistaken belief in the possibility of a monopoly on political truth, dictatorships were ultimately inferior. When properly functioning, democracy was better at linking political decision making to intellectually proficient policy making.

In addition, appreciation for democracy's epistemological virtues demanded, in Morgenthau's assessment, careful attention to the disturbing ways in which contemporary democracy, in the United States and elsewhere, failed to undergird meaningful political competition, let alone evince healthy respect for free speech and minority views. Far too often, political majorities succumbed to the arrogant view that they alone understood the major political questions at hand. Contemporary democracy was plagued by pervasive political apathy, buttressed by a constellation of power and privilege benefiting from it, and what Morgenthau lamented, in a lengthy section of *Purpose of American Politics*, as the "decline of the public realm" (*PAP*, 197–215).[41] Although Morgenthau's attempt to justify democracy as that system best suited to realizing sound policy tended to downplay the role of direct political *participation*, it preserved a key role for lively public debate and exchange. However, political competition and debate were on the decline: for example, the United States suffered from a "decline of politics . . . reminiscent of, but not identical with, the Marxist withering away of the state." An odd mirror image of orthodox Marxist ideas of communism, the United States and other advanced democracies had abandoned political debate and conflict in favor of a preoccupation with "the humdrum issue of control of the administration" (*PAP*, 200). Although rooted in objective social trends, such tendencies represented a dangerous form of political complacency which closed people's ideas to the high stakes of many of the issues confronting them – most urgently, Morgenthau reiterated in the concluding section of *Purpose of American Politics*, the specter of nuclear war.

Morgenthau also implicitly provided a corrective to Kelsen. In Kelsen's original attempt to link democracy to relativism, three different meeting points were identified. First, Kelsen had argued that democracy presupposed relativistic moral and political preferences constituting little more than subjective desires; democracy was married to *noncognitivism* in moral and political theory. Second, democracy only made sense given the rejection of the dubious thesis that any individual or group possessed infallible knowledge of moral and political affairs; democracy and *fallibilism* were intermeshed. Third, Kelsen occasionally suggested that democracy itself could only be justified in a relative or *conditional* manner; the choice in favor of democracy itself depended on other normative preferences which one might plausibly reject.[42] Even though his language occasionally confused matters, Morgenthau only endorsed Kelsen's second and soundest claim that democracy and fallibilism were integrally linked, while rejecting Kelsen's noncognitivism as well as his worrisome caution regarding a firmly grounded defense of democracy.

Moral and political truths, in Morgenthau's view, were universally binding; the dilemma at hand was that no single group could ever be absolutely sure that they had been properly identified, or were being achieved in the right way at the right time. A traditionalistic endorsement of universal moral and political verities meshed well with fallibilism and the recognition of necessary limits to our cognitive capacities. Perhaps the greatest peril facing democracy was the tendency among politically dominant groups to reject any standards other than their own. In the process, they succumbed to a moral and political relativism that conflated partisan preferences with fundamental democratic principles: "the relativism of majority rule, denying the existence of absolute, transcendent truth independent of the majority will, tends toward the immanent absolutism of a tyrannical or totalitarian majority, while the pluralism of genuine democracy assumes as its corollary the existence of such truth limiting the will of the majority" (*PAP*, 252–3). The great accomplishment of the liberal tradition had been its inflexible insistence on the verity of *objective* and even *transcendental* norms, and thus an immutable framework within which democracy might thrive. Fidelity to the fundamental liberal belief in the "integrity, happiness, and self-development" of the individual, for example, was necessary if democracy were to avoid succumbing to a decadent relativism in which competing political majorities periodically set up their own partisan political preferences as universal and permanent truths (*PAP*, 252). The Jacobin tradition, which purportedly treated popular opinion (but in reality always by necessity a mere political *majority*) as the "voice of god," repeatedly made this mistake; the Anglo-American model had avoided it. As the latter tradition properly grasped, conventional liberal and constitutional restraints on majority power – including protections for free speech – naturally played a decisive role in maintaining the vitality of democracy. A pluralistic conception of political truth was to be distinguished not only from a crude relativism according to which *every* political idea, however hackneyed, possessed equal cognitive merit, but also from a confused denial of democracy's dependence on fundamental normative commitments.

As in his earlier contributions to political ethics, Morgenthau never provided a sufficient systematic justification for liberal democracy's objective or transcendent normative foundations. He seemed to believe that basic liberal democratic normative commitments (for example, the ideal of respect for the individual) still continued to appeal to large numbers of people; perhaps this rendered philosophical justification, in his eyes, superfluous. More important from his perspective was the recognition that democracy was a fragile creation whose own close links to relativism risked generating self-destructive misunderstandings:

> If both the majority and the minority remain within this relativistic ethos of democracy [meaning that they reject a monopolistic idea of political truth], while at the same time respecting those absolute, objective principles that are beyond the ken of that relativism, the vitality of their contest will accrue to the vitality of democracy. Otherwise, they will strain the delicate ties that keep a democratic society together, and they will risk destroying it while trying to keep it alive.[43]

Whatever its limitations as a contribution to systematic normative theory, Morgenthau's creative recourse to Kelsen permitted him to tackle some of the internal theoretical dilemmas generated by his earlier anti-democratic reflections from the 1940s and 1950s. *Purpose of American Politics* now at least sometimes suggested that it was not democracy per se that was responsible for the irrationalities of US foreign policy, but instead democratic *decay*. Never mincing his words, Morgenthau claimed that the United States was already a decadent democracy that had taken disturbing steps in the direction of totalitarianism. Political competition was under attack and political debate trivialized, minorities were forced to kowtow to a conformist political mindset, and commitments to basic liberal safeguards – Morgenthau discussed McCarthyism at great length – were proving frighteningly fragile. The modern mass media were fundamentally conformist because their success was "measured by the support they are able to obtain from advertisers and the consuming public." Although economic inequality remained substantial in the United States and other advanced democracies, open class antagonism was muted, and there was a widespread sense in political life of an "absence of great issues worth fighting for" (*PAP*, 255). In reality, the major issues – first and foremost, nuclear proliferation – were simply more intractable and *distant* from everyday experience than previous ones. The Jacobin faith in the infallibility of majority opinion was now on the ascent even in the Anglo-American democracies, where political leaders diligently followed the latest expressions of public opinion as calculated by scientifically trained polling experts. Subservience to public opinion polls, however, overlooked the fact that they often captured little more than a passing mood or inclination.

Docility to polling data and the increasingly commonplace view of political leadership as a form of public relations work were also responsible for the repeated failure of US policy makers to think creatively about novel global challenges. The final section of *Purpose of American Politics* addressed the nuclear peril and the need for the USA to help to construct a historically unprecedented supranational system of nuclear controls and regulation.[44] Here again, the "second image" of politics shaped international politics: US foreign policy was badly flawed in part because Americans had abandoned their sensible preference for republican representative government in favor of the Jacobin view that political leaders, willy-nilly, should obediently follow transient majoritarian moods. Only by revitalizing their own homegrown Anglo-American conception of liberal democracy could Americans salvage their foreign policy and contribute to the new supranational system of nuclear oversight essential to human survival.

Some of Morgenthau's reflections on so-called "degenerate" democracy referred specifically to US trends; others alluded to general tendencies at work in democracy at large. Only by zeroing in on the US national purpose was Morgenthau able to focus successfully on America's particular ills. In many surprising ways, *Purpose of American Politics* anticipated Hannah Arendt's renowned *On Revolution* (1962).[45] Like Arendt, Morgenthau believed that contemporary Americans had forgotten something fundamental about their political identity. Consequently, it had fallen to a German-Jewish émigré who had once been an outsider, but had since enthusiastically adopted America as his home, to recall them. A fundamentally flattering portrait of US political traditions was contrasted favorably with pathological continental and specifically Jacobin ideas about democracy. Echoing *On Revolution*, Morgenthau's volume provided clear evidence both of his deep emotional attachment to the United States, and of his fears that something had gone badly wrong in his new home. Reminiscent of Arendt in this respect as well, *Purpose of American Politics* offered an uneasy mix of eulogistic and occasionally idealized reminiscences about the American past, along with incisive observations about America's contemporary course.

Like Arendt's *On Revolution*, Morgenthau tended to downplay the role of slavery, as well as a terrible history of violence against native peoples.[46] More significant was that the US national purpose consisted of a special version of the liberal democratic aspiration for equality in freedom. Eclectically weaving together writers like Tocqueville and Fredrick Jackson Turner, Morgenthau saw little originality in the *intellectual* contributions of the US framers. The American founders were children of the European Enlightenment; US political thought, for the most part, was derivative. The originality of the US national purpose instead stemmed from its successful application of liberal democratic ideals: the Americans may have been second-rate political *thinkers*, but the special conditions of North America allowed them to *realize* and *practice* equality in freedom to a degree unmatched elsewhere. Like no other nation, the United States had achieved substantial "equal opportunity with a minimum of political control" (*PAP*, 31). In part because it faced no serious military threats, the Americans had got by with a limited and unusually democratic government. The open frontier and relatively dynamic social conditions meant that its social life was egalitarian. For much of its history, the United States had been spared the pathologies of a rigid European class system. In nineteenth-century America, those who failed economically simply picked up their meager belongings and looked elsewhere – most likely, further west – for material prosperity and success. The possibility of internal migration, in short, was essential to both vertical and horizontal social mobility.[47] "No master within, no enemy without; equality, opportunity, freedom, power for the individual": US society was in many ways imperfect, yet it had realized these aspirations to a higher degree than others (*PAP*, 44). No wonder, Morgenthau commented with sympathy, that untold millions had looked to the United States as a moral and political exemplar, as a beacon of light to those down on their luck and downtrodden, and that so many had migrated to America to try their luck. Consequently, its national purpose "carries within itself a meaning that transcends the national boundaries of America and addresses itself to all other nations of the world" (*PAP*, 34). The American experiment in self-government was of more than mere provincial significance: it provided a practical and in many ways unusually successful realization of the great Enlightenment aspiration for equality in freedom.

Purpose of American Politics then quickly shifted into a critical gear, however. Morgenthau rightly worried more that an appreciation for America's accomplishments might open the door to hubristic self-satisfaction and patriotic drum rolls. Too often, US foreign policy had taken on irrational and even messianic contours. The United States could no longer afford to repeat such mistakes in the atomic age, however.

First, Morgenthau noted that the US national purpose, in contrast to that of other nations, was strikingly open-ended. Appropriately described as "procedural," as a form of minimal consensus, it entailed no commitment to a single substantive purpose (*PAP*, 21). The predominance of commercial pursuits and relative economic fluidity had helped to allow Americans to pursue "equality of competition for undefined goals with a minimum of political interference" (*PAP*, 57). The open-endedness of the national purpose constituted a wellspring of dynamism and liberty. Yet it was also a source of vulnerability. During periods of crisis and self-doubt, Americans had regularly surrendered to bouts of conformism and jingoism, as they rushed to escape a dynamic social world that abruptly and unexpectedly appeared alienating and hostile; a long history of xenophobic and anti-liberal movements had offered easy but fake remedies. Like Tocqueville, Morgenthau saw an intimate link between democracy and conformism: *Purpose of American Politics* repeatedly echoed the former's worries about the prospect of a novel form of mass-based or democratic despotism, in which individuality and creativity would be subjected to authoritarian popular pressures. Democratic institutions might continue to operate, but their liberal and freedom-enhancing spirit would have dissipated. For Morgenthau, as for Tocqueville, conformism was a common mechanism by which dynamic democratic societies countered deeply rooted trends towards disintegration and alienation.

Second, *Purpose of American Politics* focused on the repeated crises facing the national purpose. Shifting dramatically from his eulogistic portrayal of nineteenth-century America, Morgenthau offered a critical account of twentieth-century political and social trends, vividly highlighting social and political transformations undermining American exceptionalism. As the frontier closed and modern corporate capitalism replaced the classical free market, social mobility was stymied. Propelled into world affairs, and forced to deal with the harsh realities of class society, classical liberal anti-statism no longer made sense. The only appropriate answer, Morgenthau argued, was far-reaching social and political reform: substantial state intervention alone could salvage equal opportunity and thereby preserve the national purpose. At least in the domestic arena, the polity had faced the challenges head-on; Roosevelt's New Deal was praised for mitigating the harshest features of modern economic life and helping to preserve some measure of equal opportunity. In foreign affairs, however, policy makers for the most part had demonstrated ineptness at getting to grips with the novelties generated by the United States' rise to global preeminence, as well as the nuclear revolution.

The core message of *Purpose of American Politics* remained anxious. Despite notable efforts, Americans had yet to figure out how to preserve their special national purpose amid social and political conditions utterly dissimilar to those in which it had first been declared. Notwithstanding the New Deal, the United States remained an economically stratified society in which talk of equal opportunity and social mobility seemed ever more illusory. State intervention had dramatically expanded, yet creative mechanisms for effective political and legal accountability lagged beyond its expansion. A new feudalism fusing public and private power had emerged: reformers had failed to make the welfare and interventionist state sufficiently compatible with basic libertarian impulses.[48] America's materialistic orientation had always made up a core element of the national purpose. Regrettably, the national purpose now risked getting reduced to crass commercialism: equality in freedom as nothing more than consumer choice in the marketplace (*PAP*, 215–17). *Purpose of American Politics* articulated a far-reaching assault on contemporary capitalism, not only lamenting its resulting material inequalities, but bluntly describing it as a wasteful and inefficient system based on the irrational principle of "ever increased production for its own sake" (*PAP*, 219). Although quick to distinguish his position from those who favored socialist-style planning, Morgenthau announced that present-day capitalism no longer satisfied real economic and human needs, favored novelty and diversity in consumer goods even when wasteful and counterproductive, generated massive concentrations of wealth thus far impermeable to democratic control, and contributed directly to widespread civic privatism (*PAP*, 215–22).

What then was to be done? *Purpose of American Politics* advocated an extension of the New Deal and the welfare state, openly admitting that doing so would require a substantial expansion of state power. Nonetheless, only a strong state could check the untrammeled concentrations of private economic power that made a mockery of the national purpose. Americans would need to move beyond the blind worship of the founders which plagued political consciousness and think anew about necessary forms of state regulation that could be made congruent with the unfinished quest to realize equality in freedom. In this view, innovative state activity required institutional creativity, but by no means an abandonment of liberalism's original emancipatory spirit. Domestic reform would also have to be coupled with far-reaching international reform. As we saw in chapter 5, the USA might begin building a supranational order by first constructing an association of like-minded liberal democratic states. America's special national purpose had always implicitly spoken to peoples elsewhere, even if US political leaders too often had mistakenly interpreted this universal appeal as a clarion call for a proselytizing foreign policy and military expansion. But such an association, Morgenthau cautiously suggested, might allow the USA to "share its purpose with its associates," at least to the extent that they were also struggling to achieve a form of socially responsible liberal democracy committed to the realization of equality in freedom: "The national interest and the national purpose of America would then merge with their interests and purposes" (*PAN*, 309).

Yet *Purpose of American Politics* concluded on a pessimistic note. The final safeguard of popular power, the possibility of armed revolution, had been rendered anachronistic by the awesome military asymmetry obtaining between governments and their subjects (*PAP*, 267). Although the nuclear revolution called for the revitalization of popular politics and a new global order, it instead was working to produce technological elites over whom the electorate and its representatives exercised limited control. Admittedly, some scientific and technological matters were less complex than political and scientific elites preferred to admit. As Morgenthau noted in a related 1964 article, however, "[i]n the eyes both of the political authorities and the public at large, the scientific elites appear as the guardian of the *arcanii imperii*, the secret remedies for public ills."[49] Political conflict was now intermeshed more deeply than ever before with complex matters of scientific and technological expertise. Too often they overwhelmed the average voter. In short, there were myriad reasons for doubting that Americans would ever succeed in updating their national purpose in accord with new conditions. Morgenthau's implicit warning to the citizens of his adopted country was clear enough: like countless political communities in the past, they might soon join the ranks of those morally uninteresting peoples – like the Huns and Mongols – who had failed to represent anything special or distinctive about the human condition.

Social reform and international politics

Looking back at the trajectory of the US polity since the 1960s, it seems difficult to dismiss Morgenthau's worries, let alone discount his prediction that the Vietnam debacle was destined to leave devastating political scars. Despite substantial racial and gender advances, and some noteworthy but ultimately fragile attempts at social reform, economic inequality in the United States has swelled since Morgenthau's days, political apathy remains rampant, and the political system seems even more in need of a far-reaching overhaul. Vietnam indeed badly tarnished America's image abroad, and then numerous succeeding foreign policy mishaps – most recently, the invasion of Iraq – have further weakened the United States. In Vietnam, US brutality trampled on the once popular perception of America as a beacon to the dispossessed and downtrodden. After the Iraq War, Abu Ghraib, and Guantanamo Bay, any US citizen who dares talk of her country's exceptional and morally outstanding national purpose legitimately risks getting laughed offstage. The fact that Morgenthau's otherwise critical reflections on the United States today likely seem naïve speaks volumes about the self-destructive trajectory of US politics in recent decades. In his reflections on Vietnam and the general crisis of American democracy, Morgenthau's tone was occasionally shrill, and his argumentation at times simplistic and repetitive. Yet his remained a prophetic voice whose warnings too often rang true.

This chapter has tried to defend two main claims. First, Morgenthau's writings from the 1960s and 1970s refused to decouple international politics from domestic political and social conditions, instead highlighting how the "second image" of politics shaped international events. US success abroad depended on the degree to which Americans actually lived up to the latent normative promise of their special national purpose. Domestic pathologies were at least one major causal factor behind the irrationalities of foreign policy. From this perspective, it would be mistaken to try to separate surgically the analysis of the international system from domestic political and social conditions. Only a concrete empirical analysis can demonstrate whether domestic or international factors are more significant, in particular cases, for understanding foreign relations.

Second, Morgenthau's spirited ethical critique of the Vietnam War, which gained him massive public attention, built on his writings from the late 1950s and 1960s. Although radicalized by Vietnam, his earlier reflections were preoccupied as well with the problems of social and political reform. At least for this Realist, moral and normative matters consistently remained at the top of the intellectual and political agenda. Not surprisingly, in his topical pieces on the Middle East and the plight of Jews in the Soviet Union published in the years prior to his death in 1980, special attention was paid to domestic as well as the usual international factors. In response to Kissinger's criticism that those hoping to employ US policy to force the Soviets to improve the treatment of Jews were succumbing to a misplaced idealism, for example, Morgenthau insisted that shaping Soviet domestic policy was of "vital importance" to US foreign policy. Because shifts in Soviet policy were essential if the USA could ever hope to depend on the Russians to uphold their international agreements, humanitarian criticisms of Russian domestic policy were legitimate if "survival in the nuclear age" were to be secured.[50] Here as well, the domestic and international were intimately intertwined.

Revealingly, Morgenthau's renewed appreciation for the centrality of distinctive US political ideals did not lead him, as it has recent neoconservatives, to advance a reckless foreign policy based on a morally smug view of US superiority.[51] Neoconservatives have recently argued that a Realist conception of the national interest should be fused with an open acknowledgment of America's exemplary moral and political ideals. At first glance, this intellectual move reproduces some features of *Purpose of American Politics*. Echoing Morgenthau's attempt to integrate the concept of the national purpose into Realism, neoconservatives assert that Realism offers many valuable insights – *except* that it (supposedly) ignores America's special and indeed universal moral and political ideals. For Charles Krauthammer, a proponent of so-called "Democratic Realism," Realism "can only take you so far," since Realists like Morgenthau miss the fact that the United States was built on distinctive liberal democratic ideals which now must be aggressively protected "against the existential enemy, the enemy that poses a mortal threat to freedom," namely "Arab-Islamic Totalitarianism."[52]

This is not the place to discuss the problems posed by describing the real threats engendered by contemporary terrorism as "Arab-Islamic Totalitarianism." Krauthammer's reading of Morgenthau is incorrect: Morgenthau certainly *did* attempt to see US foreign policy as intimately related to the defense of key moral and political ideals. More importantly, the differences between Morgenthau and neoconservatives like Krauthammer remain profound. Morgenthau thought that, even if the US quest for equality in freedom contained *universal* ideals transcending their national origins, healthy skepticism about any attempt to extend them by violent means was typically in order. Too often, as in Vietnam, the quest to do so instead counterproductively *destroyed* what made the US national purpose distinctive and thus attractive in the first place. In an important chapter of *A New Foreign Policy for the United States* entitled "To Intervene or Not to Intervene," Morgenthau criticized both the USA and the USSR for mechanically acting on a shared belief in a universal "duty to intervene in the affairs of other nations on behalf of an overriding moral principle" (*NFP*, 113). Contemporary neoconservatism arguably has built directly on this problematic cold war legacy and simply applied it to the novel problems of contemporary terrorism. A familiar theme in Morgenthau's political ethics, of course, was that even morally sound ideals are undermined when pursued inappropriately; contemporary neoconservatives seem to have forgotten the ABCs of Realist political ethics. From Morgenthau's perspective, neoconservatism endorses a simplistic view of the roots of national power which dangerously overstates its military sources. Theirs is ultimately a hubristic foreign policy in which Morgenthau's sober commitment to the foreign policy virtues of humility, moderation, and prudence is thrown overboard – from the massive naval vessels now positioned offshore of Iraq.

Morgenthau indeed argued on behalf of the special and even universal traits of the US national purpose. Yet *Purpose of American Politics* noted that many other political communities had made distinctive contributions to human existence. The United States, in short, was only one "universal" nation among others: other countries also possessed a special moral significance for humankind at large. In addition, Morgenthau developed the idea of the national purpose in part for the sake of igniting progressive political and social reform. Within his thinking, it functioned as a way to mobilize his fellow US citizens to pursue equality in freedom in new and creative ways, thereby giving others elsewhere sound reason to look up again to the USA as a positive model from which something useful might be learned. In turn, Morgenthau cautiously hoped, this would allow the USA to lead the way in building a supranational political order. In contrast, contemporary US neoconservatives speak of America's universal values neither in order to advance overdue social reform nor to strengthen transnational political organization. On the contrary, their narrow interpretation of US political identity is employed as a weapon *against* reform both home and abroad, as well as an ideological cover for a unilateralist foreign policy hostile even to the barest rudiments of international law.

Conclusion
Morgenthau as classical Realist?

This study has paid special attention to the complicated twists and turns of Morgenthau's trajectory, beginning with his debut as a young politically progressive Weimar lawyer and scholar of international law, and covering his initial years in the United States as a defender of a morally rigorous political ethics, his subsequent transformation into the hard-headed Realist author of influential works like *In Defense of the National Interest* and *Politics Among Nations*, then his role as a critic of the nuclear arms race and defender of world government, and finally as an opponent of the Vietnam War worried about the fate of American democracy. In the face of the widespread tendency to provide one-dimensional and even simplistic views of Morgenthau's thinking, this book has consciously erred on the side of emphasizing his multiple intellectual perspectives. Yet it remains noteworthy that we can still identify striking parallels between his early and late writings. Just as revealing, these continuities seem relatively unrelated to the conventional image of Morgenthau as a "classical Realist." In his earliest years, Morgenthau emerged as a legal reformer, influenced by socialist intellectuals, with whom he at least initially shared the so-called "idealistic" view that change on the international scene should be linked to social reform. In *Purpose of American Politics*, we again find Morgenthau articulating a forceful critique of the social and political status quo, endorsing a forthrightly leftist critique of capitalism, though hesitating to draw conventional socialist conclusions about the virtues of state planning.[1] His advocacy of reforming both social and economic conditions and the Westphalian system mirrored Morgenthau's earlier ideas from the 1920s and 1930s. His writings on Vietnam, with their unabashed advocacy for radical political and social reform, similarly offered a resounding echo of his youthful reformist spirit. Morgenthau began his career as a lawyer associated with leftist circles in Frankfurt. He finished it in the 1970s as an outspoken New York intellectual and academic, a distinguished faculty member teaching, perhaps appropriately, at two of America's most politically progressive universities, the City University of New York and then the New School for Social Research.

At the very least, the interpretation proffered in these pages raises critical questions about the conventional categorization of Morgenthau as a classical Realist. Although I cannot sufficiently defend this thesis here, my hunch is that Morgenthau's complicated relationship to Realism is mirrored in the intellectual biographies of other writers similarly grouped under its rubric. Among so-called classical Realists (e.g. E. H. Carr, John Herz, Reinhold Niebuhr, and Arnold Wolfers) who influenced mid-century political discourse, it is striking that a large number of them had been socialists and social democrats at crucial junctures in their intellectual trajectories, and were deeply versed in left-wing social, political, and legal theory. The so-called "German tradition" out of which early Realism emerged was hardly that of Bismarck or conservative *Realpolitik* but instead arguably that of the interwar Weimar left. Some – most prominently, Wolfers – were directly linked to an influential group of self-described (non-Marxist) "religious socialists," Protestant and Jewish Weimar leftists who astutely pointed to the normative gaps of classical Marxism and sought a creative synthesis of socialism and religion;[2] others like Herz were the intellectual offspring of social democratic jurists like Hans Kelsen, and active in socialist émigré politics in the 1930s; yet others – Carr is the obvious example – sought inspiration from left-leaning social theorists like Mannheim. As in the case of Morgenthau, the conventional view that these authors simply imported the tradition of conservative Germanic power politics into English-speaking political discourse, updating it in accordance with cold war political needs, misconstrues a vastly more complicated intellectual history. The history of the relationship between Realism and the Left remains unwritten. I hope that this study, despite its limitations, can help shatter ossified preconceptions which get in the way of a more accurate assessment of that relationship.

Morgenthau's widely noted critical remarks about the morally self-satisfied but politically counterproductive "world-embracing gesture of the international reformer" in *Scientific Man* also take on fresh significance when reexamined in the context of his *own* typically overlooked reformist political impulses. Behind the defender of global reform, Morgenthau commented,

> is likely to hide an inhibited reformer of domestic affairs. He who signs a petition, makes a speech, writes an article, or simply attends a meeting in support of international understanding experiences the satisfaction of having done something for a worthwhile cause. That the good deed does not entail any sacrifices, incur any risks, or bring about any changes in the actual conditions of the actor's life makes the action only the more attractive. Conversely, the international reformer, if he is not exceptionally courageous and wise, will stay clear of tackling the conditions, ideas, and policies in his own country, upon whose transformation international understanding at least partially depends. One will find that the urgency of domestic reform in a certain period is to a certain extent proportionate to the quantity of panaceas offered for the ills of the world in general, and to the insistence with which they are offered. (*SM*, 98)

Easily mistaken for enmity to international reform, as further evidence for the institutionally quiescent core of Morgenthau's Realism, his comments should now be read in a different light. During his illustrious career, Morgenthau in fact regularly defended *both* the quest for new forms of supranational rule *and* reform at home. Morgenthau opposed neither far-reaching international nor domestic reform, but instead misplaced efforts at politically naïve international reforms which he thought too often functioned as compensation for a failure to deal with pressing political and social problems at home.

To be sure, the intensification of globalization within recent decades might have encouraged Morgenthau to tone down the harsh character of his comments. Far more than his recent Realist and Neorealist offspring, he recognized that contemporary conditions required a novel global order as well as new ways of thinking about international politics. His international theory provides many rich and potentially useful insights about which anyone concerned with international politics and indeed the fate of humanity will continue to argue. Yet he undoubtedly was justified in insisting that models of global reform should be expected to represent more than politically unrealistic and morally painless escapes from pressing domestic reforms. As we work to build a new and more just cosmopolitan order, we would do well to keep Morgenthau's warning in mind.

Notes

Introduction: Morgenthau's uneasy Realism

1 According to one major scholar, Realism has been the dominant perspective on foreign relations among Japanese political elites, for example (Kenneth B. Pyle, *Japan Rising: The Resurgence of Japanese Power and Purpose* [New York: Public Affairs, 2007]).

2 Jonathan Haslam, *No Virtue Like Necessity: Realist Thought in International Relations Since Machiavelli* (New Haven: Yale University Press, 2002).

3 John J. Mearsheimer, "Hans Morgenthau and the Iraq War: Realism versus Neoconservatism" (www.opendemocracy.net/democracy-americanpower/morgenthau_2522.jsp), posted May 19, 2005.

4 See, for example, Jack Donnelly, *Realism and International Relations* (Cambridge: Cambridge University Press, 2000), 6–42.

5 Michael Joseph Smith, *Realist Thought from Weber to Kissinger* (Baton Rouge: Louisiana State University Press, 1986), 1.

6 I am grateful to Bill Rasch for this formulation.

7 Stanley Hoffmann, *Janus and Minerva: Essays in the Theory and Practice of International Politics* (Boulder: Westview Press, 1987), 6. Hoffmann's attribution to Morgenthau of papal status is quoted in Martin Griffiths, *Realism, Idealism & International Politics: A Reinterpretation* (London: Routledge, 1995), 35.

8 John A. Vasquez, *The Power of Power Politics: From Classical Realism to Neotraditionalism* (Cambridge: Cambridge University Press, 1998).

9 Henry Kissinger, "Hans Morgenthau: A Gentle Analyst of Power," *New Republic* (August 2 and 9, 1980), 12–14.

10 See, most recently, Jürgen Habermas, *The Divided West* (Cambridge: Polity, 2006), 166–93.

11   See, for example, Jan Willem Honig, "Totalitarianism and Realism: Hans Morgenthau's German Years," in Benjamin Frankel (ed.), *Roots of Realism* (London: Frank Cass, 1996), 283–313; Alfons Söllner, "German Conservatism in America: Morgenthau's Political Realism," *Telos*, 72 (1987), 161–72.

12   Others have recently challenged conventional readings of Morgenthau. See Murielle Cozette, "Reclaiming the Critical Dimension of Realism: Hans J. Morgenthau on the Ethics of Scholarship," *Review of International Studies*, 34 (2008), 5–27; Campbell Craig, *Glimmer of a New Leviathan: Total War in the Realism of Niebuhr, Morgenthau, and Waltz* (New York: Columbia University Press, 2003); Richard Ned Lebow, *The Tragic Vision of Politics: Ethics, Interests and Orders* (Cambridge: Cambridge University Press, 2003); Alastair J. H. Murray, *Reconstructing Realism: Between Power Politics and Cosmopolitan Ethics* (Edinburgh: Keele University Press, 1997); Vibeke Schou Tjalve, *Realist Strategies of Republican Peace: Niebuhr, Morgenthau, and the Politics of Patriotic Dissent* (New York: Palgrave, 2008); Michael C. Williams, *The Realist Tradition and the Limits of International Relations* (Cambridge: Cambridge University Press, 2005). Greg G. Russell's *Hans J. Morgenthau and the Ethics of American Statecraft* (Baton Rouge: Louisiana State University, 1990) remains helpful, as does Christoph Rohde, *Hans J. Morgenthau und der weltpolitische Realismus* (Wiesbaden: Verlag für Sozialwissenschaften, 2004).

13   Morgenthau always worried about widespread misunderstandings of his work. In the third (1960) edition of *Politics Among Nations*, for example, he claimed to find "solace in Montesquieu's similar experience, to bemoan the fate of authors 'to be criticized for ideas one has never held.' I am still being so criticized. I am still being told that I believe in the prominence of the international system based upon the nation state, although the obsolescence of the nation state and the need to merge it into supranational organizations of a functional nature was already one of the main points of the first edition of 1948. I am still being told that I am making success the standard of political action . . . And, of course, I am still being accused of indifference to the moral problem in spite of abundant evidence, in this book and elsewhere, to the contrary" (*PAN*, 3rd edn., II).

14   Morgenthau's teaching, it is worth noting, typically included courses on the political philosophies of Aristotle and Abraham Lincoln.

15   See, for example, David Held, *Democracy and the Global Order: From the Modern State to Cosmopolitan Governance* (Stanford: Stanford University Press, 1995).

16   Those seeking additional biographical details should consult Christoph Frei's illuminating *Hans J. Morgenthau: An Intellectual Biography* (Baton Rouge: Louisiana State University Press, 2001).

17   Rice, "Campaign 2000: Promoting the National Interest," *Foreign Affairs* (January/February 2000), 45–62.

Chapter 1 Radical roots of Realism

1 Held, *Democracy and the Global Order*, 74–5.
2 Morgenthau's biographer Frei discusses Sinzheimer's influence, but he downplays his impact (*Hans J. Morgenthau: An Intellectual Biography*, 39, 168). Martti Koskenniemi similarly mentions Sinzheimer and the left-wing jurists with whom Morgenthau worked, but claims, without much evidence, that Morgenthau remained a conservative (*The Gentle Civilizer of Nations: The Rise and Fall of International Law, 1870–1960* [Cambridge: Cambridge University Press, 2001], 447).
3 The *Referendariat* entailed a legal apprenticeship undertaken under the auspices of a senior lawyer. It was a required component of professional legal training.
4 Sinzheimer was an outspoken critic of traditional German "power politics." In 1917, he published a monograph on international law and foreign policy in which he advocated Kantian reforms of the interstate system, criticized power politics and "reason of state" approaches to foreign affairs, and defended the establishment of a united pacific Europe (*Völkerrechtsgeist. Rede zur Einführung in das Programm der Zentralstelle "Völkerrecht"* [Leipzig: Verlag Naturwissenschaften, 1917]).
5 Morgenthau, "Fragment of an Intellectual Autobiography: 1904–1932," in Kenneth Thompson and Robert J. Myers (eds.), *Truth and Tragedy: A Tribute to Hans J. Morgenthau* (New Brunswick: Transaction Books, 1984), 10, where he discusses at length his debt to Sinzheimer. See also the extensive correspondence between Morgenthau and Sinzheimer and members of Sinzheimer's family (HJM-B54, B197, Library of Congress). As Frei notes, "[t]heir relations must in fact have been very close, as their shared professional life occasionally carried over into private life. At times, Morgenthau stayed entire days in the house of his boss, not infrequently also as a baby sitter" (*Hans J. Morgenthau: An Intellectual Biography*, 168).
6 Frei, *Hans J. Morgenthau: An Intellectual Biography*, 61.
7 Ernst Fraenkel to Gertrud Mainzer (Sinzheimer's daughter), February 25, 1975, HJM-B54, Library of Congress. It is not clear that Morgenthau was able to attend, however.
8 Mannheim probably makes his most important appearance in Morgenthau's work in his discussion of the "ideological elements in international politics" (*PAN*, 2nd edn., 80). There Morgenthau acknowledged that he borrowed from Mannheim's concept of "particular ideology" in *Ideology and Utopia* (New York: Harcourt, Brace and Company, 1936), 49.
9 Bernard Johnson, "Bernard Johnson's Interview with Hans J. Morgenthau," in Thompson and Myers (eds.), *Truth and Tragedy*, 349. Ernst Fraenkel (1898–1975) became a prominent political scientist in

postwar Germany; Otto Kahn Freund (1900–53) was a leading figure in labor and comparative law in the UK; Franz L. Neumann (1900–53) was the resident political and legal theorist of the "Frankfurt School" when in New York exile, and then an influential professor of political theory at Columbia University. All, like Morgenthau, were Jews; all shared a deep life-long admiration for Sinzheimer and described their years under his mentorship as decisive for their intellectual development. See, for example, Fraenkel, "Hugo Sinzheimer," in Falk Esche and Frank Grube (eds.), *Reformismus und Pluralismus* (Hamburg: Hoffmann und Campe, 1973), 131–42.

10 Susanne Knorre, *Soziale Selbstbestimmung und individuelle Verantwortung. Hugo Sinzheimer (1875–1945). Eine politische Biographie* (Frankfurt: Peter Lang, 1991), 116–17.

11 Cited in Frei, *Hans J. Morgenthau: An Intellectual Biography*, 168.

12 Morgenthau, "Fragment of an Intellectual Autobiography," 9–10.

13 My brief summary is drawn from a useful German-language collection: Hugo Sinzheimer, *Arbeitsrecht und Rechtssoziologie. Gesammelte Aufsätze und Reden*, ed. Otto Kahn Freund and Thilo Ramm, Vols. I–II (Frankfurt: EVA, 1976).

14 Knorre, *Soziale Selbstbestimmung und individuelle Verantwortung*, 116.

15 This paraphrase, taken from Marx, appears repeatedly in Sinzheimer's writings. More generally on this point, see Kahn Freund, "Hugo Sinzheimer 1875–1945," in Roy Lewis and Jon Clark (eds.), *Labour Law and Politics in the Weimar Republic* (Oxford: Basil Blackwell, 1981), 78.

16 Karl Renner, *The Institutions of Private Law and Their Social Functions*, ed. Otto Kahn Freund (London: Routledge, 1949).

17 Kahn Freund, "Hugo Sinzheimer 1875–1945," 98.

18 Kahn Freund, "Hugo Sinzheimer 1875–1945," 99. Sinzheimer's most prominent left-wing disciples closely followed their mentor. Kahn Freund, Fraenkel, and Neumann each synthesized Weber and Marx, similarly flavoring the recipe with a substantial dose of Renner's critical sociology of law. Like Sinzheimer, their inquiries placed special weight on the historical or dynamic character of the relationship between social reality and law. Neumann and Fraenkel, for example, argued in the 1930s that the changing contours of capitalist development transformed the significance of the traditional liberal commitment to general law. In classical capitalism, general law was not only legally desirable but also economically rational since individual legal interventions violated the principle of equal competition. When massive economic concentrations dominate production, however, this original elective affinity between general law and economic reality is destroyed. In this view, the demand for general rules – arguably the mainstay of the liberal rule of law – was likely to face significant resistance from privileged economic actors, who increasingly opted for vague and open-ended legal forms more malleable to

their manipulation than the clear general legal norms favored by classical liberal jurisprudence. Only a historically minded sociology of law, in which due attention was paid to economic history and its complex impact on legal reality, would be capable of making sense of this momentous shift in the social underpinnings of the rule of law. On Neumann, see William E. Scheuerman, *Between the Norm and the Exception: The Frankfurt School and the Rule of Law* (Cambridge, Mass.: MIT Press, 1994); on Fraenkel, see Scheuerman, "Social Democracy and the Rule of Law: The Legacy of Ernst Fraenkel," in Peter Caldwell and William E. Scheuerman (eds.), *From Liberal Democracy to Fascism: Legal and Political Thought in the Weimar Republic* (Boston: Brill, 2000), 74–105; on Kahn Freund, see Lord Wedderburn of Charlton, Roy Lewis, and Jon Clark (eds.), *Labour Law and Industrial Relations: Building on Kahn-Freund* (Oxford: Clarendon Press, 1983).

19   Kahn Freund, "Hugo Sinzheimer 1875–1945," 75–7. Concerning Sinzheimer's anxieties about judicial discretion, see Knorre, *Soziale Selbstbestimmung und individuelle Verantwortung*, 15, 71, 157.

20   See Ingo Mueller, *Hitler's Justice: The Courts of the Third Reich* (Cambridge, Mass.: Harvard University Press, 1991).

21   This untitled piece appears to have been unsuccessfully submitted to a legal journal (HJM-B110, Library of Congress). The translation here, as of other German texts unless otherwise noted, is my own.

22   *IRWG* garnered strong endorsements from major figures in the field. See, for example, the comments by Hersch Lauterpacht, who praised Morgenthau's first book in a review of Morgenthau's closely related 1933 *La Notion du "politique" et la théorie des différends internationaux* (Paris: Libraire du Recueil Sirey, 1933): "Dr. Morgenthau has won for himself through his book [from 1929] a prominent place among international lawyers engaged in clarifying the character of disputes among states and in enquiring into the limits of their compulsory settlement" (*Zeitschrift für Sozialforschung*, 3 [1934], 461). Morgenthau would rely on some of its key arguments throughout his career.

23   The contemporary Realist Danilo Zolo similarly worries about the "freezing of the world's political, and economic, and military map" via international law (*Cosmopolis: Prospects for World Government* [Cambridge: Polity Press, 1997], 13). However, Zolo apparently sees this as an unavoidable attribute of international law, whereas the young Morgenthau believed that it might be modified.

24   Sinzheimer's *Völkerrechtsgeist* similarly drew a parallel between the "juridical abstraction" of individual freedom within the context of private law and the "juridical abstraction" of absolute state sovereignty (6). In both cases, law tends to obscure the existence of relations of inequality.

25   Hans J. Morgenthau, "Genfer Antrittsvorlesung" (Geneva, unpublished, 1932) (HJM-B110, Library of Congress), esp. 4–6. On the Morgenthau–Kelsen nexus, see Niels Amstrup, "The 'Early' Morgenthau: A Comment

on the Intellectual Origins of Realism," *Cooperation and Conflict*, 3 (1978), 163–75; G. O. Mazur, "Confirming the Geopolitics of Primitive Law," in Mazur (ed.), *One Hundred Year Commemoration to the Life of Hans Morgenthau* (New York: Semenenko Foundation, 2004), 237–51. Morgenthau's biographer reports that he was fascinated by Friedrich Meinecke's *Machiavellism: The Doctrine of Raison d'Etat and its Place in Modern History* (New York: Praeger, 1965) when it first appeared in German in 1925 (see Frei, *Hans J. Morgenthau: An Intellectual Biography*, 122–3). As we will see in chapter 2, however, Morgenthau in fact was critical of what he deemed the one-sided character of reason of state.

26 Hans J. Morgenthau, "Die Wirklichkeit des Völkerbunds," *Neue Zürcher Zeitung* (April 2, 1933), 3.

27 See, for example, Franz L. Neumann, "The Change in the Function of Law," in William E. Scheuerman (ed.), *The Rule of Law Under Siege: Selected Essays of Franz L. Neumann and Otto Kirchheimer* (Berkeley: University of California Press, 1996), 101–41.

28 Morgenthau, "Fragment of an Intellectual Autobiography," 13.

29 *IRWG*, esp. 2, 14, 89–90, 98–130. Koskenniemi obscures this traditionalistic element of Morgenthau's thinking by attributing legal "anti-formalism" to him (Koskenniemi, *Gentle Civilizer of Nations*, 459).

30 Morgenthau also echoed his teacher's ideas about the autonomous (i.e., non-statist) origins of labor law, according to which legal regulation first emerged among non-state actors. Morgenthau argued against those who directly linked the concept of international jurisdiction to the sovereign state, noting that international juridical and arbitral bodies operated with some effectiveness despite the *lack* of a shared sovereign (*IRWG*, 17–19). In a crucial 1940 article, he also criticized the mainstream of international lawyers for succumbing to a "monistic statism" that leads them unduly to see international law in terms of the express written law of the state, according to which the only valid rules are those found in court decisions and formally ratified treaties. However, "all rules embodied in written documents are not valid international law, and, on the other hand, there are valid rules . . . other than the rules embodied in written documents" ("PFIL," 265).

31 Hans J. Morgenthau, "Stresemann als Schöpfer der deutschen Völkerrechtspolitik," *Die Justiz*, 5 (1929/30), 169–76.

32 Morgenthau, "Stresemann," 172.

33 Hans J. Morgenthau, "Die Völkerrechtlichen Ergebnisse der Tagung der deutschen Gesellschaft für Völkerrecht," *Die Justiz*, 4 (1929), 621–4.

34 Hans J. Morgenthau, "Der Selbstmord mit gutem Gewissen. Zur Kritik des Pazifismus und der neuen deutschen Kriegsphilosophie" (Frankfurt, unpublished ms., 1931) (HJM-B96, Library of Congress). The manuscript – which includes a detailed critique of both prewar

German pacifism and the "new bellicose philosophy" of Ernst Jünger – was submitted unsuccessfully for publication to the major German publisher Rowohlt. Morgenthau's critique of pacifism was biting yet in some crucial respects sympathetic: "old" prewar or traditional pacifism had failed miserably and should be jettisoned for a new (i.e., more realistic) theory and practice that might prove more successful at warding off the horrors of war.

35 "Bernard Johnson's Interview with Hans J. Morgenthau," 352–5.

36 Francis Anthony Boyle, *World Politics and International Law* (Durham, NC: Duke University Press, 1985), 12. The article in question appeared in *AJIL*, 34 (1940), 260–84. It brings together many of Morgenthau's key ideas from the prewar period. Morgenthau applied this theoretical framework to debates about neutrality in "The Problem of Neutrality," *University of Kansas City Law Review*, 7 (1939), 109–28.

37 They typically built on Karl Renner's influential ideas about the "functional transformation of private law" in *The Institutions of Private Law and Their Social Functions*, which was originally published in German in 1929.

38 Hans Kelsen, *Reine Rechtslehre* (Darmstadt: Scientia Verlag 1985 [1934]). Morgenthau's critique of Kelsen mirrored that of other members of the Sinzheimer circle.

39 Morgenthau, *La Réalité des normes, en particulier des norms du droit international* (Paris: Felix Alcan, 1934).

40 In "The Machiavellian Utopia" (*Ethics*, 55, 2 [1945]), Morgenthau criticized Kelsen's pure theory for missing the fact that "at the basis of the legal order there is a moral order" (147).

41 The method of immanent critique looms large in various forms of social criticism. For a general discussion, see Michael Walzer, *The Company of Critics: Social Criticism and Political Commitment in the Twentieth Century* (New York: Basic Books, 1988). On its role within recent critical theory, see Seyla Benhabib, *Critique, Norm, and Utopia: A Study of the Foundations of Critical Theory* (New York: Columbia University Press, 1986).

42 Justin Rosenberg, *The Empire of Civil Society: A Critique of the Realist Theory of International Relations* (London: Verso, 1994), 13. In his early writings, Morgenthau frequently cited Max Huber's *Die Soziologischen Grundlagen des Völkerrechts* (Berlin: Rothschild, 1928) as an exemplar of the sociological or realistic approach to international law. Much of Huber's study was devoted to an analysis of the impact of economic factors on the operations of law.

43 There is now a significant cottage industry on Morgenthau's relationship to Schmitt. See Scheuerman, *Carl Schmitt: The End of Law* (Lanham, Md.: Rowman & Littlefield, 1999), 225–52; Scheuerman, "Carl Schmitt and Hans Morgenthau: Realism and Beyond," in Michael C. Williams (ed.), *Realism Reconsidered: The Legacy of Hans J. Morgenthau in International Relations* (Oxford: Oxford University Press, 2007), 62–92; and also

Chris Brown, "'The Twilight of International Morality'? Hans J. Morgenthau and Carl Schmitt on the End of the *Jus Publicum Europaeum*," in Williams (ed.), *Realism Reconsidered*, 42–61; Koskenniemi, *Gentle Civilizer of Nations*, 413–509; Karl-Heinz Pichler, "The Godfathers of 'Truth': Max Weber and Carl Schmitt in Morgenthau's Theory of Power Politics," *Review of International Studies*, 24 (1997), 185–200. In both "Fragment of an Intellectual Autobiography" and "Bernard Johnson's Interview with Hans J. Morgenthau," Morgenthau speaks at great length about his Weimar-era conversation with Schmitt. However, Oliver Jütersonke is absolutely right to warn against overstating Schmitt's impact on Morgenthau, a mistake which I committed in some earlier publications (see Jütersonke, "The Image of Law in *Politics Among Nations*," in Williams (ed.), *Realism Reconsidered*, pp. 93–117).

44 On Schmitt's theory of international politics, see Scheuerman, *Carl Schmitt: The End of Law*, 141–74.

45 Morgenthau, "Stresemann," 176.

46 Carl Schmitt, "Der Begriff des Politischen," *Archiv für Sozialwissenschaft und Sozialpolitik*, 58 (1927), 1–33.

47 Morgenthau, "Fragment of an Intellectual Autobiography," 16.

48 Schmitt, *The Concept of the Political*, trans. George Schwab (New Brunswick: Rutgers University Press, 1976 [1932]).

49 Morgenthau, "Fragment of an Intellectual Autobiography," 16.

50 Comparing Schmitt to the infamous Nazi anti-semite Julius Streicher, Morgenthau asserted that under the Nazis he would try to become the "Streicher of the legal profession" (Morgenthau, "Fragment of an Intellectual Autobiography," 15–16).

51 Morgenthau, "Genfer Antrittsvorlesung," 23–7.

52 Morgenthau, *La Notion du "politique" et la théorie des différends internationaux*. The Library of Congress Hans J. Morgenthau Papers also include a number of fragmentary texts from this period focusing on Schmitt.

53 Hans J. Morgenthau, "Die Krise der metaphysischen Ethik von Kant bis Nietzsche" (Geneva, unpublished manuscript, 1935) (HJM-B112, Library of Congress).

54 He describes the 1933 *La Notion du "politique" et la théorie des différends internationaux*, for example, as a "sociological" contribution meant to deepen the analysis provided by his earlier 1929 study. Yet its main novelty, at least in terms of Morgenthau's own theoretical development, probably lies in its extended reflections about "the political." In this prewar work, as in many others, the crucial fact of social life is politics, and thus his discussion of the complex facticity of social power ultimately takes the form of an analysis of "the political."

55 See Helmuth Plessner, *Macht und menschliche Natur. Ein Versuch zur Anthropologie der geschichtlichen Weltansicht* (Berlin: Junker und Duennhaupt, 1931), which was similarly fascinated with Schmitt's concept of the political.

56 Morgenthau's early engagement with Freud was another product of the eventful years in liberal-minded Frankfurt, where, in contrast to many other German cities and universities, Freud was taken quite seriously. He describes his early interest in Freud in "Fragment of an Intellectual Autobiography," 13–14. While at Frankfurt, Morgenthau may have encountered the young Erich Fromm, who lectured at the Institute for Social Research in the late 1920s and 1930s. Fromm, like Morgenthau, was preoccupied with understanding what he also described as a psychologically rooted "lust for power" (see, for example, *Escape from Freedom* [New York: Henry Holt, 1969 (1941)], 4), and, at least for a period of time, the young Morgenthau, like Fromm, hoped to build on Freud to explain its origins. See especially "Über die Herkunft des Politischen aus dem Wesen der Menschen" (Frankfurt, 1931, unpublished, HJM-B151, Library of Congress), where Morgenthau tried to construct a Freud-inspired political theory. Many years later, Morgenthau attacked Fromm's reflections on warfare as resting on a crude "psychologism" ("Comment on War Within Man," in Erich Fromm, *War Within Man: A Psychological Enquiry Into the Roots of Destructiveness* [Washington, DC: American Friends Service Committee, 1963), 34–5. On Morgenthau's debts to Freud, see Robert Schuett, "Freudian Roots of Political Realism: The Importance of Sigmund Freud to Hans J. Morgenthau's Theory of International Politics," *History of the Human Sciences*, 20 (2007), 53–78.
57 Morgenthau, "Der Selbstmord mit gutem Gewissen," 44–6. Morgenthau's argument on this point anticipates some elements of Danilo Zolo's "weak pacifism" as described in *Cosmopolis*, 146–63.
58 As Koskenniemi accurately points out, Morgenthau's early works describe the political as a sociological fact: "But '[w]hat is common to such sociological facts is that they all have their basis, as a psychological factor, in the will to power' . . . Facts about states, too, are ultimately determined by the psychology of individuals. In social life the principle of desire is translated into the lust for power" constitutive of political experience (*Gentle Civilizer of Nations*, 454). The translated passage comes from *La Notion du "politique" et la théorie des différends internationaux*, 43. Political conflict is best understood, it appears, on the basis of the deep psychological drives generating it.
59 For an example of the former, see Kenneth Waltz, *Man, the State, and War* (New York: Columbia University, 1954). For the latter, Annette Freyberg-Inan, *What Moves Man: The Realist Theory of International Relations and Its Judgment of Human Nature* (Albany, NY: SUNY Press, 2004), 63–90.
60 Schmitt, *Concept of the Political*, 35.
61 Heinrich Meier, *Carl Schmitt and Leo Strauss: The Hidden Dialogue* (Chicago: University of Chicago Press, 1985), 41. Meier sees overlap between Schmitt and Strauss on this point.

Chapter 2　Morality, power, and tragedy

1　The volume grew out of a lecture given at the New School in New York, in the summer of 1940, immediately following France's defeat. Some sections were also presented originally as lectures given in 1944 at the University of Chicago.

2　Jerome Frank, "Review of *Scientific Man vs. Power Politics*," *University of Chicago Law Review*, 15 (1948), 462–78; Sidney Hook, "The Philosophic Scene: Scientific Method on the Defensive," *Commentary*, 1 (1945), 85–90; Ernest Nagel, "Review of *Scientific Man vs. Power Polities*," *Yale Law Journal*, 56 (1947), 906–9; Michael Oakeshott, "Scientific Politics," in Timothy Fuller (ed.), *Religion, Politics, and the Moral Life* (New Haven: Yale University Press, 1993). Oakeshott's review originally appeared in the *Cambridge Journal* in 1947. It initiated a respectful but spirited letter from Morgenthau to Oakeshott, where the former admitted that he may have failed to "make clear distinctions between rationalism and rational inquiry, scientism and science" (Morgenthau to Oakeshott, May 22, 1948, HJM-B44, Library of Congress). The Oakeshott–Morgenthau nexus is the basis of a thoughtful essay by Nicholas Rengger (see "Realism, Tragedy and the Anti-Pelagian Imagination in International Political Thought," in Williams (ed.), *Realism Reconsidered*, 118–36.

3　Richard Ned Lebow, *The Tragic Vision of Politics*, 216.

4　The end of the Second World War unleashed an impressive but somewhat naïve movement of "one-worlders" in favor of world government (see Lawrence Wittner, *One World or None: A History of the World Nuclear Disarmament Movement Through 1953* [Stanford: Stanford University Press, 1993]). This context is important for interpreting Morgenthau's harsh comments about global reform. Unfortunately, his polemics masked the complexity of his own ideas as well as the fact that he actually endorsed the notion of a world state (see chapter 4 below).

5　Karl Popper directed this criticism against Morgenthau without justifying it (see *Conjectures and Refutations: The Growth of Scientific Knowledge* [New York: Basic Books, 1962], 340).

6　See, for example, Morgenthau, "The Revival of Objective Standards: Walter Lippmann" [1955], in *DDP*, 380–1.

7　Morgenthau became a close friend of Arendt's, traveling abroad with her and perhaps even at one juncture hoping to marry her. Most importantly, they shared ideas over the course of many years. Perhaps one basis of their intellectual friendship was a shared interest, despite the vast differences separating them, in salvaging political action in a world both felt was increasingly hostile to it. See Morgenthau's eloquent eulogy to Arendt in *Political Theory*, 4 (1976), 5–8, as well as his article "Hannah Arendt on Totalitarianism and Democracy," *Social Research*, 44 (1977), 127–31.

8   An expanded edition is now available from Princeton University Press (2004).

9   The many writings of Chantal Mouffe are revealing in this context.

10 When later asked to list his favorite books, he mentioned Arendt's *The Human Condition* (Chicago: University of Chicago Press, 1958).

11 Morgenthau also listed Nietzsche alongside Mussolini and Hitler as someone who embraced "unrestrained manifestations" of the will to power (*PAN*, 2nd edn., 206). In a 1945 essay, Morgenthau also remarked critically about Nietzsche that he "hid his morbidity and despair behind the mask of affected brutality" (see "The Political Philosophy of Prussianism," in *DDP*, 221). Unfortunately, Frei's (see *Hans J. Morgenthau: An Intellectual Biography*) otherwise creative attempt to underscore Morgenthau's Nietzschean theoretical impulses ignores such comments. Even more fundamentally, it obfuscates the fact that Morgenthau, unlike Nietzsche, was in many respects a defender of key traditional moral ideas, and that he never embraced an unfettered "will to power." Morgenthau clearly rejected Nietzsche's reading of Christianity, liberalism, democracy, and socialism as "slave moralities." As a young student, he may have been fascinated by Nietzsche, but his political ethics – and international political theory as a whole – abandoned Nietzsche. Note also his 1958 "Introduction" to *DP*, where he lists Nietzsche alongside Kierkegaard, Marx, and Freud as thinkers who "attacked . . . the very foundations of Western civilization," thereby leaving "the received systems of thought empty of content and, in any event, without conviction" (3). Although acknowledging that the intellectual revolution wrought by Nietzsche and others cannot be reversed, Morgenthau speaks of the "need for the restoration" of the "timeless elements" of the western moral and political tradition. Characteristically, here as well he seems to acknowledge that they cannot be justified any longer by traditionalistic appeals to religion, metaphysics, or natural law. Consequently, any political theory which tries to salvage what is best of the western tradition without being able to appeal to conventional forms of justification inevitably leaves us with results that are necessarily "tentative and fragmentary" (4).

12 Morgenthau, "National Socialist Doctrine of World Organization" [1941], in *DDP*, 245.

13 Carl Schmitt, "The Age of Neutralizations and Depoliticizations," trans. John P. McCormick and Matthias Konzett, *Telos*, 96 (1993), 119–30.

14 Schmitt, "The Age of Neutralizations and Depoliticizations," 138.

15 Hans J. Morgenthau, "Diplomacy," *Yale Law Journal*, 55 (1946), 1078.

16 See chapter 6 below.

17 Hans J. Morgenthau, "Military Displacement of Politics" [1952; 1955], in *DDP*, 337–8. In later years, Abraham Lincoln played the role of an

exemplary statesman in Morgenthau's writings. See (the unfinished) "The Mind of Abraham Lincoln: A Study in Detachment and Practicality," in Kenneth Thompson (ed.), *Essays on Lincoln's Faith and Politics* (Lanham, Md.: University Press, 1983), 3–101.

18 Michael W. Doyle, *Ways of War and Peace* (New York: Norton, 1997), 106. Anatol Lieven and John Hulsman read Morgenthau as an "ethical realist" as well (see *Ethical Realism: A Vision For America's Role in the World* [New York: Pantheon, 2006]).

19 Hans J. Morgenthau, "The Scientific Solution of Social Conflicts," in Lyman Bryson, Louis Finkelstein, and Robert MacIver (eds.), *Approaches to National Unity* (New York: Harper & Bros., 1945), 437.

20 Hans J. Morgenthau, "The Moral Dilemmas of Political Action" [1950], in *DDP*, 253.

21 Morgenthau, "Dilemmas of Political Action," 247.

22 Morgenthau, "Dilemmas of Political Action," 249. Morgenthau was by no means the only postwar US intellectual who, traumatized by the 1930s and 1940s, aspired to develop a "realistic" version of liberalism equipped with an appropriate sense of tragedy (see Ira Katznelson, *Desolation and Enlightenment: Political Knowledge After Total War, Totalitarianism, and the Holocaust* [New York: Columbia University Press, 2003]).

23 Morgenthau, "Diplomacy," 1080.

24 Freyberg-Inan, *What Moves Man*, 71.

25 Hans J. Morgenthau, "Christian Ethics and Political Action" [1960], in *DDP*, 375.

26 Morgenthau, "Christian Ethics and Political Action," 376.

27 Morgenthau, "Christian Ethics and Political Action," 376.

28 Hans J. Morgenthau, "The Political Science of E. H. Carr," *World Politics*, 1 (1948), 128.

29 Morgenthau, "Political Science of E. H. Carr," 134.

30 Morgenthau, "Political Science of E. H. Carr," 133.

31 Morgenthau deeply admired Niebuhr, whom he generously praised on many occasions. See, in particular, Hans J. Morgenthau, "Niebuhr's Political Thought," in Harold R. Langdon (ed.), *Reinhold Niebuhr: A Prophetic Voice in our Time* (Greenwich, Conn.: Seabury, 1962), 99–109, where Morgenthau declared that "I have always considered Reinhold Niebuhr the greatest living political philosopher of America" (109). Morgenthau's essay points to parallels between Niebuhr's thinking and his own. The unpublished correspondence between them is revealing on this score as well. For example, Morgenthau in 1970 responded to an earlier letter from Niebuhr by stating that "you raise the question 'whether all my insights are not borrowed from Hans Morgenthau.' I have asked myself the same question with reference to you, and I am sure I have by far the better of the argument" (Hans J. Morgenthau to Reinhold Niebuhr, November 13, 1970, HJM-B44, Library of Congress). Morgenthau seems to have believed that he

could endorse many of the chief points of Niebuhr's religiously based political theory, thereby preserving Niebuhr's healthy respect for a rigorous model of morality, *without* holding onto Niebuhr's theological banisters. Like Morgenthau, Reinhold was an ex-leftist who by the 1940s was increasingly skeptical of his previous socialist dreams. Yet what he arguably preserved, like Morgenthau, was an abiding faith in the centrality of a rigorous model of morality as a necessary feature of political action, along with a hard-headed view of politics as inevitably agonistic and conflict-laden. Both also maintained deep sympathies for a left-liberal domestic reform agenda. For an excellent discussion of Niebuhr and his development, see Richard Wightman Fox, *Reinhold Niebuhr* (Ithaca: Cornell University Press, 1985). On Morgenthau and Niebuhr, see R. L. Shinn, "The Continuing Conversation Between Hans Morgenthau and Reinhold Niebuhr," in Mazur (ed.), *One Hundred Year Commemoration to the Life of Hans Morgenthau*, 65–87.

32 Morgenthau never offers a systematic discussion of either philosopher, despite their obvious importance to his thinking here. Interestingly, Morgenthau's teacher, Sinzheimer, was influenced by German-speaking Kantian socialists, for whom Kant's idea of humankind as an "end in itself" provided a moral signpost. The fact that Kant provides important inspiration to Morgenthau here suggests that he fits badly into the category of "classical Realism," in light of Realism's deep antipathy to Kant.

33 Even those sympathetic to Morgenthau noted that this vision of the moral life might be too demanding to permit a satisfactory model of political action. Niebuhr, for example, worried that it conceded "too much to the perfectionist versions of Christianity," which might erroneously lead the believer to "declare the responsibilities of the magistrate to be incompatible with the moral life." He suggested that Morgenthau's reading of Christianity reduced it to "the absolute demands of the Sermon on the Mount." Even "self-righteous idealists such as William Gladstone and Woodrow Wilson" deserved credit for struggling "in some degree [to] handle power, responsibility, and interest in some community or another." Morgenthau, of course, was far less conciliatory towards such "self-righteous idealists." See Niebuhr, "Response," in Harold R. Langdon (ed.), *Reinhold Niebuhr: A Prophetic Voice in our Time* (Greenwich, Conn.: Seabury, 1962), 121–2.

34 M. Benjamin Mollov, *Power and Transcendence: Hans J. Morgenthau and the Jewish Experience* (Lanham, Md.: Lexington, 2002).

35 Hans J. Morgenthau, "The Rediscovery of Imagination and Religion: Arnold Toynbee" [1955], in *DDP*, p. 374.

36 Morgenthau, "The Rediscovery of Imagination and Religion: Arnold Toynbee," 374. See also the transcript of a discussion with Morgenthau at the Council for Religion and Foreign Affairs, in which he asserted

that he could not "postulate a plausible moral code without a theological foundation" (Morgenthau, *Human Rights and Foreign Policy* [New York: Council on Religion and International Affairs, 1979], 10).

37 Morgenthau, "On Trying to be Just," *Commentary*, 35 (1963), 420–3; also, "Justice and Power," *Social Research*, 41 (1974), 164–75.

38 Morgenthau first encountered Weber's ideas as a young student in a seminar taught by Karl Rothenbücher at the University of Munich during 1926–7. Many commentators have rightly emphasized Weber's influence on Morgenthau (see, for example, Stephen Turner and Regis Factor, *Max Weber and the Dispute Over Reason and Value: A Study in Philosophy, Ethics, and Politics* [London: Routledge, 1984]). Morgenthau himself tended to emphasize Weber's influence (see, for example, "Fragment of an Intellectual Autobiography," 7). Nonetheless, it would be mistaken then to underplay the role of others – e.g. Kelsen, Schmitt, or Sinzheimer – in direct response to whom Morgenthau's international theory first emerged. The best recent discussion of Morgenthau's relationship to Weber is probably Stephen Turner's "Morgenthau as a Weberian," in Mazur (ed.), *One Hundred Year Commemoration to the Life of Hans Morgenthau*, 88–114. Turner is also right to underscore the Weberian core of Morgenthau's vision of the social sciences ("Morgenthau as a Weberian Methodologist," *European Journal of International Relations* [forthcoming]).

39 Freyberg-Inan, *What Moves Man*, 103.

40 See also Morgenthau, "Scientific Solution of Social Conflicts," 431.

41 The classic attempt to interpret Realism in this fashion probably remains Martin Wight, *International Theory: The Three Traditions* (New York: Holmes & Meier, 1992).

42 Hans J. Morgenthau, "About Cynicism, Perfectionism, and Realism in International Affairs" [1945], in *DDP*, 128.

43 Morgenthau, "About Cynicism, Perfectionism, and Realism in International Affairs," 130.

44 Morgenthau, "The Machiavellian Utopia," 145. Recent Realists tend to overlook this version of Morgenthau's critique of the United Nations, instead selectively relying on his ideas to criticize the UN's defenders for closing their eyes to many ways in which it reproduces a traditional quest to institutionalize the hegemonic status of a handful of great powers (see, for example, Zolo, *Cosmopolis*, 8).

45 John Mearsheimer, *The Tragedy of Great Power Politics* (New York: Norton, 2001), 365.

46 Mearsheimer, *The Tragedy of Great Power Politics*, 365.

47 Hans J. Morgenthau, "The Problem of Sovereignty Reconsidered," *Columbia Law Review*, 48 (1948), 364. Morgenthau, by the way, generally considered the United States to be a nation state, though he acknowledged many of its distinct attributes.

48 Hans J. Morgenthau, "Nationalism" [1957], in *DDP*, 187.

49 Hans J. Morgenthau, "The Twilight of International Morality," *Ethics*, 58 (1948), 82. Note the early usage of the term "national interest" here, where policy makers are actually praised for overriding it.
50 Morgenthau, "Twilight of International Morality," 87.
51 Morgenthau, "Twilight of International Morality," 96.

Chapter 3   Defending the national interest

1 Both cited in Hans J. Morgenthau, "The Conquest of the United States by Germany," *Bulletin of the Atomic Scientists*, 6 (1950), 21–2.
2 Morgenthau, "Conquest of the United States by Germany," 24.
3 Morgenthau, "Conquest of the United States by Germany," 23.
4 For useful surveys of this period in Morgenthau's thought, see Michael Cox, "Hans J. Morgenthau, Realism, and the Rise and Fall of the Cold War," in Williams (ed.), *Realism Reconsidered*, 166–94; Craig, *Glimmer of a New Leviathan*, 54–73, 93–116; Jaap W. Nobel, "Morgenthau's Struggle with Power: The Theory of Power Politics and the Cold War," *Review of International Studies*, 21 (1995), 61–85; Smith, *Realist Thought from Weber to Kissinger*, 134–64.
5 Morgenthau, "Conquest of the United States by Germany," 25.
6 Morgenthau, "Power Politics," in Freda Kirchway (ed.), *The Atomic Era – Can It Bring Peace and Abundance?* (New York: Medill McBride, 1950), 37.
7 Morgenthau, "Conquest of the United States by Germany," 25.
8 Morgenthau, "Power Politics," 36. With the advantages of hindsight, it might seem attractive to deem this position as overstated. If one recalls that the cold war very nearly did become "hot" on many occasions, however, Morgenthau's worries remain sound. We probably survived the cold war because of luck and contingencies to a greater extent than it is now fashionable to admit.
9 Hans J. Morgenthau, "The H-Bomb and After" [1950], in *RAP*, 120, 126–7.
10 Morgenthau, "The H-Bomb and After," 127.
11 See especially Hans J. Morgenthau, "On Negotiating With the Russians," *Bulletin of the Atomic Scientists* 6 (May 1950, 143–8; "The Case for Negotiation: History's Lesson," *Nation* (December 16, 1950), 587–91. Much of the argument was then reproduced in *IDNI*, along with the appeals by Toynbee, Churchill, and the Vatican. See also Morgenthau, "The Lessons of World War II's Mistakes," *Commentary*, 14 (1952), 326–33. Morgenthau's account of the Russians oscillated, however, at times stressing the ideological attributes of Soviet communism over the traditional pursuit of regional hegemony especially in Eastern Europe (see Smith, *Realist Thought from Weber to Kissinger*, 152–3). For reasons I outline later in this chapter, this tension may have been generated by the ambiguities of Morgenthau's own concept of the

national interest, which necessarily rested on controversial political values and norms to a greater degree than he typically conceded.

12 Morgenthau, "The H-Bomb and After," 127.

13 On his domestic political preferences, see, for example, *IDNI*, 80–1. The more alarmist contours of some of Morgenthau's comments in the 1950s about the Soviet build-up suggest that he may have succumbed to the overestimations of Soviet military prowess that were commonplace during the cold war. See Richard Rhodes, *Arsenals of Folly: The Making of the Nuclear Arms Race* (New York: Alfred Knopf, 2007).

14 Morgenthau, "Power Politics," 38.

15 Morgenthau, 'Power Politics," 49.

16 Writing in 1950, Morgenthau was already skeptical that much could be gained as far as Eastern Europe was concerned: "As concerns the satellites, they are already integrated . . . and they slipped from our hands long ago" (Morgenthau, "On Negotiating With the Russians," 147). The one possible exception was Yugoslavia. Morgenthau believed that it was the "moralistic" and "legalistic" foreign policy of the Americans that played a decisive role in permitting postwar Russian hegemony in Eastern Europe in the first place.

17 See chapter 6 below.

18 In "The Revolution We are Living Through" [1955], he called for the West to engage "in the active support of indigenous revolutionary movements" in the developing world (*IAFP*, 250).

19 Hans J. Morgenthau, "Should We Negotiate Now?" [1958] and "Krushchev's New Cold War Strategy" [1959], both in *IAFP*, 168–92.

20 A. J. P Taylor, "No Illusions and No Ideas," *Nation* (September 8, 1951), 196–7.

21 Raymond Aron, "En quête d'une philosophie de la politique étrangère," *Revue Française de Science Politique*, 3 (1953), 81–3.

22 Hans J. Morgenthau, "The Revolution in United States Foreign Policy" [1957], in *IAFP*, 41.

23 Hans J. Morgenthau, "The Policy of the U.S.A.," *Political Quarterly*, 22 (1951), 56.

24 Hans J. Morgenthau, "National Interest and Moral Principles in Foreign Policy: The Primacy of the National Interest," *American Scholar*, 18 (1949), 210. The concept of the "national interest" first takes on a special analytic status in this essay. The term "Realism" is reintroduced and redefined in publications from 1950 and 1951, including a co-edited (with Kenneth W. Thompson) volume, *Principles and Problems of International Politics* (New York: Alfred Knopf, 1950), in which the soon-familiar distinction between Idealist and Realist theories was first employed in a systematic fashion. The volume included excerpts from classical and recent writings in international thought and the social sciences, as well as political speeches and policy statements; it was intended to demonstrate the superiority of the Realist approach.

The Idealist/Realist contraposing was soon employed by a famous colleague at Chicago, Leo Strauss, who praised the "idealism" of classical natural right (as articulated by Plato, Aristotle, and Aquinas) in opposition to what he considered to be the decadent but "realistic" approach of modern natural right, as formulated by Hobbes and other modern thinkers. Hobbes' "realistic" method, Strauss argued, forced him "to lift all restrictions on the striving for unnecessary sensual pleasures or, more precisely . . . for power." The dangerous consequences were that "reason of state" inexorably replaced the noble classical quest for what Strauss described as "the best regime" (see *Natural Right and History* [Chicago: University of Chicago Press, 1953], 189; also 191). Although ignored by most scholarship, Strauss can easily be read as undertaking to respond to Morgenthau's 1950s resuscitation of Realism. Morgenthau, by the way, reportedly helped bring Strauss to Chicago. Not surprisingly, in light of their many intellectual and political differences, they soon fell out over a variety of matters.

25 Hans J. Morgenthau, "Another 'Great Debate': The National Interest of the United States," in Harold Karan Jacobson (ed.), *America's Foreign Policy* (New York: Random House, 1965), 119. The article appeared originally in the *American Political Science Review* (1952).

26 Morgenthau, "Another Great Debate," 125.

27 Morgenthau, "Another Great Debate," 119. See chapter 4 below.

28 Kenneth W. Thompson, *Political Realism and the Crisis of World Politics* (Princeton: Princeton University Press, 1960), 36.

29 Morgenthau, "Another Great Debate," 119–20.

30 Morgenthau, "Another Great Debate," 119.

31 For example, when he identified the national interest with an unchanging set of interests (see, for example, Morgenthau, "Commitments of a Theory of International Politics" [1959], in *DDP*, 58).

32 Morgenthau, "Another Great Debate," 118.

33 Morgenthau, "Another Great Debate," 119.

34 Morgenthau, "What is the National Interest of the United States?" *Annals of the American Academy of Political and Social Science*, 282 (1952), 2.

35 See, for example, Morgenthau, "Another Great Debate," 132–3, where the USA is described as pursuing a more flexible foreign policy than the Soviet Union because of underlying ideological differences. Morgenthau's ambiguities on the status of norms and ideals in the composition of the national interest has provided an easy opening to critics on both the left and right. The constructivist theorist Alexander Wendt, for example, criticizes Realism for obscuring the extent to which the national interest is always constituted by ideas and norms (*Social Theory of International Politics* [Cambridge: Cambridge University Press, 1999], 113–15). Neoconservatives also accuse Morgenthau of ignoring political ideals and values, arguing that any idea of the

national interest must be linked to questions of political identity (see Michael C. Williams, "Morgenthau Now: Neoconservatism, National Greatness, and Realism," in Williams [ed.], *Realism Reconsidered*, 216–40).

36 Morgenthau, "Another Great Debate," 120.

37 Morgenthau, "Another Great Debate," 121.

38 Morgenthau, "Another Great Debate," 120.

39 Morgenthau, "Another Great Debate," 124.

40 Morgenthau, "The Yardstick of National Interest," *Annals of the American Academy of Political and Social Science*, 296 (1954), 77–84.

41 Hans J. Morgenthau, "Diplomacy" [1956], in *RAP*, 198–208.

42 Smith, *Realist Theory from Weber to Kissinger*, 160.

43 Robert W. Tucker, "Professor Morgenthau's Theory of Political 'Realism,'" *American Political Science Review*, 46 (1952), 217. Raymond Aron noted the same tension in Morgenthau's thinking in his mammoth *Peace and War: A Theory of International Relations* (New York: Doubleday, 1966), 598–600. Aron was often a perceptive critic of Morgenthau; at other times, his discussions were disappointingly heavy-handed. The same, unfortunately, may be said of Morgenthau's comments about Aron's far-flung writings. In a piece from this period (see "Foreign Policy: The Conservative School," *World Politics*, 7 [1955], 284–6), for example, Morgenthau described Aron's work as fragmentary, impressionistic, and unsystematic.

44 See especially Morgenthau, "What is the National Interest of the United States?" 6–7.

45 Smith, *Realist Theory from Weber to Kissinger*, 160.

46 See especially Hans J. Morgenthau, *Purpose of American Politics* (New York: Alfred Knopf, 1960).

47 Morgenthau, "The Lessons of World War II's Mistakes," 328.

48 For an excellent critical discussion of Niebuhr's dualism and, by implication, Morgenthau's (whose *Scientific Man*, the author rightly noted, "bears the imprint of Niebuhr's influence" [p. 168]), see Kenneth Thompson, "Beyond National Interest: A Critical Evaluation of Reinhold Niebuhr's Theory of International Politics," *Review of Politics*, 17 (1955), 167–88. Useful as well is Robert C. Good, "The National Interest and Political Realism: Niebuhr's 'Debate' with Morgenthau and Kennan," *Journal of Politics*, 22 (1960), 597–619.

49 Wilson D. Miscamble, *George F. Kennan and the Making of American Foreign Policy, 1947–50* (Princeton: Princeton University Press, 1992). For Morgenthau's own reminiscences, see "Bernard Johnson's Interview with Hans J. Morgenthau," 372–4. With the installation of the Eisenhower Administration, Morgenthau's consulting duties came to an end. Craig exaggerates Morgenthau's role in policy making when he claims that Morgenthau shaped US cold war policy "like perhaps no other American intellectual of his day" (Craig, *Glimmer of a New Leviathan*, 59). With the exception of the brief interlude as an advisor

to Kennan, Morgenthau was pretty much an outsider to Washington policy making, though he certainly desired a greater role in it. Even when working with Kennan, his views seem to have been pretty much ignored. Most of Morgenthau's political writing in the 1950s and 1960s for liberal journals like the *Bulletin of the Atomic Scientists, Commentary*, the *New Republic*, and the *New York Times Sunday Magazine* in fact consisted of attacks on most major development in US foreign policy. He was uncomfortable even with Kennan's relatively modest formulation of containment policy, criticizing it in a review of the latter's *American Diplomacy: 1900–1950* (see Morgenthau, "American Diplomacy: The Dangers of Righteousness," *New Republic* [October 22, 1951], 117–19). It is inaccurate to place Morgenthau among a group of sage "bipartisan" political analysts who helped to develop US cold war foreign policy, as Anatol Lieven and John Hulsman misleadingly assert in *Ethical Realism: A Vision for America's Role*. After Dean Acheson was fired as Secretary of State by Eisenhower, Morgenthau became friendly with Acheson, working closely with him in the late 1950s to begin articulating an alternative set of foreign policies for a Democratic "opposition" which both men believed to be very much in need of one (see Douglas Brinkley, *Dean Acheson: The Cold War Years* [New Haven: Yale University Press, 1992], 57, 105; David S. McLellan and David C. Acheson (eds.), *Among Friends: Personal Letters of Dean Acheson* [New York; Dodd, Mead & Co., 1980], 121–2). In Morgenthau's generally appreciative remarks about Acheson, he was depicted as a Realist at heart but unable – because of the US political climate – consistently to pursue Realist policies.

50 Hans J. Morgenthau, "The Moral Dilemma in Foreign Policy," in *Year Book of World Affairs 1951* (New York: Praeger, 1951), 14–15.
51 Hans J. Morgenthau, "The Mainsprings of American Foreign Policy: The National Interest vs. Moral Abstractions," *APSR*, 44 (1950), 854.
52 Hans J. Morgenthau, "Nationalism" [1957], in *DDP*, 181–95.
53 Morgenthau, "Another Great Debate," 136.
54 For Weber's discussion of both the ethics of conscience and the ethic of responsibility, see especially "The Profession and Vocation of Politics" [1919], in Max Weber, *Political Writings*, ed. Peter Lassman and Ronald Speirs (Cambridge: Cambridge University Press, 1994), 309–69.
55 Morgenthau, "National Interest and Moral Principles in Foreign Policy," 210.
56 Morgenthau, "Another Great Debate," 135.
57 Morgenthau, "National Interest and Moral Principles in American Foreign Policy," 210.
58 Morgenthau, "National Interest and Moral Principles in American Foreign Policy," 210–11.
59 Morgenthau, "National Interest and Moral Principles in American Foreign Policy," 211.
60 Morgenthau, "Another Great Debate," 136.

61 Weber, "The Nation State and Economic Policy" [1895], in *Political Writings*, 16. See also, for Weber's general position on Germany's overall role in international politics, "Between Two Laws" [1916], 75–9, in the same volume.

62 Morgenthau, "What is the National Interest of the United States?" 4.

63 Morgenthau, "The Mainsprings of American Foreign Policy: The National Interest vs. Moral Abstractions," 854.

64 The first commentator to identify the Hegelian overtones of the argument was probably George Lichtheim, *The Concept of Ideology and Other Essays* (New York: Random House, 1967), 143.

65 In short, Stanley Hoffmann was right on the mark when he observed that "Morgenthau's conviction that a realistic policy was also a moral one – that his map served as a normative as well as empirical theory – was particularly troublesome" (Hoffmann, *Janus and Minerva*, 72).

Chapter 4   Politics among nations and beyond

1 Frei, *Hans J. Morgenthau: An Intellectual Biography*, 73. The literature on *PAN* is vast, but see particularly the special issue of *International Studies Notes* (24, 1 [1999]) devoted to it, and the interesting essays by Kenneth Thompson, Thomas Walker, John Vasquez, and others.

2 For a provocative account of this trajectory, see Richard K. Ashley, "Political Realism and Human Interests," *International Studies Quarterly*, 25 (1981), 204–36.

3 See the various essays reprinted in *DDP*, 16–126.

4 Hannah Arendt later criticized this definition of power, clearly influenced by Weber, in *On Violence* (New York: Harcourt, Brace & Jovanovich, 1970).

5 Michael J. Smith has accurately observed that *PAN* mixed "ideal-type definition[s] and frankly practical advice" (*Realist Thought from Weber to Kissinger*, 143). In his political writings, Weber had done the same. As Sean Molloy has noted, "*Politics Among Nations* represents itself as offering a science of international politics. Yet this is not necessarily a science based on ... the natural sciences ... Morgenthau's understanding of theory as a scientific endeavor is in the sense of the *Geisteswissenschaften* of the German academy" (*The Hidden History of Realism* [New York: Palgrave, 2006], 148).

6 This theme was developed at length by John H. Herz, *International Politics in the Atomic Age* (New York: Columbia University Press, 1959).

7 Smith, *Realist Thought from Weber to Kissinger*, 142.

8 Smith, *Realist Thought from Weber to Kissinger*, 143.

9 Lebow, *The Tragic Vision of Politics*, 227.

10 John H. Herz, *The Nation-State and the Crisis of World Politics* (New York: David McKay, 1976).

11 Morgenthau did concede that the development of a substantial bloc of uncommitted or "non-aligned states" complicated this picture (*PAN*, 3rd edn., 351–5).

12 The phrase comes from Nicholas Wheeler's *Saving Strangers: Humanitarian Intervention in International Society* (Oxford: Oxford University Press, 2000), 24, where he contrasts the English School view of international law to Realism's. However, much of what he has to say about the English School also describes Morgenthau's ideas. In contrast to some present-day Realists, Morgenthau's view of international law was never crudely instrumentalist.

13 For examples of the communitarian and republican positions, see Richard Bellamy and Dario Castiglione, "Between Cosmopolis and Community: Three Models of Rights and Democracy within the European Union," in Daniele Archibugi, David Held, and Martin Köhler (eds.), *Re-Imagining Political Community: Studies in Cosmopolitan Democracy* (Stanford: Stanford University Press, 1998), 152–79. See also the debates collected usefully in Daniele Archibugi (ed.), *Debating Cosmopolis* (London: Verso, 2003).

14 Morgenthau thereby anticipated fundamental attributes of what more recent scholars have described as "globalization."

15 Hans J. Morgenthau, "Threat to – and Hope for – the United Nations" [1961], in *RAP*, 279.

16 Danilo Zolo, *Cosmopolis*, 8–9.

17 On Schmitt's views of international politics, see Scheuerman, *Carl Schmitt: The End of Law*, 141–74.

18 Hans J. Morgenthau, "What Can the United States Do to Strengthen the United Nations?" [1954], in *RAP*, 275. Morgenthau's ideas about the "new diplomacy" appeared as early as 1953, in his "Political Limitations of the United Nations," in George Lipskey (ed.), *Law and Politics in the World Community* (Berkeley: University of California Press, 1953), 151–2.

19 Morgenthau, "Threat to – and Hope for – the United Nations," in *RAP*, 282–4.

20 Hans J. Morgenthau, "The New United Nations and the Revision of the Charter," *Review of Politics*, 16 (1954), 18; also "Law, Politics, and the United Nations," *Commercial Law Journal*, 70 (1965), 121–4, 135; "The U.N. of Dag Hammarskjold is Dead," *New York Times Sunday Magazine* (March 14, 1965), 32–8.

21 Morgenthau, "The New United Nations and the Revision of the Charter," 19.

22 This reform demand, of course, is still widely voiced today.

23 See, for example, Mearsheimer, *The Tragedy of Great Power Politics*, xii.

24 Yet as Richard Little notes, there are many parallels between the English School of international relations (and writers like Hedley Bull), which famously underscored the importance of international

society, and Morgenthau. He is also right to observe that the "social element" of international relations underscored both by early Realists like Morgenthau and by the English School is "missing from modern American Realism" ("The English School vs. American Realism: A Meeting of Minds or Divided by a Common Language?" *Review of International Studies*, 29 [2003], 445).

25 This question has been pointedly raised by Jürgen Habermas in *The Divided West*, 132–5.

26 Craig goes too far, however, when he accuses Morgenthau of not having made any "serious attempt to show how such a world state might eventuate" (*Glimmer of a New Leviathan*, 132).

27 Some of these have been recognized as well by contemporary defenders of cosmopolitan global democracy. See, for example, Held, *Democracy and the Global Order*.

28 See the now classic discussion by James N. Rosenau, "Governance, Order, and Change in World Politics," in James N. Rosenau and Ernst-Otto Cziempiel (eds.), *Governance without Government: Order and Change in World Politics* (Cambridge: Cambridge University Press, 1992), 1–29.

29 Morgenthau excoriated the newly independent countries of the developing world for repeating the errors of European nationalism. See his "Nationalism" [1957], in *DDP*, 181–95.

30 James P. Speer, "Hans Morgenthau and the World State," *World Politics*, 20 (1968), 215.

31 Speer, "Hans Morgenthau and the World State," 222.

32 David Mitrany, *A Working Peace System: An Argument for the Functional Development of International Organization* (London: National Peace Council, 1946). Morgenthau wrote an enthusiastic introduction to a subsequent US edition (Chicago: Quadrangle Books, 1966) in which he declared that "the future of the civilized world is intimately tied to the future of the functional approach to international organization" (11). For a rare exception to the general tendency to ignore Morgenthau's debts to Mitrany, see David Fromkin, "Remembering Hans Morgenthau," *World Policy Journal*, 10 (1993), 81–8. When he first arrived in the USA, Morgenthau described his own preferred method as "functionalist." That usage, however, had little in common with Mitrany's, despite the subsequent alliance between the two authors.

33 For biographical details, see Cornelia Navari, "David Mitrany and International Functionalism," in David Long and Peter Wilson (eds.), *Thinkers of the Twenty Years' Crisis: Inter-War Idealism Reassessed* (Oxford: Clarendon Press, 1995), 214–31.

34 For instance, the New Dealers never tried to secure the welfare state by expressly amending the US Constitution.

35 Mitrany, *Working Peace System*, 6.

36 Mitrany, *Working Peace System*, 35.

37 Mitrany, *Working Peace System*, 11.

38 Mitrany, *Working Peace System*, 37.
39 Morgenthau mentioned a predecessor organization, the International Trade Organization (*PAN*, 2nd edn., 492).
40 Mearsheimer, *The Tragedy of Great Power Politics*, p. 366, where he declares, in the context of his discussion of European politics, and in striking contrast to Morgenthau's views, that "there is no good reason to think that the sovereign state's time has passed."
41 Mitrany is widely taken to be a forebear of an influential body of scholarship which applied his ideas to Europe. He expressed a number of reservations about this appropriation of his ideas by those who sought to advance European integration, however (Navari, "Mitrany and International Functionalism," 233).
42 Hans J. Morgenthau, "Four Designs for Tomorrow's Europe," *New York Times Sunday Magazine* (May 17, 1964), 18–20.
43 One can imagine Morgenthau endorsing the ideas of more recent Realist-inspired writers like Glyn Morgan, who argue that it is now time for the European Union to expand common defense and security policies and unambiguously take the form of a "superstate" (Morgan, *The Idea of a European Superstate: Public Justification and European Integration* [Princeton: Princeton University Press, 2005]).

Chapter 5 Utopian Realism and the bomb

1 Hans J. Morgenthau, "The Intellectual and Political Functions of a Theory of International Relations" [1961], in *DDP*, 77.
2 Morgenthau, "Functions of a Theory of International Relations," 76.
3 Morgenthau, "Functions of a Theory of International Relations," 76–7.
4 Morgenthau, "Functions of a Theory of International Relations," 78.
5 Craig, *Glimmer of a New Leviathan*, 132.
6 Morgenthau, "Power Politics" [1950], 37.
7 Robert Jervis, "Hans Morgenthau, Realism, and the Scientific Study of International Politics," *Social Research*, 61 (1994), 862. Morgenthau was not the only Realist theorist to rethink his ideas in the face of nuclear disaster, as Joel Rosenthal documents in his illuminating *Righteous Realists: Political Realism, Responsible Power, and American Culture in the Nuclear Age* (Baton Rouge: Louisiana University Press, 1991). Thomas L. Pangle and Peter J. Ahrensdorf also usefully discuss Morgenthau's reflections on nuclear war and the world state, but they discount his commitment to global reform by attributing their own (Straussian) anxieties about it to him (*Justice Among Nations: On the Moral Basis of Power and Peace* [Lawrence: University of Kansas Press, 1999], 236–8).
8 Morgenthau, "Power Politics," 37.
9 Hans J. Morgenthau, "Nationalism," in *DDP*, 189.

10 Morgenthau, "The H-Bomb and the Peace Outlook," in *The H-Bomb* (New York: Didier, 1950), 164.

11 Cox, "Hans J. Morgenthau, Realism, and the Rise and Fall of the Cold War," 174.

12 Hans J. Morgenthau, "Russian Technology and American Policy," *Current History*, 34 (1958), 130.

13 Smith, *Realist Thought from Weber to Kissinger*, 159. Morgenthau was disappointed by Kennedy's foreign policies, however. See "John F. Kennedy," in *TP*, 139–62. Flexible response emphasized the need for the USA to act effectively to counter aggression across the full spectrum of strategic, tactical, and conventional weaponry.

14 Hans J. Morgenthau, "The Decline of American Power" [1957], in *IAFP*, 50; also, "Russian Technology and American Policy," 132.

15 Hans J. Morgenthau, "Has Atomic War Really Become Impossible?" in *Bulletin of the Atomic Scientists*, 12 (January 1956), 8.

16 Morgenthau, "Has Atomic War Really Become Impossible?" 9.

17 Hans J. Morgenthau, "The Decline and Fall of American Foreign Policy," *New Republic* (December 10, 1956), 12.

18 Craig, *Glimmer of a New Leviathan*, 96–7.

19 Hans J. Morgenthau, "Will it Deter Aggression?" *New Republic* (March 29, 1954), 12.

20 Hans J. Morgenthau, "Atomic Force and Foreign Policy" [1957], in *RAP*, 158.

21 Morgenthau, "Atomic Force and Foreign Policy," 157.

22 Morgenthau, "Atomic Force and Foreign Policy," 158.

23 Morgenthau, "Atomic Force and Foreign Policy," 160.

24 Morgenthau, "Has Atomic War Really Become Impossible?" 8.

25 Craig, for example, misreads him as defending the possibility of a limited nuclear war (*Glimmer of a New Leviathan*, 97–101). Morgenthau toys with the possibility only in order to underscore why those foreign policies which might lead to it were fundamentally flawed.

26 Morgenthau, "Has Atomic War Really Become Impossible?" 9.

27 Morgenthau, "Atomic Force and Foreign Policy," 161.

28 Hans J. Morgenthau, "The Intellectual and Moral Dilemmas of Politics" [1960], in *DDP*, 12.

29 Hans J. Morgenthau, "Death in the Nuclear Age" [1961], in *RAP*, 25.

30 Hans J. Morgenthau, "The Nuclear Discussion: Continued," *Christianity and Crisis*, 21 (1961), 223.

31 The symposium featured Morgenthau as well as Sidney Hook, H. Stuart Hughes, and C. P. Snow, and appeared as "Western Values and Total War Symposium," *Commentary*, 32 (October 1961), 285.

32 Morgenthau, "Death in the Nuclear Age," 22.

33 See the similar argument made by Hannah Arendt in "Europe and the Atomic Bomb" [1954] in Jerome Kohn (ed.), *Essays in Understanding, 1930–54* (New York: Harcourt Brace, 1994), 418–22.

34 The term is appropriate since Morgenthau suggests (see "Death in the Nuclear Age," 23) that the nearest parallel to atomic warfare is the Nazi slaughter of millions of Jews. For a thought-provoking attempt to interpret the Holocaust as a forerunner to a prospective nuclear war, see Jonathan Schell, *The Unfinished Twentieth Century* (New York: Verso, 2003).

35 Morgenthau, "Death in the Nuclear Age," 23.

36 Morgenthau, "Death in the Nuclear Age," 24.

37 Morgenthau, "Death in the Nuclear Age," 23–4.

38 Morgenthau, "Death in the Nuclear Age," 23.

39 *Washington Post* (February 23, 1960), A16; *New York Times* (February 23, 1960), 30. The USA and USSR agreed to a limited nuclear test ban in 1963. The USA still has not ratified the Comprehensive Nuclear Test Ban, which has been signed by 177 countries.

40 "Letter from Hannah Arendt to Karl Jaspers, February 5, 1961," in *Arendt–Jaspers Correspondence, 1926–1969* (New York: Harcourt Brace, 1992), 421–2.

41 Hans J. Morgenthau, "An Atomic Philosophy," *Saturday Review* (February 18, 1961), 18–19.

42 Karl Jaspers, *The Future of Mankind*, (trans.) E. B. Ashton (Chicago: University of Chicago Press, 1961), 318. For a helpful survey of the book, see Gregory J. Walters, *Karl Jaspers and the Role of "Conversion" in the Nuclear Age* (Lanham, Md.: University Press, 1988).

43 Jaspers, *Future of Mankind*, 3.

44 Jaspers, *Future of Mankind*, 332.

45 Jaspers, *Future of Mankind*, 28, 250.

46 Jaspers, *Future of Mankind*, 335.

47 Jaspers, *Future of Mankind*, 4.

48 I rely here on a typescript of the lecture series, the Faith and Freedom Lectures, given at the American University in November 1961. Lecture 1 was entitled "The Nature of the Technological Revolution"; Lecture 2, "Politics in the Nuclear Age"; and Lecture 3, "Nuclear Power and Human Existence" ([HJM-171], Library of Congress). Morgenthau's correspondence also contains materials suggesting that the lectures hit a raw public nerve. The Executive Director of the Chicago Area Committee for SANE, a leading anti-nuclear group, wrote to Morgenthau to ask permission to distribute copies of the lectures (Letter from Morton W. Ryweck to Hans J. Morgenthau, May 21, 1962, HJM-53). SANE awarded Morgenthau the Jane Adams Peace Prize on November 12, 1966. Morgenthau's ties to some segments of the anti-nuclear movement were deeper than has been recognized. In a December 5, 1949, letter to George Kennan, for example, he urged Kennan to consult with the prominent nuclear physicist turned antiwar activist Leo Szilard, noting that the "other day I discussed with him the problem of the international control of atomic energy. I was greatly impressed with the originality and force of Professor Szilard's arguments" (HJM-

B33, Library of Congress). In a letter of June 1, 1964, to Szilard's widow, Morgenthau said that "Leo Szilard has set an example which has had a profound and lasting influence upon my attitude toward public issues" (HJM-B56, Library of Congress).

49 See, especially, ch. 3 of *Science: Servant or Master?* (New York: Meridian, 1972), whose title – "The Future of Man" – was probably taken directly from Jaspers, whose relevance is discussed at great length.

50 Lecture 1 – "The Nature of the Technological Revolution," 15.

51 See also "Functions of a Theory of International Relations," 71.

52 Hans J. Morgenthau, "Another Legacy of Hiroshima: The Partially Scientific Mind," *Bulletin of the Atomic Scientists*, 18 (June 1962), 35. For further criticisms of Kahn, see Morgenthau's "Understanding Military Strategy" [1965], in *TP*, 279–82.

53 Lecture 1 – "The Nature of the Technological Revolution," 13. As Lawrence Freedman has more recently observed, one "reason why a strategy of nuclear deterrence was adopted in the mid-1950s was a degree of confidence that it would not be put to the test" (*Deterrence* [Cambridge: Polity, 2004], 40).

54 Lecture 1 – "The Nature of the Technological Revolution," 14.

55 Lecture 2 – "Politics in the Nuclear Age," 6.

56 Hans J. Morgenthau, "The Four Paradoxes of Nuclear Strategy," *American Political Science Review*, 58 (1964), 24. The analysis of the four main paradoxes was updated and became chapter 8 of Morgenthau's *A New Foreign Policy for the United States* (New York: Praeger, 1969), 207–40.

57 See also, "Western Values and Total War," 286.

58 Morgenthau, "Four Paradoxes of Nuclear Strategy," 27.

59 Counterforce strategy emphasized the virtues of nuclear attacks on enemy military targets.

60 Morgenthau, "Four Paradoxes of Nuclear Strategy," 35.

61 Lecture 2 – "Politics in the Nuclear Age," 14–15. Morgenthau typically described them as the "Acheson-Baruch-Lilienthal" proposals to underscore Dean Acheson's role in them. Robert Oppenheimer, the nuclear physicist who oversaw the Manhattan Project, is also generally seen as having played a decisive role in them. For a useful overview of the proposals, see Leneice N. Wu, *The Baruch Plan: U.S. Diplomacy Enters the Nuclear Age* (Washington, D.C.: US Government Printing Office, 1972). They still inspire creative thinking about the nuclear threat, as evinced, for example, by Daniel H. Deudney's fascinating recent discussion (*Bounding Power: Republican Security Theory from the Polis to the Global Village* [Princeton: Princeton University Press, 2007], 256–7).

62 Hans J. Morgenthau, "Disarmament" (statement before the Senate Committee on Foreign Relations, January 10, 1957), in *RAP*, 143. This was a frequent refrain in Morgenthau's writings. See, for example, "What the Big Two Can, and Can't, Negotiate," *New York Times Sunday*

Magazine (September 20, 1959), 9, 88–90; "An Approach to the Summit" [1960], in *RAP*, 290–1; *A New Foreign Policy for the United States*, 243–4.

63   Lecture 2 – "Politics in the Nuclear Age," 15.

64   Morgenthau, "What the Big Two Can, and Can't, Negotiate," 89.

65   "Western Values and Total War," 298. Morgenthau referred here to recent US foreign policy debacles in Latin America and Southeast Asia.

66   Hans J. Morgenthau, 'International Relations" [1961], in *RAP*, 175.

67   Hans J. Morgenthau, "A World State?" *Pax Romana*, 1 (1963), 14.

68   "Hans J. Morgenthau, On Solzhenitsyn, Sakharov" (exchange with Harrison Salisbury), *War/Peace Report*, 13 (October 1974), 11. See also the earlier exchange with Reinhold Niebuhr, "The Ethics of War and Peace in the Nuclear Age," *War/Peace Report*, 7 (February 1967), 6–7, where Morgenthau agreed with Niebuhr that it would be wrong to try to establish a world state via a constitutional convention, but insisted that concrete steps could be taken to construct it.

69   Morgenthau, "Explaining the Failures of US Foreign Policy: Three Paradoxes," *New Republic* (October 11, 1975), 21.

70   Cited in Anonymous, "Nuclear War Possible if Arms Race Continues," *Intellect*, 105 (November 1976), 123.

71   Hans J. Morgenthau, "The Question of Détente," *Worldview*, 19 (March 1976), 12. Indeed, the US refusal to disarm has seriously jeopardized the NPT, as Jonathan Schell reports in *The Seventh Decade: The New Shape of Nuclear Danger* (New York: Metropolitan Books, 2007). Morgenthau otherwise has little to say about the NPT, which arguably constituted a major breakthrough in attempts to minimize the likelihood of nuclear war.

72   Morgenthau, "Letter to the Editor," *New York Times* (February 23, 1960), 30.

73   Schmitt defined the sovereign as "he who decides on the exception" (*Political Theology: Four Chapters on the Concept of Sovereignty*, trans. George Schwab [Cambridge, Mass.: MIT Press, 1985 (1922)], 5). Note also the personalistic contours of Schmitt's definitions, which Morgenthau reproduced.

74   He also missed the ways in which modern ideas of *popular* sovereignty broke with Absolutist notions of *state* sovereignty. See Ingeborg Maus, *Zur Aufklärung der Demokratietheorie* (Frankfurt: Suhrkamp, 1992).

75   See Matthias Lutz-Bachmann and Jim Bohman (ed.), *Perpetual Peace: Essays on Kant's Cosmopolitan Ideal* (Cambridge, Mass.: MIT Press, 1997).

76   Deudney, *Bounding Power: Republican Security Theory from the Polis to the Global Village*, 244–64. Deudney's republican ideas are sometimes closer to Morgenthau's than he admits, because he still accepts too many of the clichés about the latter.

77   Craig, *Glimmer of a New Leviathan*, xvii.

78 Hans J. Morgenthau, "Changes and Chances in Soviet–American Relations," *Foreign Policy*, 49 (1971), 437; Hans J. Morgenthau, "Four Years of Achievement and Failure: Nixon and the World," *New Republic* (January 6 and 13, 1973), 19–20; "Discussion," in George Schwab and Henry Friedlander (eds.), *Détente in Historical Perspective* (New York: Cyrco Press, 1972), 99; on the futility of the arms race, see "Defining the National Interest – Again: Old Superstitions, New Realities," *New Republic* (January 22, 1977), 50–5.

79 Hans J. Morgenthau, "Fighting the Last War," *New Republic* (October 20, 1979), 17.

80 Morgenthau, "Fighting the Last War," 16.

81 "Western Values and Total War," 292.

82 Richard Ned Lebow and Janice Gross Stein, *We All Lost the Cold War* (Princeton: Princeton University Press, 1994), 368.

83 Morgenthau, "Changes and Chances in American–Soviet Relations," 431.

84 On finite deterrence, see Lebow and Stein, *We All Lost the Cold War*, 350. At other junctures, however, Morgenthau was closer to an interpretation of deterrence as "mutually assured destruction" (MAD), according to which deterrence required the possibility of massive destruction of the enemy's population and industry.

85 Hans J. Morgenthau, "A New Foreign Policy for the United States: Basic Issues," *Bulletin of the Atomic Scientists*, 23 (January 1967), 11. See also Morgenthau, *A New Foreign Policy for the United States*, 13. A contemporary physicist and arms control specialist, W. K. H. Panofsky, has defended a similar position: "[T]he only justifiable remaining role of nuclear weapons is deterrence of the use of nuclear weapons by others. Retaining, or even searching for, other missions for nuclear weapons is shortsighted and prolongs or even exacerbates the nuclear dangers . . . [S]uch a restricted view of the mission of nuclear weapons should enable drastic reductions of the existing nuclear stockpiles" ("Peace Talk: My Life Negotiating Science and Policy," *Bulletin of the Atomic Scientists* [November–December, 2007], 53).

86 Morgenthau, "Four Years of Achievement and Failure: Nixon and the World," 19.

87 "Nuclear War Possible if Arms Race Continues," 123.

88 Morgenthau, "A New Foreign Policy for the United States," 9–10. After the UK and France acquired nuclear weapons, Morgenthau argued that such a "national nuclear deterrent is both costly and useless, and therefore ought to be abandoned." At the very least, it would make more sense to substitute a "European nuclear deterrent for a multiplicity of national ones," as a way of at least minimizing their dangers (*A New Foreign Policy for the United States*, 188).

89 Hans J. Morgenthau, "From Napoleon to Armageddon," *New York Review of Books* (February 26, 1970), 41. The Pugwash Conference is an annual meeting, inspired by a joint resolution by Albert Einstein and

Bertrand Russell, bringing together prominent scientists and scholars concerned about the dangers of nuclear weaponry. Morgenthau frequently attended (HJM-47, Pugwash Correspondence, Library of Congress).

90 Hans J. Morgenthau, "Some Political Aspects of Disarmament," in David Carlton and Carlo Schaerf (eds.), *The Dynamics of the Arms Race* (New York: Wiley and Sons, 1975), 62.

91 Kenneth Waltz, "More May be Better," in Scott D. Sagan and Waltz (eds.), *The Spread of Nuclear Weapons* (New York: Norton, 2003), 44. For an excellent critique of Waltz and other Realists supportive of proliferation, see Craig, *Glimmer of a New Leviathan*, 117–65.

92 Schell, *The Seventh Decade*, 75–82.

93 Lebow and Stein, *We All Lost the Cold War*, 376. The authors brilliantly demonstrate the many ways in which deterrence strategy helped to contribute to some of the darkest moments of the cold war.

94 Bruce G. Blair, *The Logic of Accidental Nuclear War* (Washington, D.C.: Brookings Institution, 1993).

95 Sagan, "More Will Be Worse," in Sagan and Waltz (eds.), *The Spread of Nuclear Weapons*, 47–8.

96 Joseph Cirincione, *Bomb Scare: The History & Future of Nuclear Weapons* (New York: Columbia University Press, 2007), 103–4.

97 Morgenthau, "Some Political Aspects of Disarmament," 62.

98 On these and other criticisms of deterrence theory, see Derek D. Smith, *Deterring America: Rogue States and the Proliferation of Weapons of Mass Destruction* (New York: Cambridge University Press, 2006), 16–42.

99 We also now know, or should know, better than Morgenthau that nuclear warfare is only one path to human extermination. Global warming, for example, may be another. See Furio Cerutti, *Global Challenge for Leviathan: A Political Philosophy of Nuclear Weapons and Global Warming* (Lanham, Md.: Lexington, 2007).

Chapter 6   Vietnam and the crisis of American democracy

1 Jennifer See, "A Prophet Without Honor: Hans Morgenthau and the War in Vietnam, 1955–65," *Pacific Historical Review*, 70 (2001), 445. The survey was taken after opposition to the war had undergone a far-reaching radicalization. In the early years of the antiwar movement, Morgenthau was probably more influential than Chomsky. Morgenthau debated Chomsky in "The National Interest and the Pentagon Papers," *Partisan Review*, 29 (1972), 336–75, where he accused him, with good reason, of advancing an economistic view of US foreign policy.

2 Arthur Schlesinger recommended Morgenthau to Kennedy as a possible foreign policy advisor. National Security Advisor McGeorge Bundy, a longstanding nemesis to Morgenthau, apparently torpedoed

the suggestion, as he allegedly had earlier attempts to recruit Morgenthau to Harvard. See Ellen Glaser Rafshoon, "A Realist's Moral Opposition to the War: Hans J. Morgenthau and Vietnam," *Peace & Change*, 26 (2001), 61.

3 Histories of the antiwar movement make frequent reference to Morgenthau's involvement. See, for example, Adam Garfinkle, *Telltale Hearts: The Origins and Impact of the Vietnam Antiwar Movement* (New York: St. Martin's, 1995). One of the leading early opponents of the war in the Senate, J. William Fulbright, apparently had read Morgenthau's pieces (see, "A Prophet Without Honor," 438).

4 Morgenthau often wrote and spoke bitterly about the Johnson Administration's attempt to harass him. He claimed, for example, that his tax returns were subject to special scrutiny, he was dismissed as a consultant to the Defense Department because of his unpopular views, figures close to the Administration helped to undertake a smear campaign against him, and even that his son, Matthew, was drafted because of his opposition to the war (see Johnson, "Bernard Johnson's Interview with Hans J. Morgenthau," 382–5). Of course, some of these accusations are difficult to prove. Yet the FBI did carefully monitor his activities, and there is no question that the Johnson Administration took a special interest in trying to discredit him. The famous gossip columnist, Joseph Alsop, for example, attacked him publicly as an "appeaser" (see Rafshoon, "A Realist's Moral Opposition to the War," 64–9). A heated exchange took place in the *New Leader*, a liberal journal with which Morgenthau had been associated, but which was sympathetic to Johnson and the war (see especially Morgenthau, "Freedom, Freedom House, and Vietnam," *New Leader* [January 2, 1967], 17–19).

5 Alan Gilbert, *Must Global Politics Constrain Democracy? Great Power Realism, Democratic Peace, and Democratic Internationalism* (Princeton: Princeton University Press, 1999); Rafshoon, "A Realist's Moral Opposition to the War"; also See, "A Prophet Without Honor."

6 Waltz, *Man, the State, and War*, 80.

7 Morgenthau, "What Ails America?" in *TP*, 39.

8 Johnson, "Bernard Johnson's Interview with Hans J. Morgenthau," 382.

9 Morgenthau, "The Unfinished Business of American Foreign Policy," in *IAFP*, 13; see also his comments in the symposium on "The Cold War and the West," *Partisan Review*, 297 (1962), 54, where he argued that the USA should support revolutionary groups when at all possible.

10 Morgenthau, "The Revolution We Are Living Through" [1955], in *RAP*, 249.

11 Morgenthau, "Asia: The American Algeria" [1961], in *RAP*, 351–8.

12 This is a central theme of many of the short political essays reprinted in *TP*.

13 Morgenthau, "The Nuclear Option: What Price Victory?" *New Republic* (February 20, 1971), 21–3. Morgenthau's private correspondence with Kissinger from this period, not surprisingly, was often acerbic (HJM-B33, Library of Congress).

14 See chapter 4 above.

15 Morgenthau, "The Present Tragedy of America," *Worldview*, 12 (September 12, 1969), 14–15.

16 Morgenthau, 'The Nation as Exemplar," *Center Magazine*, 12 (1974), 69.

17 Morgenthau, "The Present Tragedy of America," 15.

18 Morgenthau, "Foreword," in Arnold Kaufman, *The Radical Liberal: New Man in American Politics* (New York: Atherton, 1968), x–xi. On Kaufman and the New Left, see James Miller, *Democracy is in the Streets: From Port Huron to the Siege of Chicago* (New York: Simon & Schuster, 1987), 44, 94–5, 111, 119, 142, 180. Kaufman's book contained a devastating critique of what he called "pseudo-realism" – which, interestingly, reads like the conventional account of Morgenthau as a Hobbesian thinker for whom "the ultimate test of the propriety of policy is its contribution to national interest" (43). Like his friend Arendt, Morgenthau resisted being pigeonholed into conventional "left" and "right" categories; both worried that the traditional division obfuscated the great issues of our day (see his questions to her on this matter as part of a discussion published in Melvyn A. Hill (ed.), *Hannah Arendt: The Recovery of the Public World* [New York: St. Martin's, 1979], 333–4). Yet, like Arendt, his sympathies in the 1960s were clearly on the side of those who desired far-reaching social and political reform. In *Purpose of American Politics*, Morgenthau revealingly praised America's idiosyncratic fusion of a "revolutionary" national purpose (see discussion below) with a conservative "method," which held that "the world, imperfect as it is from the rational point of view, is the result of forces inherent in human nature. To improve the world, one must work with those forces, not against them." The conservative method recognized that abstract principles were "at best approximated through the ever temporary balancing of interests," sought the lesser evil rather than the absolute good, and saw in the idea of checks and balances "a universal principle for all pluralist societies." This so-called "conservatism," which recapitulated some core elements of Morgenthau's own thinking, was unrelated to reverence for the status quo or traditional defenses of political and economic privilege (*PAP*, 296).

19 See various articles in *TP*, but especially pp. 37–8, 51–5, 190. Also Morgenthau, "Watergate and the Future of American Politics: The Aborted Nixon Revolution," *New Republic* (August 11, 1973), 17–19; "Power and Powerlessness: Decline of Democratic Government," *New Republic* (November 9, 1974), 14.

20 Morgenthau, "Wild Bunch," *New York Review of Books*, 16 (February 11, 1971), 40.

21 Morgenthau, "The Coming Test of American Democracy," in *TP*, 213.

22 Morgenthau, "Introduction," in H. J. Morgenthau (ed.), *The Crossroad Papers: A Look Into the American Future* (New York: Norton, 1965), 10.

23 Morgenthau, "Prologue," 7, and "The Principle of Propaganda," 319, both in *TP*.

24 Morgenthau, "Prologue," in *TP*, 6.

25 Morgenthau, "Prologue," in *TP*, 5. The prologue appeared simultaneously in the *New York Review of Books*, for which Morgenthau wrote widely in the 1960s, under the revealing title "Reflections on the End of the Republic" (*New York Review of Books*, 15 [September 24, 1970], 38–41).

26 Morgenthau, "Introduction," *Crossroad Papers*, 9–16. In 1968 he seems to have supported the insurgent antiwar campaign of Eugene McCarthy; in 1972 he toured the country on behalf of George McGovern's unsuccessful campaign for the presidency.

27 Morgenthau, "Nixon vs. Humphrey: The Choice," in *TP*, 199–206.

28 Morgenthau, "Prologue," in *TP*, 6–7.

29 Morgenthau, "Epilogue," in *TP*, 436–7. Transcripts of Morgenthau's discussions with graduate students at the New School in the early 1970s, in which he respectfully engaged their oftentimes radical positions, are also revealing. See Anthony Lang (ed.), *Political Theory and International Affairs: Hans J. Morgenthau on Aristotle's* Politics (Westport: Praeger, 2004).

30 Morgenthau, "Epilogue," in *TP*, 439.

31 Morgenthau, "Epilogue," in *TP*, 437.

32 Rafshoon, "A Realist's Moral Opposition to the War," 57.

33 In many short essays from the 1950s as well, the dominant tendency is to highlight the perils posed by democracy to the rational pursuit of the national interest.

34 Miroslav Nincic, *Democracy and Foreign Policy: The Fallacy of Political Realism* (New York: Columbia University Press, 1992).

35 I am thinking of Kissinger, whose anti-democratic proclivities and historical nostalgia were always more pronounced than Morgenthau's.

36 Nincic, *Democracy and Foreign Policy*, 167.

37 Some of his reflections seem to echo Herder and John Stuart Mill.

38 But the extent of the debt only becomes clear in his lectures – for example, from those given at the New School in the early 1970s and now reprinted in Lang (ed.), *Political Theory and International Affairs*, 86, where he refers to Kelsen's "beautiful statement" on democratic theory, *Vom Wesen und Wert der Demokratie* (Tübingen: Mohr, 1929). *Truth and Power* was dedicated "to Hans Kelsen, who has taught us through his example how to speak Truth to Power" (v). Although his 1929 book was never translated, Kelsen usefully summarized his main

ideas in "Foundations of Democracy," *Ethics*, 66 (1955), 1–101. Kelsen's work on democracy was hugely influential in central Europe and among émigrés who left Germany; it is hardly surprising that Morgenthau built on it.

39 Morgenthau, "The Dilemmas of Freedom," *APSR*, 51 (1957), 716.

40 As articulated by Joseph Schumpeter in *Capitalism, Socialism, and Democracy* (New York: Harper, 1950). Morgenthau's realism ultimately has little in common with Schumpeter's conservative "realist" democratic theory.

41 Of course, this was also a theme in Hannah Arendt's *On the Human Condition*, a book much admired by Morgenthau.

42 I follow here the excellent discussion found in Lars Vinx, *Hans Kelsen's Pure Theory of Law: Legality and Legitimacy* (Oxford: Oxford University Press, 2007), 135–8.

43 Morgenthau, "The Right to Dissent," in *TP*, 44.

44 See chapter 5 above.

45 (New York: Penguin, 1962). In the preface to *PAP*, Morgenthau thanked Arendt for commenting on an earlier draft of the manuscript.

46 He did, however, unambiguously endorse efforts to overcome racial segregation (*PAP*, 306–7).

47 Of course, many critical US historians have challenged this idyllic view of antebellum (free white) America. But Morgenthau's key point – that US conditions offered *more* political and economic liberty than its nineteenth-century competitors – arguably remains accurate.

48 See also Morgenthau, "The New Despotism and the New Feudalism," in *DDP*, 116–23, which critically dissected the welfare and interventionist states.

49 Morgenthau, "Modern Science and Political Power," *Columbia Law Review*, 64 (1964), 1386. Morgenthau frequently repeated the argument that the demise of any real chance for popular revolution undermined democracy. One can read Arendt's *On Violence*, where she underscores the possibility of defeating superior military means by non-military devices, as a response to Morgenthau's position. On the threats posed by the development of nuclear weapons to democracy, see also Morgenthau, "Decision Making in the Nuclear Age," *Bulletin of the Atomic Scientists*, 38 (1962), 7–8.

50 Morgenthau, "The Danger of Détente," *New Leader*, 56 (October 1, 1973), 7. It is inaccurate to claim that Morgenthau's policy recommendations on Soviet Jewry thus "utterly repudiated the precepts of his realism" (see Robert Kaufman, "Morgenthau's Unrealistic Realism," *Yale Journal of International Affairs*, 1 [2006], 36). His judgments on the Middle East were made through the prism of 1930s and 1940s German history, as when he crudely associated Palestinian struggles with Hitler's disingenuous 1930s appeals for self-determination for ethnic Germans in Eastern Europe ("Facing Mideast Realities," *New Leader*, 61 [April 24, 1978], 4–6).

51   For a useful critical discussion relevant to my brief comments here,
     see Brian Schmidt and Michael Williams, "The Bush Doctrine and the
     Iraq War: Neoconservatives vs. Realists," *Security Studies*, 17 (2008),
     1–30.
52   Charles Krauthammer, "Democratic Realism: An American Foreign
     Policy for a Unipolar World" (2004 Irving Kristol Lecture, February
     12, 2004, American Enterprise Institute, Washington, D.C.), available
     at www.aei.org/include/pub_printasp?pubID=19912). Krauthammer,
     by the way, was introduced by Vice-President Dick Cheney.

Conclusion: Morgenthau as classical Realist?

1   See also his comment in the 1961 symposium on "Western Values and
    Total War" in *Commentary*, where he announced that he was no social-
    ist (288). At least in a 1944 essay ("The Limitations of Science and the
    Problem of Social Planning," *Ethics*, 54 [1944], 181–6), he tried to mark
    out a middle position – clearly consistent with social democracy or
    what in the USA is still described as "New Deal liberalism" – between
    a naïve rationalistic faith in planning and an equally extreme position
    that discounts planning's potential virtues altogether.
2   The key figure in this movement was the Protestant theologian Paul
    Tillich, who was close to Wolfers, and whom Niebuhr helped to bring
    to the Union Theological Seminary in New York City, when Tillich was
    forced to leave Germany as an outspoken socialist. Niebuhr, like
    Tillich, long considered himself a "Christian Socialist."

Bibliography

Works by Morgenthau

Unfortunately, no easily accessible comprehensive bibliography of Morgenthau's writings is presently available. The list below includes his main works as well as others heavily relied on in the writing of this book. However, readers should note that Morgenthau authored other short pieces for popular outlets. Where the dating of archival materials was difficult or problematic, I have included a question mark immediately following the date supplied.

Die Internationale Rechtspflege, ihr Wesen und ihre Grenzen (Leipzig: Universitätsverlag von Robert Noske, 1929).

"Die Völkerrechtlichen Ergebnisse der Tagung der deutschen Gesellschaft für Völkerrecht," *Die Justiz*, 4 (1929), 621–4.

"Stresemann als Schöpfer der deutschen Völkerrechtspolitik," *Die Justiz*, 5 (1929/30), 169–76.

"Der Selbstmord mit gutem Gewissen. Zur Kritik des Pazifismus und der neuen deutschen Kriegsphilosophie" (Frankfurt, unpublished, 1931) (HJM-B96, Library of Congress).

"Über die Herkunft des Politischen aus dem Wesen der Menschen" (Frankfurt, unpublished, 1931) (HJM-B151, Library of Congress).

"Genfer Antrittsvorlesung" (Geneva, unpublished, 1932) (HJM-B110, Library of Congress).

"Die Wirklichkeit des Völkerbunds," *Neue Zürcher Zeitung* (April 2, 1933), 3.

La Notion du "politique" et la théorie des différends internationaux (Paris: Libraire du Recueil Sirey, 1933).

La Réalité des normes, en particulier des normes du droit international (Paris: Felix Alcan, 1934).

"Die Entstehung der Normentheorie aus der Zusammenbruch der Ethik" (Geneva, unpublished, 1934/35?) (HJM-B199, Library of Congress).

"Über den Sinn der Wissenschaft in dieser Zeit und über die Bestimmung des Menschen" (Geneva, unpublished, 1934/35?) (HJM-B151, Library of Congress).

"Die Krise der metaphysischen Ethik von Kant bis Nietzsche" (Geneva, unpublished, 1935) (HJM-B112, Library of Congress).

"Théorie des sanctions internationales," *Revue de Droit International et de Législation Comparée*, 16 (1935), 474–503.

"Das Problem des Rechtssystems" (Madrid, unpublished, 1935/36?) (HJM-199, Library of Congress).

"Positivisme mal compris et théorie réaliste du droit international," in Silvio A. Zavala (ed.), *Colección de estudios históricos, jurídicos, pedagógicos y literarios. Homenaje a D. Rafael Altamira y Crevea* (Madrid: C. Bermejo, 1936), 446–65.

"The End of Switzerland's 'Differential' Neutrality," *American Journal of International Law*, 32 (1938), 558–62.

"The Problem of Neutrality," *University of Kansas City Law Review*, 7 (1939), 109–28.

"The Resurrection of Neutrality in Europe," *American Political Science Review*, 33 (1939), 473–86.

"Positivism, Functionalism, and International Law," *American Journal of International Law*, 34 (1940), 260–84.

"Implied Limitations on Regulatory Powers in Administrative Law," *University of Chicago Law Review*, 11, 2 (1944), 91–116.

"The Limitations of Science and the Problem of Social Planning," *Ethics*, 54 (1944), 181–6.

"The Machiavellian Utopia," *Ethics*, 55, 2 (1945), 145–7.

"The Scientific Solution of Social Conflicts," in Lyman Bryson, Louis Finkelstein, and Robert MacIver (eds.), *Approaches to National Unity* (New York: Harper & Bros., 1945), 419–37.

"Diplomacy," *Yale Law Journal*, 55 (1946), 1067–80.

Scientific Man Vs. Power Politics (Chicago: University of Chicago Press, 1946).

Politics Among Nations: The Struggle for Power and Peace (New York: Alfred Knopf, 1948, 1954, 1960, 1967, 1973, 1978).

"The Political Science of E. H. Carr," *World Politics*, 1 (1948), 127–34.

"The Problem of Sovereignty Reconsidered," *Columbia Law Review*, 48 (1948), 341–65.

"The Twilight of International Morality," *Ethics*, 58 (1948), 79–99.

"National Interest and Moral Principles in Foreign Policy: The Primacy of the National Interest," *American Scholar*, 18 (1949), 207–12.

"On Negotiating With the Russians," *Bulletin of the Atomic Scientists*, 6 (May 1950), 143–8.

"Power Politics," in Freda Kirchway (ed.), *The Atomic Era – Can It Bring Peace and Abundance?* (New York: Medill McBride, 1950), 36–50.

"The Case for Negotiation: History's Lesson," *Nation* (December 16, 1950), 587–91.

"The Conquest of the United States by Germany," *Bulletin of the Atomic Scientists*, 6 (January 1950), 21–6.

"The H-Bomb and After," *Bulletin of the Atomic Scientists*, 6 (March 1950), 76–9.

"The H-Bomb and the Peace Outlook," in *The H-Bomb* (New York: Didier, 1950), 160–74.

"The Mainsprings of American Foreign Policy: The National Interest vs. Moral Abstractions," *American Political Science Review*, 44 (1950), 833–54.

(ed.) (with Kenneth W. Thompson), *Principles and Problems of International Politics* (New York: Alfred Knopf, 1950).

"American Diplomacy: The Dangers of Righteousness," *New Republic* (October 22, 1951), 117–19.

In Defense of the National Interest: A Critical Examination of American Foreign Policy (New York: Alfred Knopf, 1951).

"The Moral Dilemma in Foreign Policy," in *Year Book of World Affairs 1951* (New York: Praeger, 1951), 12–36.

"The Policy of the U.S.A.," *Political Quarterly*, 22 (1951), 43–56.

"The Lessons of World War II's Mistakes," *Commentary*, 14 (1952), 326–33.

"What is the National Interest of the United States?" *Annals of the American Academy of Political and Social Science*, 282 (1952), 1–7.

"Political Limitations of the United Nations," in George Lipskey (ed.), *Law and Politics in the World Community* (Berkeley: University of California Press, 1953), 151–2.

"The New United Nations and the Revision of the Charter," *Review of Politics*, 16 (1954), 3–21.

"The Yardstick of National Interest," *Annals of the American Academy of Political and Social Science*, 296 (1954), 77–84.

"Will it Deter Aggression?" *New Republic* (March 29, 1954), 11–14.

"Foreign Policy: The Conservative School," *World Politics*, 7 (1955), 284–92.

"The Impact of Loyalty–Security Measures on the State Department," *Bulletin of the Atomic Scientists*, 11 (April 1955), 134–40.

"Has Atomic War Really Become Impossible?" *Bulletin of the Atomic Scientists*, 12 (January 1956), 7–9.

"The Decline and Fall of American Foreign Policy," *New Republic* (December 10, 1956), 11–16.

"Der Pazifismus des Atomzeitalters," *Der Monat*, 10 (October 1957), 3–8.

"The Dilemmas of Freedom," *American Political Science Review*, 51 (1957), 714–23.

Dilemmas of Politics (Chicago: University of Chicago Press, 1958).

"Power as a Political Concept," in Roland Young (ed.), *Approaches to the Study of Politics* (Evanston: Northwestern University Press, 1958), 66–77.

"Russian Technology and American Policy," *Current History*, 34 (1958), 129–35.

"The Permanent Values in the Old Diplomacy," in Stephen Kertesz and M. A. Fitzsimons (eds.), *Diplomacy in a Changing World* (South Bend, Ind.: University of Notre Dame Press, 1959), 10–20.

"What the Big Two Can, and Can't, Negotiate," *New York Times Sunday Magazine* (September 20, 1959), 9, 88–90.

"Our Thwarted Republic: Public Power vs. the New Federalism," *Commentary*, 29 (1960), 473–85.

The Purpose of American Politics (New York: Alfred Knopf, 1960).

"An Atomic Philosophy," *Saturday Review* (February 18, 1961), 18–19.

"Faith and Freedom Lectures" (Lectures at American University, November 1961) (HJM-171, Library of Congress).

"The Nuclear Discussion: Continued," *Christianity and Crisis*, 21 (1961), 223.

"Another Legacy of Hiroshima: The Partially Scientific Mind," *Bulletin of the Atomic Scientists*, 18 (June 1962), 34–6.

"Decisionmaking in the Nuclear Age," *Bulletin of the Atomic Scientists*, 18 (December 1962), 7–8.

The Decline of Democratic Politics (Chicago: University of Chicago Press, 1962).

"Niebuhr's Political Thought," in Harold R. Langdon (ed.), *Reinhold Niebuhr: A Prophetic Voice in our Time* (Greenwich, Conn.: Seabury, 1962), 99–109.

The Impasse of American Foreign Policy (Chicago: University of Chicago Press, 1962).

The Restoration of American Politics (Chicago: University of Chicago Press, 1962).

"A World State?" *Pax Romana*, 1 (1963), 7–11, 14.

"Comment on War Within Man," in Erich Fromm, *War Within Man: A Psychological Enquiry Into the Roots of Destructiveness* (Washington, D.C.: American Friends Service Committee, 1963), 34–5.

"On Trying to be Just," *Commentary*, 35 (1963), 420–3.

"Four Designs for Tomorrow's Europe," *New York Times Sunday Magazine* (May 17, 1964), 18–20.

"Modern Science and Political Power," *Columbia Law Review*, 64 (1964), 1386–1409.

"The Four Paradoxes of Nuclear Strategy," *American Political Science Review*, 58 (1964), 23–35.

"The Impartiality of the International Police," in Salo Engel (ed.), *Law, State, and International Legal Order: Essays in Honor of Hans Kelsen* (Knoxville: University of Tennessee Press, 1964), 210–23.

"Another 'Great Debate': The National Interest of the United States," in Harold Karan Jacobson (ed.), *America's Foreign Policy* (New York: Random House, 1965), 107–36.

"Law, Politics, and the United Nations," *Commercial Law Journal*, 70 (1965), 121–4, 135.

"The U.N. of Dag Hammarskjold is Dead," *New York Times Sunday Magazine* (March 14, 1965), 32–8.

Vietnam and the United States (Washington, D.C.: Public Affairs Press, 1965).

(ed.) *The Crossroad Papers: A Look into the American Future* (New York: Norton, 1965).

"Introduction," in David Mitrany, *A Working Peace System* (Chicago: Quadrangle, 1966).

"A New Foreign Policy for the United States: Basic Issues," *Bulletin of the Atomic Scientists*, 23 (January 1967), 7–11.

"Arguing About the Cold War," *Encounter*, 28 (May 1967), 37–41.

"Freedom, Freedom House, and Vietnam," *New Leader* (January 2, 1967), 17–19.

"To Intervene or Not to Intervene," *Foreign Affairs* (April 1967), 425–36.

"The Ethics of War and Peace in the Nuclear Age" (exchange with Reinhold Niebuhr), *War/Peace Report*, 7 (February 1967), 3–8.

"Foreword," in Arnold Kaufman, *The Radical Liberal: New Man in American Politics* (New York: Atherton, 1968), x–xi.

A New Foreign Policy for the United States (New York: Praeger, 1969).

"The Present Tragedy of America," *Worldview*, 12 (September 12, 1969), 14–15.

"Der Friede im nuklearen Zeitalter," in Oskar Schatz (ed.), *Der Friede im nuklearen Zeitalter. Eine Kontroverse zwischen Realisten und Utopisten* (Salzburg: Manz Verlag, 1970), 34–62.

"From Napoleon to Armageddon," *New York Review of Books* (February 26, 1970), 38–43.

Truth and Power: Essays of a Decade, 1960–70 (New York: Praeger, 1970).

"Changes and Chances in Soviet–American Relations," *Foreign Affairs*, 49 (1971), 429–41.

"Show of Support," *New Republic* (March 13, 1971), 10–11.

"The Nuclear Option: What Price Victory?" *New Republic* (February 20, 1971), 21–3.

"Thought and Action in Politics," *Social Research*, 38 (1971), 143–65.

"Wild Bunch," *New York Review of Books*, 16 (February 11, 1971), 38–41.

"Détente: Reality and Illusion," in George Schwab and Henry Friedlander (eds.), *Détente in Historical Perspective* (New York: Cyrco Press, 1972), 71–9.

"Discussion," in George Schwab and Henry Friedlander (eds.), *Détente in Historical Perspective* (New York: Cyrco Press, 1972), 96–106.

"Remarks on the Validity of Historical Analogies," *Social Research*, 39 (1972), 360–4.

Science: Servant or Master? (New York: Meridian, 1972).

"The National Interest and the Pentagon Papers" (exchange with Noam Chomsky), *Partisan Review*, 29 (1972), 336–75.

"The Web of Falsehood," *New Leader*, 55 (December 11, 1972), 15–16.

"Four Years of Achievement and Failure: Nixon and the World," *New Republic* (January 6 and 13, 1973), 17–20.

"The Danger of Détente," *New Leader*, 56 (October 1, 1973), 5–7.

"The Geopolitics of Israel's Survival," *New Leader*, 61 (December 24, 1973), 46.

"Watergate and the Future of American Politics: The Aborted Nixon Revolution," *New Republic* (August 11, 1973), 17–19.

"Henry Kissinger, Secretary of State," *Encounter*, 43 (November 1974), 57–60.

"Justice and Power," *Social Research*, 41 (1974), 164–75.
"On Solzhenitsyn, Sakharov" (exchange with Harrison Salisbury), *War/Peace Report*, 13 (October 1974), 7–13.
"Power and Powerlessness: Decline of Democratic Government," *New Republic* (November 9, 1974), 13–18.
"The Moral Dilemma in the Middle East" (exchange with Daniel Berrigan), *Progressive* (March 1974), 31–4.
"The Nation as Exemplar," *Center Magazine*, 12 (1974), 69.
"Explaining the Failures of US Foreign Policy: Three Paradoxes," *New Republic* (October 11, 1975), 16–21.
"Some Political Aspects of Disarmament," in David Carlton and Carlo Schaerf (eds.), *The Dynamics of the Arms Race* (New York: Wiley and Sons, 1975), 57–63.
"The Decline of the West," *Partisan Review*, 42 (1975), 508–16.
"The Elite Protects Itself," *New Republic* (May 3, 1975), 20–1.
"Hannah Arendt, 1906–75," *Political Theory*, 4 (1976), 5–8.
"The Question of Détente," *Worldview*, 19 (March 1976), 7–13.
"Defining the National Interest – Again: Old Superstitions, New Realities," *New Republic* (January 22, 1977), 50–5.
"Hannah Arendt on Totalitarianism and Democracy," *Social Research*, 44 (1977), 127–31.
"Pathology of American Power," *International Security*, 1 (December 1977), 3–20.
"Facing Mideast Realities," *New Leader*, 61 (April 24, 1978), 4–6.
"Vietnam and Cambodia" (exchange with Noam Chomsky, Michael Walzer), *Dissent*, 25 (Fall 1978), 386–91.
"What Solzhenitsyn Doesn't Understand," *New Leader*, 61 (July 3, 1978), 12–13.
"Fighting the Last War," *New Republic* (October 20, 1979), 15–17.
Human Rights and Foreign Policy (New York: Council on Religion and International Affairs, 1979).
"The Mind of Abraham Lincoln: A Study in Detachment and Practicality," in Kenneth Thompson (ed.), *Essays on Lincoln's Faith and Politics* (Lanham, Md.: University Press, 1983), 3–101.
"Fragment of an Intellectual Autobiography: 1904–1932," in Thompson and Myers (eds.), *Truth and Tragedy*, 1–20.

Other works

Amstrup, Niels, "The 'Early' Morgenthau: A Comment on the Intellectual Origins of Realism," *Cooperation and Conflict*, 3 (1978), 163–75.

240 *Bibliography*

Archibugi, Daniele (ed.), *Debating Cosmopolis* (London: Verso, 2003).

Arendt, Hannah, *The Human Condition* (Chicago: University of Chicago Press, 1958).

On Violence (New York: Harcourt, Brace & Jovanovich, 1970).

"Europe and the Atomic Bomb," in Jerome Kohn (ed.), *Essays in Understanding, 1930–54* (New York: Harcourt Brace, 1994), 418–22.

Aron, Raymond, "En quête d'une philosophie de la politique étrangère," *Revue Française de Science Politique*, 3 (1953), 69–91.

Peace and War: A Theory of International Relations (New York: Doubleday, 1966).

Ashley, Richard K., "Political Realism and Human Interests," *International Studies Quarterly*, 25 (1981), 204–36.

Bellamy, Richard and Castiglione, Dario, "Between Cosmopolis and Community: Three Models of Rights and Democracy within the European Union," in Daniele Archibugi, David Held, and Martin Köhler (eds.), *Re-Imagining Political Community: Studies in Cosmopolitan Democracy* (Stanford: Stanford University Press, 1998), 152–79.

Benhabib, Seyla, *Critique, Norm, and Utopia: A Study of the Foundations of Critical Theory* (New York: Columbia University Press, 1986).

Bonante, Luigi, *Ethics and International Affairs* (Cambridge: Polity Press, 1995).

Boyle, Francis Anthony, *World Politics and International Law* (Durham, N.C.: Duke University Press, 1985).

Brinkley, Douglas, *Dean Acheson: The Cold War Years* (New Haven: Yale University Press, 1992).

Brown, Chris, "'The Twilight of International Morality?' Hans J. Morgenthau and Carl Schmitt on the End of the *Jus Publicum Europaeum*," in Williams (ed.), *Realism Reconsidered*, 42–61.

Bull, Hedley, "Hobbes and International Anarchy," *Social Research*, 48 (1981), 717–38.

Carr, E. H., *The Twenty Years' Crisis, 1919–39* (New York: Harper & Row, 1964).

Cerutti, Furio, *Global Challenge for Leviathan: A Political Philosophy of Nuclear Weapons and Global Warming* (Lanham, Md.: Lexington, 2007).

Chwaszcza, Christine and Kersting, Wolfgang (eds.), *Politische Philosophie der internationalen Beziehungen* (Frankfurt: Suhrkamp, 1998).

Cirincione, Joseph, *Bomb Scare: The History & Future of Nuclear Weapons* (New York: Columbia University Press, 2007).

"The Cold War and the West," symposium in *Partisan Review*, 29, 1 (1962), 51–6.

Cox, Michael, "Hans J. Morgenthau, Realism, and the Rise and Fall of the Cold War," in Williams (ed.), *Realism Reconsidered*, 166–94.

Cozette, Murielle, "Reclaiming the Critical Dimension of Realism: Hans J. Morgenthau on the Ethics of Scholarship," *Review of International Studies*, 34 (2008), 5–27.

Craig, Campbell, *Glimmer of a New Leviathan: Total War in the Realism of Niebuhr, Morgenthau, and Waltz* (New York: Columbia University Press, 2003).

Deudney, Daniel, *Bounding Power: Republican Security Theory from the Polis to the Global Village* (Princeton: Princeton University Press, 2007).

Donnelly, Jack, *Realism and International Relations* (Cambridge: Cambridge University Press, 2000).

Doyle, Michael W., *Ways of War and Peace* (New York: Norton, 1997).

Fox, Richard Wightman, *Reinhold Niebuhr* (Ithaca: Cornell University Press, 1985).

Fraenkel, Ernst, "Hugo Sinzheimer," in Falk Esche and Frank Grube (eds.), *Reformismus und Pluralismus* (Hamburg: Hoffmann und Campe, 1973), 131–42.

Frank, Jerome, "Review of *Scientific Man vs. Power Politics*," *University of Chicago Law Review*, 15 (1948), 462–78.

Freedman, Lawrence, *Deterrence* (Cambridge: Polity, 2004).

Frei, Christoph, *Hans J. Morgenthau: An Intellectual Biography* (Baton Rouge: Louisiana State University Press, 2001).

Freyberg-Inan, Annette, *What Moves Man: The Realist Theory of International Relations and Its Judgment of Human Nature* (Albany, N.Y.: SUNY Press, 2004).

Fromkin, David, "Remembering Hans Morgenthau," *World Policy Journal*, 10 (1993), 81–8.

Garfinkle, Adam, *Telltale Hearts: The Origins and Impact of the Vietnam Antiwar Movement* (New York: St. Martin's, 1995).

Gilbert, Alan, *Must Global Politics Constrain Democracy? Great Power Realism, Democratic Peace, and Democratic Internationalism* (Princeton: Princeton University Press, 1999).

Gilpin, Robert, "The Richness of the Tradition of Political Realism," in Keohane (ed.), *Neorealism and Its Critics*, 301–21.

Good, Robert C., "The National Interest and Political Realism: Niebuhr's 'Debate' with Morgenthau and Kennan," *Journal of Politics*, 22 (1960), 597–619.

Griffiths, Martin, *Realism, Idealism & International Politics: A Reinterpretation* (London: Routledge, 1995).

Guzzini, Stefano, *Realism in International Relations and International Political Economy* (London: Routledge, 1998).

Habermas, Jürgen, *The Divided West* (Cambridge: Polity, 2006).

Haslam, Jonathan, *The Vices of Integrity: E. H. Carr, 1892–1982* (London: Verso, 2000).

No Virtue Like Necessity: Realist Thought in International Relations Since Machiavelli (New Haven: Yale University Press, 2002).

Held, David, *Democracy and the Global Order: From the Modern State to Cosmopolitan Governance* (Stanford: Stanford University Press, 1995).

Herz, John H., *Political Realism and Political Idealism* (Chicago: University of Chicago Press, 1951).

International Politics in the Atomic Age (New York: Columbia University Press, 1959).

The Nation-State and the Crisis of World Politics (New York: David McKay, 1976).

Hill, Melvyn A. (ed.), *Hannah Arendt: The Recovery of the Public World* (New York: St. Martin's, 1979).

Hoffmann, Stanley, "The Limits of Realism," *Social Research*, 48 (1981), 653–9.

Janus and Minerva: Essays in the Theory and Practice of International Politics (Boulder: Westview Press, 1987).

Honig, Jan Willem, "Totalitarianism and Realism: Hans Morgenthau's German Years," in Benjamin Frankel (ed.), *Roots of Realism* (London: Frank Cass, 1996), 283–313.

Hook, Sidney, "The Philosophic Scene: Scientific Method on the Defensive," *Commentary*, 1 (1945), 85–90.

Huber, Max, *Die soziologischen Grundlagen des Völkerrechts* (Berlin: Rothschild, 1928).

Jaspers, Karl, *The Future of Mankind*, trans. E. B. Ashton (Chicago: University of Chicago Press, 1961).

Jervis, Robert, "Hans Morgenthau, Realism, and the Scientific Study of International Politics," *Social Research*, 61 (1994), 853–76.

Johnson, Bernard, "Bernard Johnson's Interview with Hans J. Morgenthau," in Thompson and Myers (eds.), *Truth and Tragedy*, 333–86.

Jütersonke, Oliver, "The Image of Law in *Politics Among Nations*," in Williams (ed.), *Realism Reconsidered*, 93–117.

Katznelson, Ira, *Desolation and Enlightenment: Political Knowledge After Total War, Totalitarianism, and the Holocaust* (New York: Columbia University Press, 2003).

Kaufman, Robert, "Morgenthau's Unrealistic Realism," *Yale Journal of International Affairs*, 1 (2006), 24–38.

Kelsen, Hans, *Vom Wesen und Wert der Demokratie* (Tübingen: Mohr, 1929).

Law and Peace in International Relations (Cambridge, Mass.: Harvard University Press, 1942).

"Foundations of Democracy," *Ethics*, 66 (1955), 1–101.

Reine Rechtslehre (Darmstadt: Scientia Verlag, 1985 [1934]).

Keohane, Robert (ed.), *Neorealism and its Critics* (New York: Columbia University Press, 1986).

Kissinger, Henry, "Hans Morgenthau: A Gentle Analyst of Power," *New Republic* (August 2 and 9, 1980), 12–14.

Knorre, Susanne, *Soziale Selbstbestimmung und individuelle Verantwortung. Hugo Sinzheimer (1875–1945). Eine politische Biographie* (Frankfurt: Peter Lang, 1991).

Knutsen, Torbjorn L., *A History of International Relations Theory* (Manchester: Manchester University Press, 1997).

Koskenniemi, Martti, *The Gentle Civilizer of Nations: The Rise and Fall of International Law, 1870–1960* (Cambridge: Cambridge University Press, 2001).

Krauthammer, Charles, "Democratic Realism: An American Foreign Policy for a Unipolar World" (2004 Irving Kristol Lecture, February 12, 2004, American Enterprise Institute, Washington, D.C.) (www.aei.org/include/pub_printasp?pubID=19912).

Kuklick, Bruce, *Blind Oracles: Intellectuals and War from Kennan to Kissinger* (Princeton: Princeton University Press, 2006).

Lang, Anthony (ed.), *Political Theory and International Affairs: Hans J. Morgenthau on Aristotle's* Politics (Westport: Praeger, 2004).

Lebow, Richard Ned, *The Tragic Vision of Politics: Ethics, Interests and Orders* (Cambridge: Cambridge University Press, 2003).

Lebow, Richard Ned and Stein, Janice Gross, *We All Lost the Cold War* (Princeton: Princeton University Press, 1994).

Lichtheim, George, *The Concept of Ideology and Other Essays* (New York: Random House, 1967).

Lieven, Anatol and Hulsman, John, *Ethical Realism: A Vision For America's Role in the World* (New York: Pantheon, 2006).

Little, Richard, "The English School vs. American Realism: A Meeting of Minds or Divided by a Common Language?" *Review of International Studies*, 29 (2003), 443–60.

Lutz-Bachmann, Matthias and Bohman, Jim (eds.), *Perpetual Peace: Essays on Kant's Cosmopolitan Ideal* (Cambridge, Mass.: MIT Press, 1997).

Mannheim, Karl, *Ideology and Utopia* (New York: Harcourt, Brace and Company, 1936).

Maus, Ingeborg, *Zur Aufklärung der Demokratietheorie* (Frankfurt: Suhrkamp, 1992).

Mazur, G. O. (ed.), *One Hundred Year Commemoration to the Life of Hans Morgenthau* (New York: Semenenko Foundation, 2004).

Mearsheimer, John, *The Tragedy of Great Power Politics* (New York: Norton, 2001).

"Hans Morgenthau and the Iraq War: Realism versus Neoconservatism" (www.opendemocracy.net/democracy-americanpower/morgenthau_2522.jsp) (May 19, 2005).

Meier, Heinrich, *Carl Schmitt and Leo Strauss: The Hidden Dialogue* (Chicago: University of Chicago Press, 1985).

Meinecke, Friedrich, *Machiavellism: The Doctrine of* Raison d'Etat *and its Place in Modern History* (New York: Praeger, 1965).

Miller, James, *Democracy is in the Streets: From Port Huron to the Siege of Chicago* (New York: Simon & Schuster, 1987).

Miscamble, Wilson D., *George F. Kennan and the Making of American Foreign Policy, 1947–50* (Princeton: Princeton University Press, 1992).

Mitrany, David, *A Working Peace System: An Argument for the Functional Development of International Organization* (London: National Peace Council, 1946).

Mollov, M. Benjamin, *Power and Transcendence: Hans J. Morgenthau and the Jewish Experience* (Lanham, Md.: Lexington, 2002).

Molloy, Sean, *The Hidden History of Realism* (New York: Palgrave, 2006).

Morgan, Glyn, *The Idea of a European Superstate: Public Justification and European Integration* (Princeton: Princeton University Press, 2005).

Mueller, Ingo, *Hitler's Justice: The Courts of the Third Reich* (Cambridge, Mass.: Harvard University Press, 1991).

Murphy, Cornelius, *Theories of World Governance: A Study in the History of Ideas* (Washington, D.C.: Catholic University of America Press, 1999).

Murray, Alastair J. H., *Reconstructing Realism: Between Power Politics and Cosmopolitan Ethics* (Edinburgh: Keele University Press, 1997).

Nagel, Ernest, "Review of *Scientific Man vs. Power Politics*," *Yale Law Journal*, 56 (1947), 906–9.

Nardin, Terry and Mapel, David R., *Traditions of International Ethics* (Cambridge: Cambridge University Press, 1992).

Navari, Cornelia, "David Mitrany and International Functionalism," in David Long and Peter Wilson (eds.), *Thinkers of the Twenty Years' Crisis: Inter-War Idealism Reassessed* (Oxford: Clarendon Press, 1995), 214–31.

Niebuhr, Reinhold, *Moral Man and Immoral Society* (New York: Scribner's, 1932).

Nincic, Miroslav, *Democracy and Foreign Policy: The Fallacy of Political Realism* (New York: Columbia University Press, 1992).

Nobel, Jaap W., "Morgenthau's Struggle with Power: The Theory of Power Politics and the Cold War," *Review of International Studies*, 21 (1995), 61–85.

Oakeshott, Michael, "Scientific Politics," in Timothy Fuller (ed.), *Religion, Politics, and the Moral Life* (New Haven: Yale University Press, 1993), 97–110.

Pangle, Thomas and Ahrensdorf, Peter J., *Justice Among Nations: On the Moral Basis of Power and Peace* (Lawrence: University of Kansas Press, 1999), 236–8.

Pichler, Karl-Heinz, "The Godfathers of 'Truth': Max Weber and Carl Schmitt in Morgenthau's Theory of Power Politics," *Review of International Studies*, 24 (1997), 185–200.

Plessner, Helmut, *Macht und menschliche Natur. Ein Versuch zur Anthropologie der geschichtlichen Weltansicht* (Berlin: Junker und Duennhaupt, 1931).

Popper, Karl, *Conjectures and Refutations: The Growth of Scientific Knowledge* (New York: Basic Books, 1962).

Rafshoon, Ellen Glaser, "A Realist's Moral Opposition to the War: Hans J. Morgenthau and Vietnam," *Peace & Change*, 26 (2001), 55–77.

Raskin, Marcus, "Morgenthau: The Idealism of a Realist," in Thompson and Myers (eds.), *Truth and Tragedy*, 85–94.

Rengger, Nicholas, "Realism, Tragedy and the Anti-Pelagian Imagination in International Political Thought," in Williams (ed.), *Realism Reconsidered*, 118–36.

Renner, Karl, *The Institutions of Private Law and Their Social Functions*, ed. Otto Kahn Freund (London: Routledge, 1949).

Rhodes, Richard, *Arsenals of Folly: The Making of the Nuclear Arms Race* (New York: Alfred Knopf, 2007).

Rice, Condoleezza, "Campaign 2000: Promoting the National Interest," *Foreign Affairs* (January/February 2000).

Rohde, Christoph, *Hans J. Morgenthau und der weltpolitische Realismus* (Wiesbaden: Verlag für Sozialwissenschaften, 2004).

Rosecrance, Richard, "The One World of Hans Morgenthau," *Social Research*, 48 (1981), 749–65.

Rosenau, James N., "Governance, Order, and Change in World Politics," in James N. Rosenau and Ernst-Otto Cziempiel (eds.), *Governance Without Government: Order and Change in World Politics* (Cambridge: Cambridge University Press, 1992), 1–29.

Rosenberg, Justin, *The Empire of Civil Society: A Critique of the Realist Theory of International Relations* (London: Verso, 1994).

Rosenthal, Joel, *Righteous Realists: Political Realism, Responsible Power, and American Culture in the Nuclear Age* (Baton Rouge: Louisiana State University Press, 1991).

Russell, Greg G., *Hans J. Morgenthau and the Ethics of American Statecraft* (Baton Rouge: Louisiana State University Press, 1990).

Sagan, Scott and Waltz, Kenneth (eds.), *The Spread of Nuclear Weapons* (New York: Norton, 2003).

Schell, Jonathan, *The Unfinished Twentieth Century* (New York: Verso, 2003).

The Seventh Decade: The New Shape of Nuclear Danger (New York: Metropolitan Books, 2007).

Scheuerman, William E., *Between the Norm and the Exception: The Frankfurt School and the Rule of Law* (Cambridge, Mass.: MIT Press, 1994).

Carl Schmitt: The End of Law (Lanham, Md.: Rowman & Littlefield, 1999).

Frankfurt School Perspectives on Globalization, Democracy, and the Law (London: Routledge, 2008).

(ed.), *The Rule of Law Under Siege. Selected Essays of Franz L. Neumann and Otto Kirchheimer* (Berkeley: University of California Press, 1996).

Schlesinger, Arthur M., Jr., "In Memoriam: Hans Joachim Morgenthau," in George Schwab (ed.), *United States Foreign Policy at the Crossroads* (Westport: Greenwood Press, 1982), ix–xvi.

Schmidt, Brian and Williams, Michael, "The Bush Doctrine and the Iraq War: Neoconservatives vs. Realists," *Security Studies*, 17 (2008), 1–30.

Schmitt, Carl, "Der Begriff des Politischen," *Archiv für Sozialwissenschaft und Sozialpolitik*, 58 (1927), 1–33.

The Concept of the Political, trans. George Schwab (New Brunswick: Rutgers University Press, 1976 [1932]).

Political Theology: Four Chapters on the Concept of Sovereignty, trans. George Schwab (Cambridge, Mass.: MIT Press, 1985 [1922]).

"The Age of Neutralizations and Depoliticizations," trans. John P. McCormick and Matthias Konzett, *Telos*, 96 (1993), 119–30.

The Nomos *of the Earth in the International Law of the* Jus Publicum Europaeum, trans. Gary Ulmen (New York: Telos Press, 2003).

Schuett, Robert, "Freudian Roots of Political Realism: The Importance of Sigmund Freud to Hans J. Morgenthau's Theory of International Politics," *History of the Human Sciences*, 20 (2007), 53–78.

Schumpeter, Joseph, *Capitalism, Socialism, and Democracy* (New York: Harper, 1950).

See, Jennifer, "A Prophet Without Honor: Hans Morgenthau and the War in Vietnam, 1955–65," *Pacific Historical Review*, 70 (2001), 419–47.

Sinzheimer, Hugo, *Völkerrechtsgeist. Rede zur Einführung in das Programm der Zentralstelle "Völkerrecht"* (Leipzig: Verlag Naturwissenschaften, 1917).

Arbeitsrecht und Rechtssoziologie. Gesammelte Aufsätze und Reden, ed. Otto Kahn Freund and Thilo Ramm, Vols. I–II (Frankfurt: EVA, 1976).

Smith, Derek D., *Deterring America: Rogue States and the Proliferation of Weapons of Mass Destruction* (New York: Cambridge University Press, 2006).

Smith, Michael Joseph, *Realist Thought from Weber to Kissinger* (Baton Rouge: Louisiana State University Press, 1986).

Söllner, Alfons, "German Conservatism in America: Morgenthau's Political Realism," *Telos*, 72 (1987), 161–72.

Speer, James P., "Hans Morgenthau and the World State," *World Politics*, 20 (1968), 207–27.

Strauss, Leo, *Natural Right and History* (Chicago: University of Chicago Press, 1953).

Suri, Jeremi, *Henry Kissinger and the American Century* (Cambridge, Mass.: Harvard University Press, 2007).

Taylor, A. J. P., "No Illusions and No Ideas," *Nation* (September 8, 1951), 196–7.

Thompson, Kenneth W., "Beyond National Interest: A Critical Evaluation of Reinhold Niebuhr's Theory of International Politics," *Review of Politics*, 17 (1955), 167–88.
Political Realism and the Crisis of World Politics (Princeton: Princeton University Press, 1960).

Thompson, Kenneth and Myers, Robert J. (eds.), *Truth and Tragedy: A Tribute to Hans J. Morgenthau* (New Brunswick: Transaction Books, 1984).

Tjalve, Vibeke Schou, *Realist Strategies of Republican Peace: Niebuhr, Morgenthau, and the Politics of Patriotic Dissent* (New York: Palgrave, 2008).

Tucker, Robert W., "Professor Morgenthau's Theory of Political 'Realism,'" *American Political Science Review*, 46 (1952), 214–24.

Turner, Stephen and Factor, Regis, *Max Weber and the Dispute Over Reason and Value: A Study in Philosophy, Ethics, and Politics* (London: Routledge, 1984).

Vasquez, John A. *The Power of Power Politics: From Classical Realism to Neotraditionalism* (Cambridge: Cambridge University Press, 1998).

Vinx, Lars, *Hans Kelsen's Pure Theory of Law: Legality and Legitimacy* (Oxford: Oxford University Press, 2007).

Walker, Thomas C. (ed.), *International Studies Notes [Special Issue: 50 Years of Politics Among Nations]*, 24, 1 (1999).

Walters, Gregory J., *Karl Jaspers and the Role of "Conversion" in the Nuclear Age* (Lanham, Md.: University Press, 1988).

Waltz, Kenneth, *Man, the State, and War* (New York: Columbia University, 1954).

Walzer, Michael, *The Company of Critics: Social Criticism and Political Commitment in the Twentieth Century* (New York: Basic Books, 1988).

Weber, Max, *Political Writings*, ed. Peter Lassman and Ronald Speirs (Cambridge: Cambridge University Press, 1994).

Wedderburn of Charlton, Lord, Lewis, Roy, and Clark, Jon (eds.), *Labour Law and Industrial Relations: Building on Kahn-Freund* (Oxford: Clarendon Press, 1983).

Wendt, Alexander, *Social Theory of International Politics* (Cambridge: Cambridge University Press, 1999).

"Western Values and Total War Symposium," *Commentary*, 32 (October 1961), 277–304.

Wheeler, Nicholas, *Saving Strangers: Humanitarian Intervention in International Society* (Oxford: Oxford University Press, 2000).

Wight, Martin, *International Theory: The Three Traditions* (New York: Holmes & Meier, 1992).

Williams, Michael C., *The Realist Tradition and the Limits of International Relations* (Cambridge: Cambridge University Press, 2005).

"The Hobbesian Theory of International Relations: Three Traditions," in Beate Jahn (ed.), *Classical Theory in International Relations* (Cambridge: Cambridge University Press, 2006), 253–76.

"Morgenthau Now: Neoconservatism, National Greatness, and Realism," in Williams (ed.), *Realism Reconsidered*, 216–40.

(ed.), *Reconsidering Realism: The Legacy of Hans J. Morgenthau* (Oxford: Oxford University Press, 2007).

Wittner, Lawrence, *One World or None: A History of the World Nuclear Disarmament Movement Through 1953* (Stanford: Stanford University Press, 1993).

Wu, Leneice N., *The Baruch Plan: U.S. Diplomacy Enters the Nuclear Age* (Washington, D.C.: US Government Printing Office, 1972).

Zolo, Danilo, *Cosmopolis: Prospects for World Government* (Cambridge: Polity Press, 1997).

Index